TH...

BEER GUIDE

• • • • • • • • • • •

EASTERN REGION

THE GREAT LAKES BEER GUIDE

• • • • • • • • •

EASTERN REGION

An Affectionate, Opinionated Guide to
the Beers of Michigan, New York,
Ohio, Ontario, Pennsylvania, Quebec
and Vermont

JAMIE MACKINNON

The BOSTON
MILLS PRESS

Published in 1997 by
Boston Mills Press
132 Main Street
Erin, Ontario, Canada N0B 1T0
Tel 519-833-2407
Fax 519-833-2195
www.boston-mills.on.ca

Distributed in Canada by
General Distribution Services Limited
30 Lesmill Road
Toronto, Canada M3B 2T6
Tel 416-445-3333
Fax 416-445-5967
e-mail customer.service@ccmailgw.genpub.com

Distributed in the United States by
General Distribution Services Inc.
85 River Rock Drive, Suite 202
Buffalo, New York 14207
Toll-free 1-800-805-1083
Fax 416-445-5967
e-mail gdsinc.genpub.com

01   00   99   98   97   1   2   3   4   5

Cataloging in Publication Data

MacKinnon, Jamie, 1952–
   The Great Lakes beer guide : an affectionate, opinionated guide to the beers of Michigan, New York, Ohio, Ontario, Pennsylvania, Quebec & Vermont

ISBN 1-55046-209-1

1. Beer – Great Lakes Region.   2. Breweries – Great Lakes Region.   3. Brewing industry – Great Lakes Region.   I. Title.

HD9397.G74M34 1997   641.230977   97-932024-0

Cover design by Gillian Stead
Design by Mary Firth
Printed in Canada

DEDICATION

This book is dedicated to my mother, Margaret, and my late father, Archie, who taught me to live well and wisely (I have not learned all they taught me), and to my two children, Genevieve and Matthew, who have started to learn that wisdom can be found in pleasure, and pleasure in wisdom.

· ·

ACKNOWLEDGMENTS

A book is an advertisement of indebtedness. A great deal of kind help was given me by brewers and brewery workers as I researched this book. I'd like to thank them all.

There's the debt of friendship. I'd like to raise a glass in appreciation of friends who, over the years, have tolerated or encouraged my enthusiasm for beer, especially Paulette and Alex Sinclair. Thanks go to Allan Cameron for helping me to better understand beer and for many pleasant beery conversations.

There's words. I owe a good deal to a variety of beer and food writers, as well as writers in other domains. Many of their names are in the bibliography.

And there's beer. I'd like to salute all the people involved in the beer renaissance of the Great Lakes region: in brewing, packaging, selling and delivering good beer, as well as those who work in our better pubs and bars. Your work nourishes better communities.

The lyrics to "The Man That Waters the Workers' Beer" (chapter 4) are published with the kind permission of the Workers' Music Association of England. Part of chapter 5 is based on a presentation I made at the 1994 Canadian Amateur Brewers Association conference in Toronto. I and other Canadians need to thank CABA for their beer education efforts over the years.

Finally, I'd like to salute the following beer-appreciation and beer-education societies: the Canadian Association for Better Ale and Lager (CABAL); L'Ordre de St-Arnould, a Canadian organization for French-speaking beer enthusiasts; the U.S.-based Association of Brewers and its subsidiary, the American Homebrewers Association, publishers of many excellent works on beer; as well as the Campaign for Real Ale (CAMRA), the U.K.-based beer drinkers' advocacy group. These groups deserve to be better known for their role in helping to revive and nurture our beer culture.

CONTENTS

FOREWORD

This book is two books in one. It's a meditation on beer: personal essays on various aspects of my favorite beverage. It also provides information on breweries and brewers, and describes and evaluates many of the beers brewed in the eastern Great Lakes region. While the essays and the evaluations may speak to different parts of the brain, they speak to the same person — the thoughtful beer drinker.

It's my hope that the essays will provide some useful analysis, while the brewery and brand descriptions will be seen as concrete reference points for the more general themes in the essays. In any worthwhile subject, one's sense and appreciation of the historical, cultural and spiritual aspects grow with increased understanding of technical and material aspects. So too with beer.

While the ratings are, of course, personal assessments, I would ask you to think of them as reports from one man's journeys in the world — in the spirit (if this isn't too grandiose a comparison) of René-Robert Cavalier de la Salle, reporting on his trips (1669–82) through the Great Lakes and down the Ohio and the Mississippi Rivers. De la Salle was hoping to find a river that flowed to the Pacific, and didn't; I was hoping to try every beer, and haven't.

I've tried to cover most of the packaged beer in Michigan, Ohio, Pennsylvania, New York and Vermont, as well as Ontario and Quebec — that is, the eastern Great Lakes region. Inevitably some breweries and beers have been missed. I've left out some breweries because they were too new to evaluate. I've covered some, but not all, regional breweries. I've tried to cover brewpubs that bottle beer, but I know I've missed a few. I've ignored draft-only beers.

As to the megabreweries, I've looked carefully (I hope) at their deleterious influence on beer culture, but I've reviewed only one beer for each of the Big Five brewers. The impact of the largest brewers on the image of beer and on markets is huge and worth noting; the beer they make, however, is generally poor and of little interest to the beer enthusiast.

As the subtitle makes clear, this guide does not cover all the Great Lakes states. Why, then, include Vermont? Simply, I suppose, because Vermont is an exciting beer state: there's more good beer in the Green Mountain state than there is in several larger states. Then too, Vermont *is* a Great Lakes state — historically, Lake Champlain was referred to as one of the Great Lakes.

It would be fair to say that this guide covers an important part of the beer world. There's more stylistic variety, I believe, in the beers brewed in the Great Lakes region than can be found in Britain, Germany, or even in North America's other great beer region, the Pacific northwest and British Columbia (Cascadia some call it, after the hop strain, perhaps). In late-night discussions of "What's the greatest beer country in the world?" I note that

Formosa Springs Brewery, original building, 1870.

more and more frequently, the United States comes up as a plausible answer. And by this, thoughtful beer drinkers aren't referring to the fact that the United States brews more beer by volume than any other country. They mean that, taken as a whole, the United States provides more stylistic variety than other countries, with the possible exception of Belgium. Canada too has become a center of brewing excellence.

In both countries, however, there are huge regional variations, and beer oases as well as beer deserts. Ontario is once again becoming a great brewing province. Within 20 miles of the city in which I grew up, Guelph, there are five breweries. Vermont and Quebec are becoming destinations for the beer tourist. Since the late 1980s, the growth of quality brewing has been explosive in New York, Ohio and Pennsylvania. And recently, Michigan has seen the good beer renaissance take hold.

Considered as a whole, then, these seven jurisdictions form one of the world's great beer regions. A respect for European tradition and a New World inventiveness make this region an exciting place for the beer lover.

A pub chain I admire uses the slogan "Think globally, drink locally." I like to drink the odd import, but I agree with the sentiment — local brew is often best. Local beer is usually fresher; less energy is used (imagine the oil required to ship beer across the ocean); and local beer nourishes a local beer culture. At the same time, I think it's great to try beers from other places. Maybe reading about the region's beers will extend, if you will, your sense of community.

And so, this guide isn't complete, it isn't up to the minute, and it isn't "objective." It provides one man's thoughts on some of the many facets of beer, and notes many of the interesting beers and breweries in a wonderful beer region.

I think most people can increase their understanding, and thus enjoyment, of beer over a lifetime, and I play with this notion throughout the book. I believe that an understanding of beer style is crucial to beer appreciation (and to intelligent brewing). I think good pubs are great community institutions. I think we've lost something (soul, for lack of another word) as our understanding of beer and other foods has become more secular.

I don't think that all the beers made by the big brewers are bad (although many are), and I don't think that all small-brewery beer is good (but much of it is). Anheuser-Busch and Molson and Miller and Coors and Labatt brew beer that a large number of people seem to want to drink, though it must be said that the large breweries spend huge sums of money creating and reinforcing this "want."

Variety-seeking beer fans are obliged, I think, to fight silly, anti-competitive laws that prevent them from buying brands brewed in neighboring jurisdictions. Variety-seeking beer fans are also obliged — fortunately — to travel, if they want to discover the glories of their neighbors' Real Ale, which doesn't travel well.

The five states and two provinces covered by this book have much in common, including a watershed. Still, proximity (and ecology and neighborliness) aside, isn't there an international boundary here? Aren't there important differences between American and Canadian beers? Well, yes. But the most important differences, at least with regard to quality beer, are brewery to brewery, not country to country.

Beer lovers wisely seek out good beer. They enjoy the familiarity of the hometown suds *and* they're curious to know what's brewing over the fence or down the road. Beer is part of the common language of neighbors. A vignette: I was sitting at a sidewalk bistro in Kingston, Ontario, one afternoon when I overheard a man, a French-speaking tourist, asking for *une bière Canadienne intéressante.*

Now the French word *intéressante* has a slightly more positive connotation than does the neutral, English "interesting," and I had an idea that the man was looking for a beer of quality and character. Therefore when I heard the waitress say "You want a Canadian?" (the best-seller from Molson) my protective (or meddling) instincts were quickened. I asked the man if I could be of help. He told me that he was looking for a beer to go with his meal, a good beer — *et, pourquoi pas, une bière excitante* — but not an import. I made a suggestion, for which he seemed grateful. It is through these small exchanges, through words both spoken and written, that beer culture is shaped.

I hope this book makes a contribution, however modest, to our evolving beer culture.

❶
A BEER DRINKER'S
BILL OF RIGHTS

Beer drinkers in the United States and Canada lack basic rights. Beer drinkers are consumers, but they lack some of the elementary protection had by consumers of other food products. Beer drinkers are also citizens, but they're not afforded the same dignity that other citizens regard as their due. Typically, large breweries and anti-drug zealots are consulted about the regulation of beer. Drinkers are seldom, if ever, consulted. It's time we were. As consumers and citizens, beer drinkers have the right to:

1 **Fair trade:** the right to buy beer in a market unfettered by trade barriers and retail monopolies.

2 **Sensible retailing:** including the right to buy beer in local stores; the right to buy beer that's been properly stored (at cool temperatures, away from fluorescent light); the right to buy single bottles of beer (having to buy 6-, 12-, or 24-packs means that beer drinkers can't choose appropriate beers for given foods, or savor limited amounts of fresh beer in various styles and flavors); and the right to buy with any legal medium of exchange, including credit cards.

3 **Honest measure in pubs:** the right to clear measures on glasses of draft; the right to see this measure on a price list; and the right to know that measures are inspected, on occasion, by government authorities.

4 **Honest taxation:** the right to fair treatment under tax law. Beer is a food and should be treated as such under tax law. If alcohol is to be taxed, beer should be taxed on a unit-*alcohol* basis, not the entire beverage on a volume basis.

5 **Beer variety:** the right to drink any kind of beer. Some American states prohibit the brewing and selling of strong beers such as barley wine. Such laws are discriminatory and must be repealed.

6 **Fair and legal access:** including the right to buy beer by or at the same age that other benefits of adulthood are conferred (to allow a citizen to vote, marry, drive a car, or use a gun — but not to buy beer — is misguided public policy; such policy ensures that beer will be seen and used as a drug); and the right of children to drink beer in a family setting.

7 **Informative labeling:** the right to know the date a given beer was packaged, the alcohol level, and all the ingredients.

8 **Honest advertising:** the right to truth in commercial language (language can be used, George Orwell noted, "to make lies sound truthful and murder respectable, and to give an appearance of solidity to pure wind." Beer drinkers deserve better. Better than "genuine draft" applied to canned or bottled beer, "pilsner" applied to beer made with adjunct, "all natural ingredients" when applied to a brand that doesn't list its ingredients — after all, arsenic and earwigs are natural).

2

BEER CULTURE

O Willie brew'd a peck o' maut,
And Rob and Allan cam to see;
Three blyther hearts, that lee lang night,
Ye wad na found in Christendie.

Robbie Burns, "Willie Brew'd a Peck o' Maut"

There's romance in beer — marvel, mystery, bosh and adventure. The profane and mystic traditions associated with beer reflect a culture that is deep and wide, a culture tied to society, season and soil. Beer is a beverage of fancy as well as of science: it's a product of custom, lore and imagination, as well as of knowledge, work and procedure. All this to say, an understanding of beer requires an understanding of context — historical, social, agricultural and culinary.

Beer is the oldest manmade beverage, at least seven millennia old, and is one of civilization's great triumphs. "Beer came before wine everywhere, and it is sometimes claimed that Dionysus became the god of wine only after reigning as Sabazios, the archaic god of beer... The famous orgies of Thrace and Phrygia used beer before wine, and when they did take to wine, they scandalized the Greeks by drinking it neat," Maguelonne Toussaint-Samat tells us in her marvelous *History of Food*.

Beer has been an essential part of diet from ancient times to the last century. It was among the foods with which Noah provisioned his ark. About 40 percent of the grain in ancient Samaria went into ale. And beer has long been regarded as a tonic. Of the 700 remedies listed in the Ebers papyrus (circa 1400 BC), 100 contained beer. Now, as the 20th century draws to a close, science is re-learning that beer can promote physical and mental health.

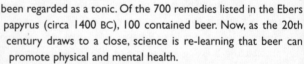

It is said that beer was born in the lands around the east end of the Mediterranean, and a good deal of research has been done on beer in ancient Egypt, Mesopotamia and Samaria. We know, for example, that eight kinds of barley ale and eight kinds of wheat ale were brewed in Samaria some three or four thousand years ago. Some of the oldest laws and regulations pertain to beer. The Code of Hammurabi, circa 1750 BC, contained various strictures against weak beer and price gouging. This first age of beer goes back into the mists of history and covers millennia.

While some accounts would have beer jump, so to speak, over an era (Greco-Roman Empire, circa 400 BC to AD 400) and a mountain range (the Alps), it would be more accurate to say that beer slipped through classical Greece (Sophocles recommended beer as part of a balanced diet) and snuck through Rome (Julius Caesar enjoyed his beer) largely unnoticed. Beer was very much in the shadow of wine. In the south of Europe, wheat (and bread), grapes (and wine), and olives (and oil) formed the key "triad which took on productive and cultural significance as a representative symbol of classical civilization itself," whereas in Germany and central Europe, meat, fish, milk (and its derivatives), wild fruits and beer were the key foods, and they too had enormous cultural significance. So we learn from Massimo Montanari's *The Culture of Food*. Wine was associated with the Greek notion of *civitas* and pride in being separate from nature, while beer flourished in a central European culture that saw man as part of nature.

As Christianity spread northward in Europe, beer took on some of the religious and cultural values that had been attached to wine. Monks often built the first brewery in a community. Perhaps because Christianity embraced and assimilated the rituals of daily life, it embraced beer. Saint Augustine of Hippo, Saint Nicholas of Myrna (Santa Claus), and Saint Luke the Physician are among the patron saints of beer. Saint Columban (who multiplied a small amount of beer) and Saint Bridget (who changed water into beer) are also associated with beer, as are many orders of monks.

Beer has more seasons than any other food. The various ingredients that go into beer have various keeping times and demand different techniques, and beer itself is both improved (over the short term) and destroyed (over the long term) by time. This fact required the brewer to be sensitive to the calendar and temperature. The brewer also had to respond to constraints in brewing technology, in keeping methods, and in the availability of ingredients. The consequence for the drinker (especially the modern drinker) is the opportunity to enjoy an extraordinary range of styles.

Another major determinant of style was spicing agent. A huge variety of agents has been used historically, including clover, horseradish, oak bark, bay, sage, myrtle and wormwood, but since the middle of the eighth century, when the Bavarians starting using them on a widespread basis, hops have reigned as the pre-eminent spicing (and preserving) agent. In 1409, Jean sans Peur, the Duke of Burgundy, created the Order of the Hop, whose motto was "*Ich Zuighe*," Flemish for "I savor."

Given beer's central role in diet, and people's propensity to cheat, it's easy to understand why the regulation of beer has always been important in European life. The 11th-century Domesday Book mentions punishments for brewers who made bad beer. In the 13th century, in parts of the northern Continent, brewers who adulterated beer were to have their right hands cut off, be banished for five years, and have their brewhouses destroyed. In Britain, the "importance of ale in the national diet was recognized in 1267, when it was subjected, like bread, to a sliding price scale based upon the seasonal cost of grain" — that is, the Assize of Ale (*Food and Drink in Britain*). In 1466, the city of Frankfurt decreed that brewers couldn't sell "green," or immature beer, that is, beer that hadn't been aged three weeks. To "foreigners," however, they could "knowingly sell younger beer."

The proclamation of the now-famous Reinheitsgebot beer law of 1516 was therefore not a break with the past, but a continuation of centuries of beer regulation. The Reinheitsgebot, originally written by the Duke of Bavaria, set prices for beer and decreed that beer could be made only from barley malt, hops and water. Adjunct was *verboten*. Under a later amendment, wheat became an acceptable ingredient. The Assize and the Reinheitsgebot were to be but two elements in a never-ending process of regulation — of quality, price, measure, allowable ingredients, disclosure of information, and of trade and competitive practices relating to beer — that has continued to this day in much of Europe.

Some historical accounts pick up the beer trail in Britain during the Roman occupation, or the early Christian epoch, but beer was brewed in Britain as early as the Celtic Iron Age. As long ago as 2000 BC, people with the charming name of Beaker Folk (for the thin, beaker-like pots they made) may have made beer. Barley was the main grain of Roman Britain. Fine pottery for the drinking of beer was being made by the third century AD.

An "important new discovery" associated with the Celts was "the use of beer barm as leaven ... The Celts of Gaul and Spain deliberately encouraged fermentation by adding beer barm to their dough, so that they had a lighter bread than the Greeks and the Romans; and we may believe that the Celts in Britain did the same" (*Food and Drink in Britain*).

As many readers will know, medieval England drank only unhopped ale, which must have been quite sweet. Hopping ale had significant impact on taste; it also had a significant impact on price, undoubtedly because of hops' preservative properties. In the early 1400s, hopped ale cost a third less than unhopped ale in London. Some ale brewers, who had their own guild, the Mystery of Free Brewers, protested when hops were first introduced from Flanders, but by 1600, hopped ale, or "beer," held sway. This major change in diet is alluded to in a wonderful rhyme:

> Turkey, Carp, Hops, Pickerel and Beer
> Came into England all in one year.

or its better-metered variation:

> Hops, Reformation, Bays, and Beer
> Came into England all in one year.

The time frame may be exaggerated, but the rhyme captures the revolutionary effects of a sudden change in diet (and in thinking) from the introduction of new foods (and ideas) from abroad. The year, perhaps, is 1524. More than a century later, when brewing with hops was the norm, lamentations for unhopped ale were still heard: "*Beere* is a Dutch boorish Liquor, a thing not knowne in *England*, till of late dayes an Alien to our Nation, till such times as Hops, and Heresies came amongst us, it is a sawcy intruder in this Land" wrote the "Water Poet" John Taylor in 1661 in "Ale Alevated into the Ale-titude." A saucy intruder indeed, but destined to stay.

Beer came to be *the* British drink. In fact, for most of central and northern Europe, "prior to the introduction of the potato, beer was second only to bread as the main source of nourishment" (*Tastes of Paradise*). In the 17th century and later, "the food value of beer was far from negligible, for it seems probable that this 'small beer' had a calorific value of about 150–200 Cal. per pint. This meant that a young boy drinking about 3 pints a day would get some 500–600 Cal. Toward his daily needs . . . homebrewed beer was a good, sound, healthful drink, and one which could not possibly do harm to children when drunk in reasonable amounts" (*The Englishman's Food*).

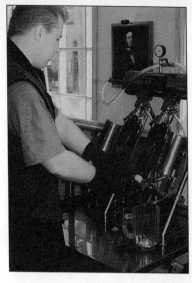

Capping bottles by hand at the Elora brewery.

Despite the growth of pubs, it was not until 1800 or so that more commercially produced beer was drunk than homebrew. All of this homebrew would have come from a pot or a barrel. Barrels, invented in Gaul in the first century AD, allowed the brewer to attain higher levels of carbonation than that afforded by pot brewing. Beer was first bottled in 1736, a wonderful event in the history of food packaging. The Dean of St. Paul's Cathedral, Alexander Nowell, is said to have been fishing when he left a bottle of ale on a riverbank. Returning a few days later and discovering the unopened bottle, he removed the stopper and found "no bottle, but a gun, so great was the sound at the opening."

When beer crossed the Atlantic, it appeared at first as if little had happened to beer or beer culture. Both were imported, mainly from France, England and Holland. In the first century of colonial life, beer was brewed sporadically and non-commercially and with limited success. In New France, brewing in the 1620s is documented, and a brewery was established by the Jesuits in 1647. In British North America, commercial brewing goes back to the 1630s in the Massachusetts Bay Colony. (This, it must be said, is a Eurocentric take on beer. Beer, notably maize beer, was brewed in parts of the Americas long before Columbus and earlier Viking visitors crossed the Atlantic.)

The real story of brewing in North America in the early days of European settlement was homebrewing. Cost and distance made importing beer expensive, and buying commercial beer was simply not possible for many a settler. On newly cleared farms, it was often pioneer women who had the job of making beer — with malt when it was available, and from other cereals, including corn, buckwheat, oats and rye. Vegetables such as pumpkin were also used, as were hops and other spicing agents, including spruce and birch.

In the cities, taverns were built. Taverns and inns made their own potables, including beer, and became important meeting places where politics, trade and community affairs could be discussed. However, perhaps owing to the general busyness of life in the New World (frontiers to be opened, deals

Andy Tveekrem at Great Lakes Brewing, Ohio.

to be made), beer lost some of the ceremonial and festive associations it had had in Europe. For the settler in the cabin or the gentleman in Philadelphia, beer simply *was* — a potable, sometimes tasty drink. In other words, it achieved a new form of invisibility.

And so the image and culture of beer changed, in many ways for the worse, in the New World. The industrious, it was widely believed, were rewarded. Indeed, to be industrious was to be moral. It isn't hard to imagine that over time, drinking might be seen as slothful, or worse, immoral. Worse than drinking in sloth would be drinking intemperately, thus combining two failings, at least to the Puritan mind.

It was against this backdrop that "temperance" societies arose. While anti-booze sentiment was not unique to the New World, it was a uniquely American version of this sentiment that was, I believe, the first aspect of alcohol culture ever to be exported from the New World to the Old.

In Michael Jackson's *The English Pub*, there's a reproduction of a poster that was circulated in England to counter the growing influence of American "teetotalism":

To Working Men & Women: "The Anti-Saloon League" of the United States —
which has now changed its name to "The World League Against Alcoholism"
has now sent a number of skilled organizers and specious speakers to our
country to help the misnamed "Temperance" Associations to ROB YOU OF
YOUR BEER. The League is supported by millionaires and has enormous
funds. . . Will you allow these Aliens to: DICTATE TO YOU, INTERFERE
WITH YOUR LIBERTIES, CLOSE YOUR PUBLIC HOUSES, HUSTLE YOU
INTO COMPULSORY TEETOTALISM? . . . SHOW THESE FUSSY ZEALOTS
THAT YOU RESENT THEIR IMPERTINENT INTRUSION.

In the New World, our understanding of beer is "deracinated," without
myth. We value busyness, conquest and individualism, not leisure, contemplation or social cohesion. We don't sing much, but when we do, it's "Ninety-nine
bottles of beer on the wall," not "John Barleycorn." Uprooted from its myth-
ic soil, beer became attached to the prohibitionist mindset and the larger
forces of secular industrialization. It is my belief that these two factors
explain, to a large extent, why and how beer has lost so much of its cultural
and spiritual vitality.

Consider the frightening notion in the phrase "In heaven there is no
beer." No beer in heaven? Reader, rejoice: in heaven there is more beer! Much
more beer, and we have every reason to believe that it is simply divine.

Wealthy Egyptians would raise a goblet and say "Here's beer for your
ghost." In medieval Denmark, "grave ales" were served at funerals to keep
ghosts away. Perhaps because we no longer cheer or fear ghosts we have an
increasingly sterile beer culture. In a sense, we are becoming dispirited.

Toussaint-Samat reminds us that "the ancient world did not see intoxication, whether induced by mead, beer or diluted wine, as reprehensible. To
some extent, it was regarded as an act of religion in the literal sense of the
word, creating a bond between man and God . . . Given a good head, you
could feel the god within you. The Greek term for ritual intoxication was
enthousiasmos, divine possession."

William James said that drinking stimulated the "mystical
faculties of human nature usually crushed by the cold facts and
dry criticism of the sober hour. Sobriety discriminates, diminishes and says no. Drunkenness expands, unites and says yes."

Drinking is a way to suspend time for a moment. It is said
that we drink to forget; often, I believe, we drink to remember. We drink to know who we are. We drink to escape not
"reality" but mechanical notions of time, the measuring, and
the parceling of time. We drink to nourish feeling, memory and
imagination. Interestingly, some of what is termed drunken behavior is a form
of anticipation; it is forward-looking. People often show diminished inhibition,
greater conviviality and even slurred speech before alcohol has time to take
effect, and even when they drink beverages they believe to be alcoholic, but
which, in fact, are not.

Let's look at beer in action. As an activity, beer drinking is at once dramatic gesture and carnal motion. It is ritual and rite.

Your hand strokes the glass. It pauses, finds the right spot, applies pressure (an embrace, so to speak) and lifts. From hand to mouth, *en passant*, the heart. A pause. You admire the head, its arctic topography. You note the bands of color above and below your thumb: the honey, the ginger, the umber. The motion resumes. The lip of the glass rests on your lower lip. Chin up slightly, the hand pushes up, and … beer in mouth … Throat … gut: alimentary motion.

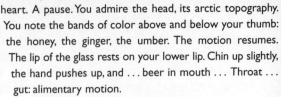

Beer tickles all the senses. Visually, it is the most attractive of all beverages. Unlike wine or whisky, beer is transformed visually and structurally when released from its bottle. It develops a dual structure, with body and head (or cap and gown) in perfect proportion. For the upper, more ephemeral part, colors range from snow, eggshell and pearl through beige and dun to chestnut and mocha. For the lower, more durable part, from palest straw through all the red-yellow combinations, to pitchy near-black.

The head of a beer is a visual and tactile delight, a glorious hybrid of two of the four classical elements, air and water. The texture of the head, from crinkly and effervescent to a fragile but stable meringue, is one of beer's great glories. Touching the head with your finger reveals resistance, but the least resistance one might imagine. And the foam also has feeling! Your finger leaves a depression that deepens and widens; the structure of the head is under attack from invasive traces of digital dirt and oils.

On the tongue, beer can glide or creep, stick or slide. It can be tart, acerbic, soft, unctuous, velvety or viscous.

The tactility of beer is foremost an oral sensation, but thanks to centuries of beer culture and the skills of glassmakers, drinking is also a delight for the fingers. Beer glasses — the tall, fluted pilsner style, the heavy "top hat," the classic sleeve, the stemmed tulip — any stylish glass can provide tactile as well as visual pleasure. A good beer glass has another role: that of holding and releasing aroma.

To a professional taster, aroma is, among other things, information. To a beer lover, aroma is sheer pleasure. Remember the pleasure, as a child, of smelling food when you came home from school and opened the door? Beer can afford the same pleasure, if only we'd let it. Too often, we suppress this sensual possibility; we overchill beer and strangle aroma.

One of beer's unique and underappreciated sensory aspects is its sound. From the thththththipp of the opened bottle, to the rising notes of being poured into a glass, to the delicate soundscape of a dissipating head, beer offers pleasure to the ears, and, at times, useful information as well.

Finally, flavor. Beer flavor is more varied than many people realize. Here's a spacial metaphor: the range of flavors represented by North America's top-selling ten beers is half an inch on a yardstick; the range of flavors to be found in whisky is three inches; in wine, a foot; in the world's major beer styles, the whole yardstick. Beer flavor ranges from the highly sweet to the very dry, from the hugely bitter to the shockingly sour. Like a work of art, beer flavor

Ellen Bounsall at work at McAuslan.

conjures up what *is* in the composition (grainy flavors from the malt, grassy or floral flavors from the hops) as well as what *isn't* (fruity flavors, among others).

The swallow, a kind of grab and squeeze, is a poignant wonder, and brings us back to spirit. "The esophagus is an excellent image of one of the soul's chief functions: to transfer material of the outside world in to the interior" (*Care of the Soul*).

To appreciate the sensory aspects of a single beer can take a mere 20 or 40 minutes. But "happiness," Robert Frost noted, "makes up in height what it lacks in length." There's a bittersweet side to the temporal limits of enjoying a beer. Most people (me included) deal with this by having another beer.

If beer were only a sensory pleasure, I'd still like it, I might even drink a lot of it, but I wouldn't be as engaged by it, as deeply engrossed by it as I am. Beer has a non-material side, an aspect that is cultural and spiritual, that appeals to me and feeds my long-term interest. In any glass of suds, there are aspects of history, geography, agronomy, culinary culture, business and commerce, as well as a complex social context. I also see, when I hold the glass up to the light, meta-physical glints. I see, when I've had half a pint of an excellent ale or lager, fila-ments of time and culture, threads of lore and knowledge that braid, evolve and tangle; I see molecules and words, science and spirit, physics and meta-physics.

❸
THE CHANGING IMAGE
OF BEER

I have fed purely upon ale, I have eat my ale, and I always sleep upon ale.
George Farquhar, "The Beaux' Stratagem"

Oh, the rare virtues of this barley broth!
To rich and poor it's meat and drink and cloth.
Marchant, "Praise of Ale"

Beer's a healthy drink, best regarded as our ancestors saw it, as a food and part of our culinary tradition. Like bread, which also goes back millennia to the first harvesting of grain, beer is a food in itself, an ingredient in various dishes, and a complement to other foods. In northern Europe and in much of North America, beer has, until recently, been a traditional part of a healthy diet, sometimes a major part. In other parts of the world, it still is.

In sub-Saharan Africa, where I lived for two years, burukutu, a mild, still-fermenting beer made from guinea corn, is an important source of food energy. Similar beers, often made from corn or millet, are found in much of the Third World.

If beer has traditionally been seen as a food, as an important source of nutrition and an important bond in community life, why is it that in some parts of North America, beer has suddenly become a drug? In 1996, one group, the Wisconsin Clearinghouse for Prevention Resources, distributed a poster that showed a huge, nasty-looking syringe labeled "BEER," and a caption that read: "IT'S ONLY BEER. Beer contains alcohol. Alcohol is a drug. Alcohol is the number one drug problem in this country. Not marijuana. Not cocaine. Alcohol."

We'll come back to this. But first, let's look carefully at the notion of beer as a food to see what it amounts to.

Beer, glorious food. Close your eyes, think about beer, and what comes to mind? Is it a rough-mannered stepbrother to wine or single-malt whisky? Is it a TV image: a "good times" or "lifestyle" picture? Is it the first drink you had when you weren't yet of legal age? Do you see an ice cooler, a beach, a hot summer day? Do you see yourself with certain friends? For many people in North America, the image of beer is quite different now than what it was even a generation ago. In some ways, beer has gone "upscale" and has an improved reputation; in some ways it has become ethereal, more image than substance.

It's useful to remember that this changing image isn't new. As food and

Open fermenting at Hart.

social historians are discovering, foods and drinks have undergone extraordinary vogues, only to be forgotten (or looked down upon, or made illegal) later. William Hogarth's widely reproduced engravings *Gin Lane* and *Beer Street* are known for illustrating, in an early 18th-century context, the moral degeneration and social decay associated with gin consumption, and the healthful, socially uplifting world of beer consumption. The gin drinkers are debauched; the beer drinkers are sociable and healthy. Interestingly, these two engravings illustrate something else: the gin drinkers are poor and the beer drinkers show signs of adequate income. Jump forward 200 years, join James Bond in a quiet moment, and gin is fashionable, a sociable drink; at the same time (the 1950s and '60s) beer is regarded as the drink of the lower orders.

Many of us grew up with an image of beer that would include the Great Lakes tavern: a childless, womanless, often windowless space — with smoke, a TV high in a corner, a juke box, tavern tables, salt shakers, and potato chip bags pinned to the wall. Where I grew up, in southwestern Ontario, the image included brown stubby bottles or "quart" bottles, draft glasses that were miniature versions of a pilsner-style glass, pickled eggs in an oversized jar, and, it seemed, a hockey game always on the TV. The absences of the larger world — women, children, good food — weren't noticed.

I love good food. I use the word "love" with caution, but I use it. Together with loving, reading, conversing, and cultivating life's various gardens, eating and drinking are certainly life's most central, soulful activities. And of course eating is, in a mundane sense, necessary to live. Think of the song from the musical *Oliver* — "Food, glorious food." Food *is* glorious.

Oliver Twist sang about food, when he could get it, but he doesn't mention beer. For the sake of historical accuracy, he should have. Until the mid- or late 19th century, students at English boarding schools were fed bread, porridge and "small" beer — often stale bread, thin por-

ridge and sour beer. "In the latter half of the 17th century — the period when coffee drinking was catching on among the upper classes — [an English family] consumed about three litres of beer per person daily, children included" (*Tastes of Paradise*).

In the 16th century, men who worked on a "Herring-Fishing Ship" had a daily food allowance that included "biscuit," bacon, butter, "as much fresh fish as they can eat," and "a gallon of beer a day." Life must have been more sedentary at St. Bartholomew's Hospital in London, for in 1687 rations there included only three pints of beer per day (*The Englishman's Food*).

In 1824, health and beauty guides for women were recommending a walk before breakfast, and for breakfast itself, "plain biscuits (not bread), broiled beef steaks or mutton chops, under-done, without any fat, and half a pint of bottled ale — the genuine Scots ale is the best." Now you know: the phrase "Beer — not just for breakfast any more" isn't a mere joke; it's a joke with historical resonance.

Beer, glorious food: glorious, from the Latin *gloria*, connotes praise due to God, divine happiness, as well as the more mundane sense of splendour, brilliance and excellence. "Eat, drink, and love," Lord Byron said, "the rest's not worth a fillip."

The nutritional value of beer. Given that beer is a food, what do we know about its nutritional value? If we know less than we should, perhaps it's the result of beer being marketing not as food, but as a packaged entertainment product. Perhaps too, it's the result of some brewers treating beer ingredients as a "secret." North Americans can easily find out the ingredients that have gone into a non-alcoholic drink (or even dog food) by reading a list on the package. For most of the beer they drink, they can't.

Canadian regulations permit a wide variety of wonderful things to be added to beer "during the course of manufacture," including: carbohydrate matter, such as glucose, in addition to cereal grain; salt; carbon dioxide; dextrin; caramel; class 1 preservatives, including ascorbic acid and erythorbic acid; class 2 preservatives, including potassium metabisulphite and sulphurous acid; polyvinylpyrrolidone; ammonium persulphate; dimethypolysioxane (an "antifoaming agent"); and hydrogen peroxide (a "clarification aid").

Neither the United States nor Canada has ingredient-labeling requirements for beer. And most large breweries and some small ones, unfortunately, are unwilling to tell their clients what they've put in their beers.

I think there are two reasons for this. First, ingredient listing would show how far some brewers have gone in substituting cheaper adjuncts, such as rice and corn sugars, for barley malt. Second, ingredient listing would make consumers more knowledgeable and demanding, a result that some brewers fear.

The nutritive value of beer is greater than many might think. As with any fermented or distilled beverage, beer has no cholesterol or fat. Although it has no fiber and is fairly low in protein, beer is a good source of carbohydrates. Unfiltered lagers and ales (including Real Ale) have significantly more protein than filtered beer. Beer is about 92 percent water.

Half of the calories in beer come from carbohydrates and half from ethyl alcohol. Interestingly, although the malting and fermentation processes radically transform the barley grain, beer's nutritional value largely resembles barley's. "Barley sandwich" is not an inaccurate description for a bottle of quality beer.

One way of looking at the nutritive value of beer is to compare it with spirits and wine. The following figures come primarily from *Nutritive Value of American Foods in Common Units* by Catherine F. Adams; *The Dictionary of Food and What's in It for You* compiled by Barbara Levine Gelb; *The Healthy Barmaid* by Dr. W. Gifford-Jones; "Typical Beer Analysis," published by Molson Breweries; *The Complete Food Book: A Nutritional, Medical and Culinary Guide* by Carol Ann Rinzler; and from the nutritional analysis provided for Grant's Scottish Ale (Yakima Brewing) — before the Bureau of Alcohol, Tobacco and Firearms made providing such educational information illegal!

The variety of sources account for some of the ranges in value. The ranges in value also point to the need for individual breweries to have available nutritional profiles for each beer they brew.

	Liquor (50 ml.; 40% alc./vol.)	Wine (200 ml.; 12.2% alc./vol.)	Beer (341–355 ml.; 4.5% alc./vol.)
Calories	165	170	140–150
Proteins	0	0.2 g	1.0–2.2 g
Carbohydrates	trace	8.4 g	12.7–13.7 g
Cholesterol & Fat	0	0	0
Phosphorus	0	20 mg	50–108 mg
Calcium	0	18 mg	17–50 mg
Iron	0	0.4 mg	trace–0.2 mg
Sodium	0.5mg	10 mg	14-25 mg
Potassium	1 mg	184 mg	85–300 mg
Magnesium	0	12–26 mg	36–105 mg
Vitamins A,C,D,E	0	0	0
Vitamin B1	0	trace	trace
Vitamin B2	0	0.02 mg	0.01–0.13 mg 4.6–20% RDA
Vitamin B3	0	0.2 mg	0.23–2.2 mg 13.9–50% RDA
Vitamin B6	0	0.08 mg	0.017–0.20 mg 13.9–30% RDA
Vitamin B12	0	0	0–170% RDA
Folic acid	0	0	62.5% RDA
Pantothenic acid	N/A	N/A	20% RDA

A good example of difference in nutritional profile from beer to beer is in the protein content. Generally speaking, beer is not a good source of protein, but according to Anton Piendl, beer "contain[s] more protein, especially the essential amino acids" when beer is made "from the exclusive use of malt in the brewing process, in place of such adjuncts as rice, corn and corn syrup, as properly modified malt is rich in amino acids, peptides and proteins" ("Beer as Food," *Brewers Digest*, January 1981). In other words, the top-selling beers of North America, all of which contain adjunct, are poorer sources of nutrition than most micobrewery beers, which tend to be made from 100 percent barley malt. Tables in Bowes and Churche's *Food Values of Portions Commonly Used* show how beer can vary a good deal in nutritive value, even among similar tasting mainstream beers. For example, the protein figure for Anheuser-Busch beer (presumably Budweiser) is 50 percent higher than for Coors' Premium.

Yet overall, we can see that beer is a healthy drink, a good source of carbohydrates, phosphorous and potassium, and some of the vitamin B family.

Beer is a tonic, a sedative and a laxative. Beer is also good for your mental health, and good mental health is good for physical health. According to a major study done by Johns Hopkins hospital in Baltimore, people who drink beer in moderate, regular amounts are ill 13 percent less often than the average for their age, sex and income groups.

Beer is a food; food is best when fresh, ergo . . . "If you can find the freshness dates on these labels, we'll buy the next round." So goes an ad from the Boston Beer Company. The photo shows three different beer labels. None has a "freshness date," that is, a best-before date or a date of production. Does it matter? Is there any point in knowing how old a beer is?

Yes, it does matter. As a food, beer has a limited shelf-life. Especially good beer, because it's not pasteurized, and low-alcohol beer, because alcohol is a natural preservative. More on the freshness issue in chapter 6.

Beer and cuisine. In the past ten years, beer has gained new respect as a useful food ingredient and as a flexible, food-complementary beverage. As Michael Jackson writes in the foreword to the *Great American Beer Cookbook* by Candy Schermerhorn, "The notion that wine is the only drink to accompany or to be used in the kitchen as an ingredient was always foolish and snobbish, and fortunately is now in retreat. Diners and cooks are rediscovering beer in each of these roles. . . . Today what the French and Belgians call *cuisine à la bière* is gaining ground on both sides of the Atlantic. It could be argued that the most interesting beer kitchen is now in North America."

Beer with and in food — natural extensions of the idea that beer is a food. As a food ingredient, a basic rule of thumb is neatly expressed by Robert Bourassa, a master chef who has worked in Canada's best restaurants: "Beer can replace wine in most dishes in which you want less acidity, more sweetness and nuttiness."

The malty sweetness of many ales is suited to many soups and stews. Carbonnade à la Flamande is a classic Belgian beef dish made with malty ales. Mussels can be steamed in beer. Tortes, quiches and breads can all be made with drier, hoppier lagers, or with sweeter ales.

If beer is a good food ingredient, it is as a food accompaniment that beer, with its extraordinary stylistic variety, really shines. It is perhaps the most versatile of beverages. Canada has won the International Culinary Olympics, and America has won many illustrious food awards, and both countries brew beer that wins international medals, but all too seldom do we see excellent food served with first-class beer. Having an interest in cuisine while ignoring or forgetting beer is like painting portraits or landscapes with a primary color missing from the palette.

Three rules of thumb for beer as an accompaniment. First, beer can match a dish. Complex and spicy foods warrant complex, big-flavored beers; simple and subtly flavored foods require simple and/or mildly bitter beers. Second, the reverse: beer can provide a strong contrast to a dish. For example, a simple, thirst-quenching lager to accompany a curry, or a complex bock to go with a simple soft cheese. Third, there's the idea of order. In a multi-course meal, beers should (generally) be served from light to dark, from light-bodied to full-bodied, and from lower to higher alcohol. Beer is easy to get along with, so these general guidelines should serve you well.

On occasion (actually, on many occasions), I like to see beer in a haute cuisine setting. I've attended and sometimes planned dinners — perhaps banquets would be a better term — in which beer was a prominent ingredient as well as the featured beverage.

Here are four menus drawn loosely from these dinners. The menus show beer's utility as an ingredient as well as its flexibility in matching and contrasting with food. I haven't provided any recipes, but recipes are easy to research, and you can invent your own dishes. The first three menus draw from beers described in this guide; the last menu features international beers.

MENU 1

Leek and Onion Torte	Unibroue Blanche de Chambly
Split Pea Beer Soup	Brick Kaiser Pils
Carbonade à la Flammande	Wellington County Ale
Semi-soft Cheeses	Niagara Falls Eisbock
Dessert Crepes (made with beer)	Niagara Falls Maple Wheat
Chocolate Stout Truffles	McAuslan Oatmeal Stout

MENU 2

Beer Borsch and Ale Asparagus Soup	Brooklyn Lager
Artichoke Strudel with Goat Cheese	Catamount Gold
Beer-braised Beef Brisket, with New	
Potatoes and Fiddleheads	Lift Bridge ESB
Salad with Maple Wheat Vinaigrette	Great Lakes Dortmunder

| Strawberry Millefeuille with Ale Caramel Sauce | Woodstock Big Indian Porter |

MENU 3

Lager-marinaded Shrimp, Remoulade Sauce	Penn Pilsner
Pumpkin Bisque	Motor City Pale Ale
Duck Leg Braised in Ale, with Rice and Red Cabbage	King's Crown Brown Ale
Two Cheeses and Fresh Baked Beer Bread	Stoudt's Weizen
Pears Poached in Ale	Unibroue Gaillarde
	Samuel Adams Triple Bock

MENU 4

Smoked Salmon Canapes	Schneider Weisse (Germany)
Mussels Steamed in Ale	Creemore Springs Premium (Canada)
Cheddar Ale Soup	Belhaven Ale (Scotland)
Grilled Bratwurst and Cabbage Salad	Pilsner Urquel (Czech Republic)
Cherries Jubilee	Rodenbach Alexandre (Belgium)
Chocolate-dipped Hazelnuts	Samuel Smith's Imperial Stout (England)

I hope these menus inspire some readers to try beer in a more refined context than the usual one of pizza and hamburger.

Not that I don't like pizza or hamburger. Try mixing two pounds of hamburger with half a cup of finely diced yellow pepper, two or three finely sliced green onions, two tablespoons of horseradish, two ounces (60 ml) of not-too-sweet beer, and a dash of fresh ground pepper. Grill and serve with grilled red onion. Mmm-mmm.

Beer is also great with hot dogs, pita rolls and sandwiches, grilled veggies, meat pies, perogies, pasta, chops. . . . Is there any food that can't be complemented by some style of beer? In chapter 7, along with the beer descriptions, I've made food suggestions for some of the beers.

Chefs are starting to discover that beer can complement and intensify flavors that would be overwhelmed by wine. Try Penn Pilsner with beer-marinaded shrimp, and Niagara Falls' Maple Wheat with dessert crepes. Likewise, beer can stand up to strong flavors and delight a fatigued tongue better than many a wine. Stoudt's Weizen with cheeses and fresh-baked beer bread, for example, or Unibroue's Gaillarde with pears poached in ale.

Here are some common and useful ideas for cooking with beer.

• marinading meat with beer (and oil, garlic, mustard, herbs, etc.)

- cooking rabbit or chicken or ham with a fruit beer
- braising meat in beer
- adding a dark ale to any stew
- adding ale or bock to any meat-based curry
- splashing beer into any fried or baked meat for flavor and for gravy
- glazing meats with beer barbecue sauce
- serving fish with a simple beer sauce
- using sweet beer in a fish batter
- steaming clams or mussels in beer
- baking beans in a dark ale, porter, stout or maple beer
- making a beer-cheese fondue
- making soup with beer
- making pancakes, biscuits, Yorkshire puddings, pizza crusts (or any breadlike food) with beer
- serving sandwiches or meat with a beer mustard
- poaching any firm fruit in beer
- using beer in cakes, brownies, cookies
- making sauces with strong beers for cooked fruit desserts
- making chocolate sauce, or chocolate-fruit sauce with bock or stout
- cooking any chocolate dessert with stout

The possibilities, as they say, are endless.

Beer, the dirty drug. Approaches to alcohol retailing and regulation run the gamut from the liberal or "wet," to the conservative or "neo-dry." Liberal jurisdictions, such as France, Italy, Germany and, to an extent (for beer, at least), Quebec, allow retail competition and see education and family and public culture as the best forms of problem prevention. In conservative jurisdictions, such as Pennsylvania, Vermont and Ontario, retail monopolies exist, and control is seen as the best way to prevent alcohol-related problems.

Is beer a "drug"? Should 18-year-olds be denied access to beer? Should the state prohibit pregnant women from drinking? Where do fearful or hostile attitudes to alcohol come from?

From America's and Canada's earliest days, sentiment about alcohol has reflected, to a large degree, anxieties about political power, immigration and religious practice. "Temperance" groups gained support in the 1830s, particularly among certain strands of the growing middle class. For example, Americans who immigrated to Ontario were themselves barely established in their newly adopted country when they formed Temperance Societies as a way of screening out from meetings the even more recently arrived Irish. The Americans deemed the Irish not adequately "fit and proper" to attend what were nominally public meetings, so "intemperate" drinkers were banned, meaning the Irish.

Until 1826, the temperance movement in America was opposed only to the "too free use of ardent spirits" (*Brewed in America*). In the 1830s and thereafter, despite the fact that the Episcopal, Lutheran and Roman Catholic churches weren't opposed to drinking, a peculiar "strain of social responsibility,

abstemiousness, sanctimony, do-goodism and moral severity" took hold of parts of New England. In the mid-1800s, Maine, Vermont, Michigan, New York and other states passed prohibition bills. The peak of prohibitionist legislation was 1919 to 1933, but many restrictions from this era still apply today.

The modern equivalent of a Temperance Society is the "substance abuse" agency. Such agencies call beer a drug, as in the phrase, "alcohol and other drugs."

The Bureau of Alcohol, Tobacco and Firearms, for example, holds "all therapeutic claims" for alcohol, "regardless of their truthfulness to be inherently misleading," and that "no reference should be made to calories, vitamins or other nutritional information." Interestingly, American law allows brewers to list any of the ingredients they use, but they do not have to list all the ingredients they use — a wonderful opportunity for chicanery.

Many of the modern anti-booze agencies believe that alcohol sales should be tightly controlled, because "when alcohol is made more available, consumption increases," and "when overall consumption rises, so does the number of people of who experience alcohol-related problems" (The Canadian Addiction Research Foundation). Is this true?

In the United States, Canada, Britain and many other jurisdictions, availability of alcohol has increased over the past 20 years, but per capita consumption has decreased. A telling comparison is between Quebec, which has competitive wine and beer sales, and Ontario, which sells beer only through monopoly outlets. Analysis of the introduction of wine into Quebec's grocery stores showed that such sales "created no short- or medium-term increase in wine sales of total per capita consumption."

In fact, for almost every year of the period since Quebec introduced corner-store beer and wine sales, Quebec's statistics have compared favorably to Ontario's with regard to the overall rate of alcoholism, the rate of alcohol-related deaths, the mortality rates for chronic liver disease, the rate of liquor act offenses, and the rate of juvenile offenders involved in liquor act offenses.

As to the second premise, that increased overall consumption leads to an increase in alcohol-related problems, the evidence is mixed. We do know that during the late 1960s and mid-1970s, the death rate from drunk driving fell 43 percent in the United States even as per capita consumption rose. We know that the Japanese have doubled their intake of alcohol over the past 40 years, and yet they have highest life expectancy in the world.

A good deal of evidence suggests that alcohol-related problems are as much a function of how and why alcohol is drunk, that is, its social and cultural context, as they are of absolute consumption levels.

Moderate drinkers live longer than teetotallers. In the early 1990s, the American Council on Science and Health, a non-profit public health institute, reviewed epidemiological, clinical and experimental studies on the effect of alcohol consumption on health, and concluded: "Moderate alcohol use can extend life. Most health studies on the effect of alcohol conclude that moderate or light drinkers — defined as those who consume an average of up to one or two drinks per day — have the lowest death rates. We believe that this level of alcohol intake can be consistent with good health, and is not associated with increases in those forms of death (like liver cirrhosis) which are known to be causally related to alcohol misuse."

One of the specific benefits of moderate drinking is the reduction of clot-producing fibrinogen in the blood. Reduction of fibrinogen reduces the chance of heart attack and stroke.

What is "moderate" drinking? Much depends on age, health, gender and diet (among other variables), but a good rule of thumb for beer is to divide your body weight (in pounds) by three, and then subtract 10 percent. The result is the number of ounces of mid-strength beer (4.5 to 5% alc./vol.) that you can drink per day, assuming that you don't drink other alcohol. For a 135-pound man, that's 40 ounces; for a 180-pound man, it's 54 ounces. Women should drink less per unit body weight — alcohol concentrates at higher rates in women's blood than men's. They can divide by three and subtract 25 percent. I also think it's a good idea for all drinkers to go a few days each month with no alcohol at all.

It must be emphasized that drinking is not for everyone, and that moderate drinking can cause problems for some people. Some people do not tolerate alcohol well. Drinking alcohol can stress the immune system of someone suffering from a cold or flu. Overall, however, it would appear that for most people, moderate beer drinking is not only bad, but part of a healthy life.

THE BIG BREWERIES

The Man that Waters the Workers' Beer
  Chorus:
  I'm the man, the very fat man, who waters the workers' beer
  I'm the man, the very fat man, who waters the workers' beer
  And what do I care if it makes them ill
  Or if it makes them terribly queer
  I've a car and a yacht and an aeroplane
  And I waters the workers' beer

  Now when I makes the workers' beer I puts in strych-i-nine
  Some methylated spirits and a drop of paraffin
  But since a brew so terribly strong
  Might make them terribly queer
  I reaches my hand for the water tap
  And I waters the workers' beer

  Now a drop of beer is good for a man who's thirsty & tired & hot
  And I sometimes has a drop for myself from a very special lot
  But a fat and healthy working class
  Is the thing that I fear most
  So I reaches my hand for the water tap
  And I waters the workers' beer

  Now ladies fair beyond compare and be ye maid or wife
  O sometimes lend a thought for one who leads a sorry life
  The water rates are shockingly high
  And malt is shockingly dear
  And there isn't the profit there used to be in
  Watering the worker's beer
        Traditional Irish song. Words by Paddy Ryan first published in 1939.

The large North American breweries face some serious challenges. Freer trade and more competitive markets; the mushrooming of microbrewers; decreasing per capita beer consumption; growing sophistication of beer drinkers and their demands for stylistic variety; the exponential growth of homebrewing; and finally, the decreasing effectiveness of image advertising in an age of educated, cynical consumers — these are some of the factors that are putting pressure on the national and multinational breweries. The big breweries are responding to these pressures in ways that don't always make sense.

Increasingly, the business of big breweries is the image business. Megabrewers see the world in terms of demographic segments. They spend all their energy chasing what they regard as the most profitable segment of the population:

typically, young males. Then they pay advertising firms huge sums of money to generate images that are supposed to encapsulate an ideal to which the segment is supposed to relate.

However, if you've seen any big brewery ads recently, you know that they don't show much respect for anyone's intelligence. Here's the head of a advertising agency describing beer drinkers as he sees them: "We are talking testosterone here. Rock and roll and girls. Not a lot of these guys read *Finnegan's Wake* or are into Hegelian dialectics."

"I AM currently in violation of every noise by-law ever written by city hall" is part of the text of a Molson print ad that shows a young male with his mouth open wide enough to permit entry of a truck. Molson, it seems, wants to reinforce the image of beer drinkers as noisy, inconsiderate jerks. A TV ad from Coors shows two men walking up to a bar; they're stunned to discover that the pub has a beer menu! They mock the flavor descriptions in the menu, apparently ignorant of the concept of beer style, and frightened by variety and choice.

In the United States, a lot of big brewer advertising implies the accusation they most fear: that the brewer is a drug pusher. Much of the advertising from Coors, Miller and Anheuser-Busch is actually a plea *not* to drink. Pregnant women and people who are under twenty-one are exhorted not to drink; at the same time, there is a curious lack of useful information in this advertising that might help people to see and treat beer as a food. Many American brewers (not just the big ones) don't even put the alcohol level on the label, let alone information on style and ingredients.

Of course, when beer is a third or more adjunct, when it contains preservatives, antioxidants, "stabilizing agents," foam "enhancers," and "antifoaming agents," it's easy to see why some people might think of the product as having a greater resemblance to a drug than a food. Cheap, adjunct-laden beer has a psychotropic effect due to alcohol, but little (or bad) flavor, and in comparison with an all-malt beer, little nutrition.

American brewers have introduced high-alcohol brands and marketed them directly to young males. Such brands slyly imply in their packaging that their major attribute is a high level of alcohol. The attitude implied is that young men aren't concerned with flavor or style; they just need a drug. Beer drinkers are, or want to be, "party animals," as Anheuser-Busch put it.

In the mid-1990s, Molson condemned Labatt as being irresponsible for introducing such a beer, Maximum Ice, a high-alcohol, cardboard-tasting product aimed at young males — and then introduced its own copy-cat beer a week later. The following statement by the Molson president may end up in the Corporate Ethics Hall of Fame: "We would like to see [Labatt's Maximum Ice] contained ... However, we have employees and shareholders, and if the segment continues to grow we may well need to respond with our own product."

As the big brewers grew, they lost their rootedness, their attachment to communities. Molson, once a proud, focused, and very Canadian brewery, is now 40 percent owned by Foster of Australia and 20 percent owned by Miller. Molson had "a unique Canadian heritage that offer[ed] a lot of potential," a Miller spokesman said after buying its share of Molson — "unique" and "Canadian," but easily bought, it would seem.

Anheuser-Busch has brewing interests in France, Germany, Mexico, Spain, Switzerland and China. Interbrew, owners of Labatt, owns pubs in Britain, the Latrobe brewery (Rolling Rock) of Pennsylvania, as well as operations in Hungary, China, Mexico and half a dozen other countries. This morning, Interbrew is the proud owner of the Italian brewer Moretti. This afternoon it sells it. Tonight, it will buy a Latin American brewer. For many large brewers, citizenship and culture are abstractions; reality is profit-per-dollar invested.

Some large breweries have been trying to dominate the sale of imports. Buy a bottle of Corona, and Molson as "agent" makes money. Buy Boddingtons, and money goes to Labatt-Interbrew. Buy Steinlager, money goes to Coors. Buy Carlsberg, money goes to Anheuser-Busch. Buy Kilkenny, Guinness makes a buck. In fact, Guinness dominates much of the North American import market.

Smaller breweries are being bought up by the Big Five brewers. Miller owns a major portion of the Celis brewery in Texas, the Shipyard Brewing Company of Maine, as well as other breweries. Anheuser-Busch owns 25 percent of Seattle's Redhook brewery. "Blue Moon" beers and "Killian's Irish Red" are Coors products.

Some of the brands produced by these subsidiaries are very good. But in marketing them, the big brewers face a problem. How can they promote a quality, all-malt beer without drawing unnecessary attention to the composition of their mainstream products? One way is to hide the identity of the brewer. This is exactly what Molson does with Rickards Red (not, I believe, an all-malt beer, but a reasonably flavorful one). The label of this beer indicates the brewer as the "Capilano Brewing Company." No hint of the real brewer is to be found on the label.

Other breweries are using the same tactic. Miller's Plank Road beers don't identify Miller as the brewer, although the "Plank Road Brewery" does not exist. Labatt markets its bland Kootenay Mountain Ale as a microbrewery brand. Seagram, the distiller and entertainment industry giant, and which has acquired the U.S. rights to Grolsch beer, plans to market a line of "craft beers acquired under licence from an experienced brewer." Increasingly, it's difficult to tell whether a beer is brewed by a genuine independent, or an arm of one of the giants.

I think it useful at this point to say that I'm not against big business. Nor do I think that small is good. Some small brewers make bad beer; some small brewers are unethical. To imply that there is something virtuous in the common phrase "brewed in small batches" is simply wrong. Small batches of beer are neither good nor bad; they are small.

Most of the problems in the big breweries in North America (and Britain) are not the result of bigness; they are the result of a management culture that has lost its way. The focus is not on beer, but on demographic trends, current-value analysis, focus group responses, and other financial and marketing concepts. A high value is placed on image and symbol, and the greatest achievement is a sort of reverse transubstantiation in which beer loses its substance and becomes a TV image.

In a large brewery, a minority of employees are involved in brewing; the majority are involved in counting, projecting, controlling, proceduralizing, negotiating, marketing, partnershipping, repositioning, product placement dealing, and so on. These non-brewing employees are what John Ralston Saul, in *The Unconscious Civilization*, calls "small picture experts." They inhabit a "world in which those trained to know are not permitted to look up and around." In most large breweries, the brewer is simply an employee, and certainly not, if pay is any measure, among the most important of employees. He (almost never a she) is not encouraged or even permitted to look up and around; that's the job of the MBAs and the vice-presidents, the people in finance, marketing and public relations.

From the small-picture expert's point of view, it makes sense to substitute more rice extract for barley malt; you can't argue with a spreadsheet. It makes sense from another small-picture expert's point of view to focus advertising on young males via lifestyle images and rock music; it doesn't pay (and may not even be legal) to portray beer being consumed thoughtfully, in a family setting. It makes sense when a small picture expert says that beer must be made and sold in cans with nitrogen inserts; the trend lines are clear. To yet another small-picture expert, it makes sense to try to minimize competition; competition, after all, puts pressure on the bottom line.

Many of the large brewers have a history of trying to limit competition. The result for beer drinkers is less choice and higher prices.

In *Under the Influence: The Unauthorized Story of the Anheuser-Busch Dynasty*, Peter Hernon and Terry Ganey outline some of the unethical practices employed by Anheuser-Busch to gain market share. When, in the late 1980s, two senior executives at A-B were sent to prison for fraud, one of them, Joseph Martino, vice president of sales, indicated that he didn't think he'd done anything unusual: "It was part of the corporate culture," he told the *Wall Street Journal*. He told authors Hernon and Ganey that he had "witnessed incredible greed and corruption at the highest levels of the company."

In 1889 Adolphus Busch wrote his "Dear Friend Captain Pabst" to suggest that four largest brewers stop "fighting each other and running the profits down," that is, competing, and instead fix prices in order to "realize a profit of half a million or even a million more" than was the case while they were competing. In 1977, the Securities and Exchange Commission alleged that Anheuser-Busch had paid more than $2.5 million in inducements over a three-year period. According to Hernon and Ganey, A-B told its shareholders that it made such "questionable payments" "to maintain its position in the market place." In 1978, A-B paid a $750,000 settlement to the Bureau of Alcohol, Tobacco and Firearms for "questionable payments." In 1984, it paid $2 million to "settle charges of attempting to monopolize beer sales at ball parks, racetracks and stadiums," in violation of federal law (*Under the Influence*).

Molson and Labatt have been caught a number of times in the 1990s providing "licence holders . . . with financial and material benefit in exchange for promoting the company's products" (LLBO News Release). Making these "inducements contrary to the Liquor Licence Act" (cash, kickbacks, merchandise) results in less competition and reduced choice for the beer drinker.

Nowhere has the art of competition avoidance been better perfected than in Ontario, where the largest brewers own and control a beer retail monopoly, the "Beer Store."

The Beer Store is the world's only privately owned beer retail monopoly. It is 99 percent owned and controlled by Molson (and thus Miller and Foster) and Labatt (and thus Interbrew); 1 percent is owned by Sleeman.

To help readers wrap their minds around this concept, here's the equivalent in an American context: Anheuser-Busch, Miller and Coors have a monopoly over beer retailing. Beer sales in independent stores are prohibited by law. For the privilege of selling their beer at an AnMiCo outlet, competing brewers must pay a "retail fee" to the owners, who are America's largest breweries. The fees are high, but the owners will not open the books to show how much profit they're making. They don't have to, and the government doesn't require them to. If America's smaller brewers won't pay the fee, tough. They can't sell their beer and they'll go bankrupt. Of course in the United States, such a monopoly would be illegal.

The U.S. does not, however, have a very competitive beer market. Since the megabrewers aren't allowed to monopolize retailing, they are trying to make the distribution system more to their liking.

Anheuser-Busch has recently started to flex its distribution muscles. The company gets its product to retailers via eleven distributors that it owns, as well as hundreds of independent distributors. According to *Barron's*, "40% of the company's beer rides to market through exclusive distributors who carry nothing else. Anheuser wants to increase this exclusive percentage to 70%, effectively preventing rival beers from getting what the company figures is a free ride." To entice the "independent" distributors, Anheuser will extend credit and marketing funds and make additional discounts to the distributors that sell the fewest competing beers.

Given the influence that the large brewers have over beer distribution and retailing in North America, and given their historic use of this influence, beer drinkers in the Great Lakes region would be wise to learn as much as they can about how their local beer market works, and organize to lobby for fairer, more competitive retailing.

❺
BEER STYLE

I am a stylist, and the most beautiful sentence I have ever heard is,
"Have one on the house."

Wilson Mizner

Incapable of anonymity or plainness, beer always comes in style. There's no such thing as "just plain beer." It wears the subtle and understated elegance of the pilsner style, or the soulful voluptuousness of a stout, or the stern beauty of an alt, or one of two dozen other classic styles and substyles.

And you? Do you have to be stylish to appreciate beer?

No. Or not necessarily. Or yes, perhaps. To develop a long-term relationship with beer, you have to understand and, I think, have some affection for style. It's like having as a lover a stylish person, a person who is concerned with elegance and tradition. Because this person is your lover, you can't be indifferent to style. You become more and more conscious of style, and because you're more conscious, you become more stylish yourself.

I'm using the word to connote two shades of meaning — flair and type.

As type, the concept of style is indispensable to the person who wants to be able to think coherently about beer. To be able to describe and compare beers, and to know what makes beers look, taste and smell the way they do, you need to know something about the major distinctive groups within the great family of beer. With an understanding of type, flair will follow.

The whole point of understanding a little about beer style is to be able to appreciate a beer in its proper context, and to be able to make fair and enlightening comparisons between beers. It makes sense to compare a bock with another bock, not a pale ale; it also makes sense to compare a "single" bock with another single bock, and if with an eisbock or a weizenbock, to do so knowingly. An analogy from the world of wine: you wouldn't evaluate an icewine as a "wine" (if you did, you'd call it sweet and cloying); you'd evaluate it within the parameters of the icewine style.

Developing a sense of style requires exposure to a good number of beers. To get a reasonable idea of the porter style, or the wheat beer or bock style, one would need to try four or five brands, perhaps as many as ten or twelve from each style. Learning about beer style takes time, and one usually develops knowledge of style over a lifetime.

In fact, it seems to me that beer style is one of those things that gets harder, more complex and nuanced, the more I learn about it. I don't think there is, or ever will be, a definitive manual of style. More than any other writer, Michael

Jackson has helped us all to better understand style. He does this by describing (appearance, aroma, taste), by defining some of the technical parameters for a given style, and by elucidating many of the important geographic, historic and cultural factors that play into style.

The task of explaining or understanding style is an intellectual one, similar, for example, to efforts in natural science to produce a taxonomy. In other words, when we speak about style, we're not speaking about quibbles over color, or how much stouter than porter a stout has to be to be a stout, or whether the use of steam or open fermentation merits its own style category. At least we're not speaking only about these things. We're speaking about a framework within which we can make sense of an enormous amount of information — information that is historical, geographic, social, botanical, biological and mechanical, as well as sensory and psychological.

D. H. Lawrence, the novelist, said that categories leach the surprise out of life. Well, yes. That's the point. We need categories to make sense of — that is, to take some of the surprise out of — the world. When we can't get a grip on a beer — an Ichabod Crane (U.S.) say, or a Gaillarde (Canada), or La Chouffe (Belgium) — it's often because we don't have a category for it.

But systems for categorizing beer can't mimic the periodic table, with everything neatly and unproblematically in separate but related boxes. Rather, beer style categorization is more like the layout of a supermarket. Tomato paste, ketchup and salsa might reasonably be placed together — they're all tomato-based, after all — but one might also place the salsa beside the nachos, two rows away from the tomato paste, which someone has thoughtfully shelved beside the noodles, and put the ketchup over in aisle number one with the mustard and the relish.

What style of beer is Miller Beer? Is a brown-colored beer a brown ale just because it says so on the label? Can a five percent alcohol stout really be an "imperial" stout? Does packaged "Genuine Draft" or "Pub Draft" allude to a new style, or is it a contradiction in terms? What in the world, stylistically speaking, is ice beer? Is Sam Adams' Cranberry Lambic a lambic? Can a lambic beer ever be made in North America? And if a beer writer says such-and-such is the case, does that make it more true than if Coor's public relations department says such-and-such is the case?

Should we take a clinical approach to style, that is, construct a matrix with statistical parameters — for color, for units of bitterness, for maximum percentage of wheat, for level of alcohol, and so on? Perhaps. Such a quantitative approach at least has the virtue of lending itself to debate and international use; its disadvantage is that it's not culturally bound and that it's arbitrary.

I've considered a "factor-based" approach, with the factors divided into two lists, one forward-looking (from the brewer's point of view), and one backward-looking (from the drinker's). The forward-looking list would include:

- ingredients, including yeast, and ingredient proportions
- brewing method, including equipment, heat source, mashing method, mashing and fermenting and conditioning temperatures, scheduling, and filtration
- the physical environment of the brewery
- packaging equipment and methods, and, perhaps
- the brewer's intentions and hopes, and past experience with the style

The backward-looking list of factors — the things the drinker can draw on to categorize beer after it's bottled or kegged and served — would include:

- color, head appearance, bubble size and sound, and other aspects of appearance
- aroma and flavor
- mouthfeel and body, including heft, alcohol level, viscosity and carbonation
- expectations and knowledge about the beer: what you think or know the beer to be (a label, or even a word from a companion can produce some of this information), and
- knowledge of similar beers and related beer styles

Beer style is also affected by the role of chance — or serendipity, or happenstance — as opposed to procedure and control. Think about open fermentation, or small batch brewing, and consider the role of chance. North Americans have great faith — perhaps too much faith — in control, but many Belgian brewers know in their bones that control can never be absolute, and that beer style can thus never be reduced to a mathematical formula or a statistical matrix.

One of the most interesting factors at the end of the 20th century is the role — the changing role — of geography. If you can develop a sense of beer geography — if you can internalize a kind of personal beer map — you're well on your way to building a framework for understanding and appreciating beer.

Imagine a map of North America. When you look at it, when you think about it, you're probably apt to focus on parts you know. You can fill these parts in with personal experience and acquired knowledge. But for every map, there are also parts that, on a personal level, are "This Region Is Entirely Unknown" — mysterious parts. In fact, that's part of a map's utility, to schematize both knowledge and the lack of it.

To a beer drinker, geography is important because, initially, differences in soil, sunshine, water and farming practice result in significant differences in regions' ingredients. As well, brewing method and technology vary from place to place. Then, over time, these differences become entrenched, reinforced by custom and lore, resulting in the great historic beer styles.

The soft, rounded and slightly fruity pale ales of the Trent Valley in the Birmingham area of England (such as Marston Pedigree and Bass pale ale) have their origin in the local water, which is very high in gypsum. France, with its greater warmth, and need for a beer with storage properties, arrived at the *bière de garde* style (Trois Monts, for example). Geography and history combined to develop steam beers in California, maple beers in Quebec and Ontario, and so forth. Pilsners, rye beers, wheats and whites, fruit ales — all have their origins in geographic factors.

There's an interestingly parallel with music. Just as some people have worried that American pop music will take over the world, dominating and then eliminating local music, ending with a homogenized, lowest-common-denominator, style — in a parallel fashion, many beer drinkers have worried that local beer styles may disappear as taste converges on a bland, low-bitterness, low-maltiness lager.

Fortunately, these worries appear to be unfounded. Many forms of local culture, including music, seem to be gaining strength despite the juggernaut of American popular culture. And likewise, I believe, for beer. We haven't seen one bland style of American or European beer take over the world — although it may have seemed a legitimate fear 20 years ago. Rather, we've seen extraordinary growth in indigenous beer styles, styles that draw on global influences and local culture.

As it happens, the two main ways of improving one's beer geography involve drinking beer. One way is to travel and drink. Spend a few weeks in Ohio or Quebec or Vermont (or Germany or Belgium), and discover the local brewing scene. Fall into conversation with a fellow beer drinker, and discuss the local suds. I've spent some time in Africa and Europe and the Americas, and the specifics of local beer are certainly part of my understanding of place. When I lived in Nigeria, I learned most of what I did learn about family and compound life (not to mention the local language) while drinking the guinea-corn beer, burukutu. I learned something of Scotland, its economy and some of its citizens' outlook and temperament by playing darts and drinking ale in Scottish pubs.

The second way to develop a sense of beer geography is to read, beer in hand. I've always fancied myself a lazy fellow, so I can appreciate someone like Don Quixote who liked to "journey," but "without the expense and fatigue of traveling, without suffering the inconvenience of heat, cold, hunger, and thirst." Reading a good book (a beer book, or travel book or novel with a strong sense of place) with a beer from the book's locale is a wonderful indulgence for the lazy explorer.

Of course geography ain't what it used to be. A Japanese brewer can make a fine schwartzbier; a Quebec brewer can brew a great bitter; an Ohio brewer can make an excellent pilsner. Moreover, no single brand, nor even single style, can be said to "represent" its country of origin. Increasingly, one finds a wide variety of style, and of character and profile within a style, in most of the major beer countries. And yet some beers do tell us something about their source countries.

For the most part, beer styles shade, or intergrade, into "adjacent" styles. And of course, this is part of beer's complexity and glory. As Vladimir

Nabokov, the writer and scientist, pointed out, most interesting things in this "fluid and interesting world" do intergrade. Beer styles are wonderfully fluid and intergrading, and thus complicate geography and mapmaking. Because beer styles are seldom discrete categories, it is debatable how many distinct styles there are. For example, ESBs, strong ales, old ales, and winter warmers overlap; each style blurs at the edges and shows characteristics of the adjacent style.

If I can't provide the definitive answer to the question of style — and I can't — I might at least provide a metaphor for the search.

Beer styles are typically categorized in lists, as I've done below. Sometimes ales and lagers form two groups, sometimes the order is alphabetic, sometimes color-bound, and sometimes alcohol levels play a role. More dense in the information it carries is Jackson's sideways-branching trees, one for ale, one for lager, in *The New World Guide*. I have tried in a similar fashion to sketch two trees, vertical, with the trunks being the most basic forms of ale and lager, and each branch bound in a combination of geography and history. Following this, I began to wonder if the best way to represent beer style might be a hub and spoke: Put "ale" or "ur-ale" at the center, and branch out, with distance from the central hub representing the passage of time, as well as geographic distance. But there are problems with this image too, chief among them the notion that there *is* a center of the circle. Perhaps a better graphic representation of beer style might be a net, a net whose edges are out of sight, and thus a net without a center.

The metaphor I'm working with these days is that of a garden. A beer garden! Gardens have flowers and weeds, of course, but people argue over which is which. Many gardeners garden for control. A garden, after all, is a triumph of culture over nature. Other gardeners are more apt to allow nature a role.

Gardens may have curious, out-of-fashion plants, as well as plants that are all the rage, at least this year. Long-forgotten plants get noticed, are newly nurtured and newly appreciated. Some plants have roots that can't be seen, but only guessed at. Apparently separate plants may have common roots. Some plants cross-pollinate; others propagate themselves.

And of course a garden displays variety, but a common soil and climate limit the possibilities. Not all plants can grow in any given garden, but a satisfying variety can be. The Spanish have a proverb: "In the garden more grows than the gardener sows." We might add "Or knows."

Likewise, with beer. Beer style is big enough that some aspect always escapes our ken. I'm willing to live in this imperfect state, especially if I have a beer in hand to help me in my musing.

Ale and lager. How many beer styles are there? Some wine drinkers think that there are two types of wine: red and white. Or dry and sweet. Or affordable and otherwise. So it is with beer. Some beer drinkers believe that there are two kinds of beer: mass market and micro. Or domestic and imported. Or ale and lager.

Ale and lager *are* two useful tags, partly because they're zymurgically precise, and partly because they divide the beer family into two large clans. However, to say a beer is an ale or a lager is often to say very little.

While some beer writers emphasizes yeast and top versus bottom fermentation as the key factors in distinguishing ale from lager, it is perhaps more useful to think of ale as a warm-temperature approach to beer. Ale is fermented relatively quickly at relatively warm temperatures (about room temperature), and is also best served warmer than lager (at cellar temperature, about 15–16° C or 59–61° F).

Lager is a cold-temperature approach to beer; it is often fermented at 5–12° C, then slowly "conditioned," or matured, at temperatures just above freezing. Lager is best served cooler than cellar temperature, at about 13–14° C, or 55–58° F. Lager is also, in historical terms, a "new" approach to making beer. While ale has a recorded history of thousands of years, lagering, or cool conditioning, has been employed in central Europe for mere centuries (since the 1400s or 1500s). Benno Scharl, who was born in 1741 in Bavaria, may have been the first person to describe bottom fermentation, but it wasn't until the 19th century that knowledge of yeast and of lager brewing was adequate for lagers to be brewed in a controlled fashion.

Ale is usually (but not always) fermented with *Saccharomyces cerevesiae*, the traditional ale yeast. Ales are called "top fermenting" because the yeast tends to collect near the top of the fermenting beer before it falls to the bottom of the fermenting vessel. Rapid fermentation often imparts a full, faintly fruity flavor.

Lager is fermented with *Saccharomyces cerevesiae uvarum* (or *carlsbergensis*), the traditional yeast for lagers. Cool fermentation is often followed by a cold (0–4° C) aging-conditioning period. Lagers are "bottom-fermenting" beers in that the yeast tends to work at the bottom of the fermenting vessel as it converts the sugary wort into alcohol. Lagers are often "grainier" than ales, less fruity, and often "cleaner" and/or "smoother" tasting, due in part to cold conditioning. To contradict myself, conditioning can also produce complexity as well as cleanness and smoothness.

Factors that complicate the notion of ale and lager are the use of adjunct, the strain of yeast, mashing and fermenting temperatures, and brewing method. To further complicate things, beer styles evolve, and occasionally new styles are born.

Lager production has gained and continues to gain at the expense of ales worldwide. About 90 percent of the beer in the Great Lakes region is "international-lager-style" beer (Miller, Budweiser, Labatt Blue, and so on). Sad, isn't it? It's a bit like being at a banquet, with a huge variety of foods available, but with most people wedged into a corner of the banquet hall, the corner with the soda crackers and the Colby cheese.

The following list covers some key beer styles.

ALES

Abbey beer: strong, fruity, spicy, complex and warming. In Belgium, this style is brewed by commercial brewers who model the beer on those made by the Trappist abbeys. Abbey beer examples: Maredsous, Corsendonk. **Trappist** beer examples: Chimay, Orval, St. Sixtus, and Westmalle. See **Belgian ales**.

Alt: the German word for "old," that is, the old style of beer, which was simply ale. (Lager is the new style.) Copper to mid amber in color, and light to medium in body, a German alt (usually brewed in or near Dusseldorf) has roasty, sometimes earthy tones, a wee metallic edge (almost coppery), and a very subdued fruitiness (subdued because of a long conditioning period). Bitterness of about 32 to 55 IBUs is noticeable, but delicate and well married to the malts. Wheat is sometimes used to supplement barley malt. German examples: Schlosser Alt and Hannen Alt.

Amber: a color. Color is a poor determinant of style, and thus to say a beer is an "amber" is to say little. Amber is, perhaps, an evolving North American style, a subset of the pale ale style, typically using some of the darker malts. **Red ale** is, incidentally, a real Belgian style, of which Rodenbach is a fine example. It is malty, sour and complex.

Belgian ales: a large domain of ales with extraordinary variety among them. In a North American context, it is useful to know about the **lambics**; the **whites**; and two bottle-conditioned, high-alcohol **abbey** styles — the **double** style, which is mid to dark amber, very malty, fruity-ethyly, and spicy (Chimay Red is a classic), and the **tripel** (triple) style, which is pale in color (no dark malts are used, just easily fermented pale malts and specialty sugars), lightly spicy, and delicately, cunningly hopped with British and/or German hops. Duvel and La Fin du Monde are classics. Finally, considering the increasing number of Belgian-inspired ales now being brewed in North America, perhaps the invented term "New World Belgian ale" is a useful one, covering a range of mid- to high-alcohol ales made with Belgian yeast and emphasizing spiciness.

Bitter: the most common form of beer sold in Britain, virtually always on tap. The fact that bitter is a draft beer is critical to the British, who value bitter's low carbonation. When bottled, bitter is often called **pale ale**. Usually bitter in taste from the generous use of "bittering" hops, bitter can also be marked by detectable malt sweetness. While hop bitterness is salient in the flavor, hop aroma is not. Bitters range widely in flavor and strength, with original gravities ranging from 1036 to 1055. In Britain, bitter is often categorized and priced by strength. "Ordinary" bitter (1036–1042) is lowest in price and strength; "special" bitter (1043–1049) is stronger and pricier; "extra special" bitter or **ESB** (1050+) is the strongest and most costly.

Brown ale: medium-bodied and often lower than average in alcohol, brown ales vary in color from pale to dark brown. Brown ales are historically related to **mild** ales, a very English, low-alcohol, but full-of-flavor style usually sold in draft form. Brown ales are seldom bitter or hoppy. British brown ales (Newcastle, King and Barnes, Samuel Smith Nut Brown) tend to sweetness, are often soft, nutty and malty, and may have yeasty-bready qualities. Belgian brown ales (Goudenband) are noticeably sour.

American brown ales tend to be more highly hopped, making them, perhaps, a new substyle.

Canadian ale: does this style still exist? Until the late 1960s, many would have said that Molson Export and Molson Stock exemplified a distinct style of ale — the "Canadian ale" style. The moderately bitter, husky-rough characteristic of this style was largely the result of using six-row barley (less delicate, more "husky," than the two-row variety), as well as limited corn adjunct, which, in quantities of up to 15 percent, still allowed malt flavor to predominate. Now, most mainstream Canadian ales suffer from high levels of adjunct and low levels of bitterness due to low hopping. The style is now best exemplified by Brick's Red Cap.

Cream ale: a confusing term. Cream ale can refer to an ale/lager hybrid: ale is blended with lager, with lager usually forming the bulk of the beer. The roots of this style may come from the last century when, in an effort sell to a wider market, North American brewers tried to make lighter tasting, less full-bodied beer than the ales and lagers then on the market. Cream ale can also refer to an ale that undergoes the additional cold conditioning associated with lagers, or even to a lager fermented at warm temperatures.

Kölsch: a subtle, soft, dryish, and rounded German style of ale, with some fruity elements. Usually made from barley malt only, but sometimes containing a little wheat for technical (rather than flavor) properties, Kölsch is only moderately bitter (up to 35 IBUs), using German hop strains such as Hallertau or Perle.

India Pale Ale: colonial administrators like the comforts of home, and the British in 18th- and 19th-century India were no exception. How to get British-brewed ale, a staple, to India in good shape, when the duration of the trip (months) and the temperatures (high) were working for bacteria and against the India-based ale lover? High alcohol and generous hopping, which inhibit bacteria formation, were the answer, and are two characteristics of the IPA style, which was born in the 1790s and peaked in production in the 1880s. Traditional IPAs are pale (gold to light amber), have original gravities of 1060 to 1075, and are very highly hopped, both in the boil and later. Heavy hopping produces a full, flowery aroma, as well as noticeable bitterness (40–80 IBUs). Taxation and Prohibition-induced amnesia almost put paid to this style, but there are signs of a revival in North America and Britain.

Lambic beers: not brewed in North America, but useful to know about. Actually a family of beers, lambics are made with up to 40 percent wheat and then "spontaneously" fermented; that is, the yeast that sparks the fermentation is wild (or more accurately, uncultured), found in the brewery's atmosphere. Lambic beers are typically quite sour to a North American palate. **Gueuze** is a blend of young and matured lambics resulting in a taste that is at once sour and tart with hints of butterscotchy sweetness. Lambic beers are sometimes flavored with fruit: **kriek** is a cherry lambic; **Framboise** is made with raspberries. It is likely impossible to duplicate the lambic process outside Belgium, but in Britain the Samuel Smith brewery is trying (marketed in the United States under the All Saints name), and North American brewers will, undoubtedly, follow. The **fruit beers** traditionally associated with the lambic family have inspired North American brewers to make their own non-lambic fruit beers. Lambic breweries include Boon, Cantillon, Lindemans, and Mort Subite (all Belgian).

Mild: a malty, lightly hopped ale that intergrades with the brown ale style. Mild was once very popular in England but is now often hard to find. Light to dark amber in color, its key characteristics include low alcohol, about 3 to 3.8 percent by volume; soft, malty, sometimes roasty flavors; and low hopping. Low initial gravity makes mild ideal for cask conditioning, so long as the demand ensures rapid turnover. Flavor comes from crystal malt and sometimes pinches of black malt. While milds are virtually unknown in North America, they're likely to appear as the Real Ale scene develops.

Pale ale: classic pale ales have roots in the Burton-on-Trent region of England, where hard water, containing calcium sulphate (gypsum) and carbonate mineral, helps in maintaining a hoppy character. The pale ale style encompasses a wide variety of ales ranging in color from straw to deep amber. Pale ales should have some fruity (though "rounded") qualities, and hops should be noticeable, both in aroma and taste. Pale ales are medium-bodied, medium in alcohol (4.5–5.5% alc./vol.), low to medium in maltiness, and moderately bitter (20–45 IBUs).

Porter: cola-colored (but not quite opaque) from the use of black malt, and sometimes hinting at a coffee or burnt-toast flavor from the use of roasted barley, porter owes its name to the bag carriers of 19th-century London who favored this full-flavored drink. In addition to pale and specialty malts, licorice and even molasses can be employed. Porters have less viscosity, mouthfeel and body than stouts, but are similar in other respects. Medium to heavy bittering hops balance what might otherwise be a cloying flavor. Alcohol levels of 4.8 to 5.25 percent by volume would be the norm, while bitterness levels of 30 to 55 International Bitterness Units are common.

Real Ale: not a style so much as a an article of faith for many beer enthusiasts. Real Ale is any kind of all-malt ale that is neither filtered nor pasteurized (pasteurization kills beer) and that is "cask conditioned." The result is a beer different in kind — indeed, a quantum leap away — from its kegged and artificially carbonated counterpart. To make a Real Ale, the brewer must put the beer into a cask at the end of its primary, or most vigorous, fermentation. The ale, with yeast still active, is "conditioned" at the pub or bar in which it will be served, that is, it undergoes a gentle secondary fermentation in the cask. This conditioning produces a delicate, natural carbonation, as well as more salient flavor. Drinking one's first Real Ale is a bit like seeing color for the first time in *The Wizard of Oz*: only in retrospect can you realize what you were missing. Real Ale is by definition a draft-only beer. It is a living product and is as fresh as beer can be. It has a short lifespan and optimal flavor period (no more than a few days once the cask is tapped), and it changes in flavor and character during this period. Because it is fragile and demands knowledgeable bar staff to keep and serve it, Real Ale isn't as widespread as it should be. The Wellington County brewery of Guelph, Ontario, was the first brewery in modern-time North America to produce Real Ale. It still does, and it's excellent.

Red: see amber.

Scotch ale: usually very malty and seldom hoppy, the Scotch Ale style tends to use some darker malts, which produce a grainy bitterness, unlike hop bitterness. Scotch ales are thus often dark amber in color. Examples: Belhaven, Caledonian 80/ (eighty shilling).

Stout: known to most people through exposure to the classic Irish dry stout, Guinness, stout is in itself a family of beer. The dry Irish style is one side of the family; there is also an English, somewhat sweeter style, although dry stouts are also made in England. Another stout style is the very rich, viscous, tarry and complex-flavored **imperial stout** style, which should have a high original gravity (at least 1070) and high alcohol content (usually over 7 percent alcohol by volume). **Oatmeal** is sometimes used in stouts for an oaty flavor; it can also produce a silky mouthfeel. Roasted, unmalted barley gives stouts their characteristic dark bitterness. Flaked barley can also be used. Bitterness levels in stouts can be quite high. Stout can be characterized by a good deal of fruitiness (plum, prune, fig, date, raisin). In Quebec, stout is sometimes called noire.

Strong ale: copper to deep amber in color, strong ales have from 6 to 12 percent alcohol by volume. Medium to full bodied, strong ales have a malty, sometimes fruity sweetness, vinous qualities and medium to high viscosity. **Old ale**, **winter warmer**, and **barley wine** are British terms for types of strong ale, with respectively, about 6 to 7, 7 to 8, and 8-plus percent alcohol by volume. Strong ales require long conditioning.

Wheat beer / Weisse / Weizenbier / White: a beer family in its own right, wheat beers are brewed with, in addition to barley malt, up to two-thirds wheat. The result is a very different style of beer. Belgian **witbiers** (**white** beer or, in French, **blanche**; classics include Hoegaarden White from Belgium and Blanche de Chambly from Quebec) may incorporate coriander seeds and orange peel. **Weissbier** (meaning white beer) and **weizenbier** (wheat beer) cover a lot of ground and include variations on tartness (sometimes hard fruit), citric fruitiness (lemon, grapefruit), lactic sourness, estery flavors (especially banana) and spiciness (especially cloves). **Hefe-weizens** are unfiltered and have yeast in suspension. Many wheat beers have a tart fruitiness and acidity that makes them thirst-quenching and suitable for hot summer days. Some German wheat beers are quite low in alcohol, as low as 3 percent alcohol by volume, making them even more attractive as a summer drink. **American wheat** is an evolving style, typically brewed with 50 percent wheat, and often with some breadiness and a light citric tang to it, but little or no trace of banana esters, or cloves or other forms of spiciness. Wheat beers are not terribly bitter; usually they range from 10 to 20 IBUs. They can be served neat, or with a slice of lemon, or mixed with fruit juices or concentrates.

LAGERS

Bock: often a seasonal beer, appearing at Christmas and in the springtime. Bock should be fairly strong, that is, more than 6.5 percent alcohol by volume. The aroma should have a pronounced, even intense, maltiness, and the lightly hopped flavor is sweet or semi-sweet, and malty. There are often complex dark fruity flavors, and there may be roasty hints of chocolate. The color varies from copper to dark amber. **Weizenbock** (wheat bock) is darker and stronger than a regular wheat beer, and lighter and creamier than most bocks. Higher-alcohol bocks (more than 7.5% alc./vol.) have come to be called **double bocks**. By inference, ordinary bocks are **single bocks**, though there is no clear demarcating line between them and double bocks.

Dortmunder: a dryish, somewhat grainy, moderately hoppy (that is, 20 to 25 IBUs), but not very floral lager, with medium body, low viscosity, and clean taste. It has alcohol of just over 5 percent by volume.

Dry: an international-lager-style beer, but more fully attenuated for a "cleaner" (smaller) taste.

Eisbock: an unusual, very strong (can be over 10% alc./vol) bock. The brewer starts with a high-gravity bock, ferments it, and then freezes the beer to remove ice crystals, thus some of the water, thereby increasing the alcohol concentration. The brewer may freeze the beer more than once. Eisbocks are typically amber to mahogany in color, and have a strong malty-ethyl nose. Flavors range from intense caramel-malty flavors through chocolate and fruit complexity to sherry and portlike (but never sharp) ethyl-warming flavors. Sweetness varies.  Maltiness can mask bitterness levels that are technically very high. Niagara Falls Brewing was the first North American brewer to make an eisbock.

Great Lakes lager: an invented term. Using two-row malt, and German-derived hops (Hallertau, Liberty, Mount Hood, Saaz, Tettnang), the quality lagers of the Great Lakes region exhibit the light malt profile one associates with the Pils style of Germany, but with more hop grassiness, and sometimes more viscosity.

Märzen / Oktoberfest: historically brewed in the spring (March), and conditioned over the summer at cool temperatures for consumption in the fall (October). Old gold to reddish amber in color, with maltiness dominating the hops. Overlaps with the Vienna style.

Pilsner: true pilsner needn't be brewed in Plzen, Bohemia. But many North American beers touted as "pils" or "Pilsner" or "Pilsener" are quite lacking in the essential characteristics of the true pilsner style. Pale straw to gold in color, pilsners should be delicately malty and very well hopped. "Well hopped" means two things: bittering hops to produce a high level of bitterness (often 35 to 45 IBUs, three to four times the bitterness level of most mass-market lagers), as well as the judicious use of aromatic hops, (often of the Saaz or Hallertau variety) to impart a powerful floral-hay nose (appropriately, Plzen means "green meadows"). Although bitterness is high, hoppy flavors should not be rough, or grassy-metallic. Flavor should be soft and highly nuanced, starting crisp and bitter with detectable malt, and finishing soft and bitter.

International lager style: a very pale (light straw colored), bland, "clean," unremarkable lager with less than 16 International Bitterness Units. Hops scarcely noticeable in the aroma. When made with more than 25 percent rice or corn adjunct (as are many North American best-sellers), bland becomes bad, and defects such as sake, corn and cardboard flavors are noticeable.

Schwartzbier: a black, or near-black, lager, low to medium in alcohol, malty and with varying degrees of bitterness. **Preta** is a variant that became popular in South America last century; Xingu, available in the United States and Ontario, is a fat, modern take on the style.

Vienna style: copper to red-tinged amber in color, with a medium-plus starting gravity (1050–1058, 5–5.5% alc./vol.), Vienna is related to the märzen-oktoberfest style. Using malts that are somewhat sweet, and with a lowish attenuation that leaves some of this sweetness in the beer, Viennas have a predominantly sweet malt profile, with some roastiness evident, and low, but detectable hopping.

❻
BEER APPRECIATION

The pleasures of sense are really intellectual pleasures confusedly known.
Gottfried W. Leibnitz, *Principles of Nature and Grace*

You can deepen your understanding of beer over a lifetime. You never learn all there is to know. Like fly-fishing, book collecting or the study of history — like any worthwhile passion — learning about beer never ends. The subject is boundless.

Happily, learning about beer involves some very civilized activities: drinking and thinking, discussing brews with friends, reading and notekeeping. It can also involve travel and collecting. What it amounts to is trying to develop a personal understanding of beer, of getting to know the drink on your terms. In this chapter, we'll look at beer ingredients, buying and storing beer, and savoring and evaluating beer. The chapter ends with a sketch of the beer drinker's "learning curve."

Ingredients in beer. You can put almost anything into beer, and over the centuries, almost everything has been tried. But it's generally true to say that, with the exception of wheat beers, fruit beers and Belgian ales, good beer consists largely or exclusively of four classic ingredients: water, malted barley, hops and yeast.

Some brewers draw attention to the **water** they use — "pure spring water" for example — and this is important, for beer is 90 to 95 percent water. However, I'd rather have a beer made by a good brewer from Hudson River water than a beer made by a sloppy brewer from any kind of spring or artesian water. The water used by most brewers is treated, and its provenance is of decreasing importance.

Dechlorination is standard practice for any brewer using city water. Dissolved minerals are found in water and added, as required, by brewers. Calcium and sulfate tend to increase bitterness by enhancing hop bitterness. Calcium can also help to prevent cloudiness. Sodium can enhance mouthfeel; magnesium can cause astringency; both tend to accentuate beer flavor. Chloride helps to "round out" bitterness. Different waters are therefore suited to different beer styles. In general, hard, carbonate waters (like most artesian water) are best suited to darker ales and drier, hoppier beers, while soft water (like most water from inland lakes) can carry soft delicate flavors (for example, those associated with pilsners) well.

Malted barley, usually called **malt**, is the heart of any beer. And the largest part of this heart is a pale (light in color) malt that brewers tend to use as a base, adding relatively small amounts of darker, more highly roasted malts for aroma, flavor, mouthfeel and color. The great malt-producing countries of the world are Argentina, Belgium, Canada, England, Germany, Scotland and the United States.

The malts most commonly used in most microbrewery beer are "two-row" barley malts. Some barley ears have the grain arranged in two rows, and some have it in six. Traditional European malts were almost exclusively two-row, and until recently, most North American barley was of the six-row variety. Traditionally, six-row pale malt was used by the large breweries because it was cheaper and worked well with adjunct. Most small brewers use two-row pale exclusively. Six-row malt has more of a husk flavor; two-row has more of a refined caramel and grain flavor. I bet we'll see renewed small-brewery interest in six-row malts. They can be difficult to work with (sometimes causing problems with haze), but they offer a variety of flavors. Some brewers know how to combine the two varieties with skill and subtlety.

Pale malt is the main malt out of which almost all beers are made. In either its two- or six-row guise, pale malt provides the brewer with a foundation on which to build. Pale malt usually represents more than 80 percent of the malt used in a beer.

Victory or **biscuit malt** is very pale brown. It imparts a bready, toasty or nutty flavor.

Vienna malt is also pale in color. It's used in Dortmund-style lagers, in sweeter Vienna-style beers, and a variety of North American beers.

Carastan covers a range of malts commonly called **crystal** malt in Britain and **caramel** malt in the United States (in the ingredient listings for individual beers, I have used the term given me by the brewer). Carastan is made by drying the malted barley at relatively high temperatures (up to 100° C),

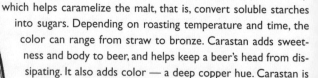

which helps caramelize the malt, that is, convert soluble starches into sugars. Depending on roasting temperature and time, the color can range from straw to bronze. Carastan adds sweetness and body to beer, and helps keep a beer's head from dissipating. It also adds color — a deep copper hue. Carastan is used in a large variety of beers.

Munich malt adds a toasty, nutty richness to beer.

Chocolate malt is deep sienna to chocolate in color. It produces a roasted grain flavor, and is used sparingly in oktoberfest beers. It is commonly used in porters, and sometimes in stouts and bocks.

Black malt is barley malt so highly roasted that it's charred. It even smells a little like charcoal. Used primarily for color, black malt also imparts a sharp dry bitterness that is prized in many stouts and porters.

Unmalted barley can help produce a creamier head and add a grainy flavor to beer. **Roasted barley** is unmalted barley that has been roasted to a very dark brown. It adds a coffeeish note to porters and stouts, but can be used sparingly in lighter-colored ales as well.

Corn and **rice**, two common adjuncts, are often converted to soluble starches before being fermented. Both adjuncts save the brewer money. Both are said to lighten the body and the flavor, especially rice. This is only partly true. Corn, used in most mass-market Canadian beer, has a sweet and maizy flavor that shows clearly when used in high proportions. It makes the aroma of a beer papery: anywhere from fine paper to newsprint to cardboard. Corn adjunct can also make the aroma suggestive of popcorn. Rice, used in some mass-market American beers, lends a ricey flavor to beer, and makes the aroma suggestive of sake, the Japanese rice wine.

Wheat tends to lighten the body of beer and make the head creamy and long-lasting. It can add a "toasty" flavor and can produce lemon or grapefruit skin hints. Some wheat beers have distinct notes of lemon, banana, cloves and/or cinnamon, partly because of the wheat, and partly because of the yeast and the brewing method.

Hops add so much to beer it's hard to imagine a brewer going without them. Hops add bitterness, thus balancing the sweetness than comes from malt. They can add spicy and herbal flavors, and they contribute greatly to aroma as well — often a grassy, or haylike, or floral bouquet. In addition, hops help head retention and prolong shelf-life. Beer is fragile, and generally deteriorates from the moment it's bottled, but hops, a natural preservative, diminish the rate at which this deterioration occurs. Hops' preservative nature gives them an important role in beers that gain balance and "roundedness" through long conditioning, IPAs, for example.

At various points in history, people have made a tea by infusing hop cones in hot water (hops, or *humulus lupulus*, are related to marijuana and hemp). The result is a medicinal drink with sedative qualities. Hops have been used in bread making. Hop shoots that come up in the spring are used in salads. Hop leaves (as opposed to the cones) have been used as a medicine for skin problems, and in poultice form, as an analgesic for pain and stiffness. Dried hops have been used to stuff pillows; George the Third of England was one person who slept with a hop pillow.

The major commercial hop growing centers are Germany, England, Australia, and the American northwest. British Columbia also produces some hops.

Hops are perennials. They grow on vines, flower in early summer, and are harvested in the fall. Whole hops flowers, or "cones," provide the best aroma. For practical reasons, many brewers use hop "plugs" (compressed flowers), hop pellets (pulverized and compressed flowers) or hop extracts (liquids that may have only some hop components). Hops are **dioecious** (from the Greek, meaning two dwellings); the plants are either male or female. Only the female plants provide the cones used by brewers. Male plants are eliminated from the hop yard, except in sexy England, where they are permitted to cavort with the females.

Hops can be added at almost any time in the brewing process, from early in the "boil" to just before bottling. The timing is critical to the effect that hops will have on

beer. Generally, "bittering" hops, added early in the boil, provide bitterness and have limited effect on the beer's aroma. The later that hops are added to the other ingredients — that is "finishing" hops or "aromatic" hops — the more hoppy the flavor and the more impact on aroma. Adding hops when the beer is almost fully fermented is called "dry hopping," and can produce a marked hoppy aroma and taste.

Hop bitterness is noticed most by the beer drinker at the back of the tongue. Hop bitterness is largely the result of "alpha acids," or humulons, being converted during the boil to isohumulons. "High alpha" hops produce a high degree of bitterness. Many such hop strains have been developed in recent years.

It's useful for beer drinkers to know some of the major hop strains, especially those that have aromatic as well as bittering properties. Fuggles and Goldings are two classics used in ales. They come from England and have rich, soft, herbal, earthy, and lightly spicy aromatics and flavors. Styrian Goldings is a Fuggles derivative grown in central Europe. Willamette is a seedless "daughter" of Fuggles.

In lagers, two classic hop strains are Hallertau and Saaz. Hallertau is grassy-spicy, but never harsh; Saaz is floral and vaguely peppery-spicy, but in a delicate fashion. Liberty and Mount Hood hops are North American derivatives of the Hallertau strain. Tettnang (or Tettnanger) is another good lager hop with spicy, herbal aromatics as well as bittering properties.

Cascade, Cluster and Perle are moderately bitter hops commonly used in North American lagers and sometimes in ales. Challenger and Northern Brewer are also moderately bitter (deemed to be, respectively, spicy and "minty"), and are used in ales and sometimes lagers. Bullion is moderately bitter and is used in dark ales.

Some of the most bitter bittering hops cultivated in North America are Centennial, Chinook, Galena and Nugget (ales and lagers), and Eroica, Progress and Target (mostly ales).

Yeast. Is yeast an ingredient? In two important ways, it is. First, while most brewers filter out yeast, some brewers don't filter at all, or filter so loosely that yeast is visible and tastable in the beer. "Bottle-conditioned" beer (or "beer on lees") and "unfiltered" draft beer contain yeast, which tends to add flavors that range from bready to dry to woody-bitter. Second, even in filtered beer, yeast leaves a ghostly trace of its earlier visit. Each yeast strain imparts its own characteristics to the beer.

However, it's also useful to view yeast as a catalyst as opposed to an ingredient. It is actually classified as a one-celled fungus, and belongs to the genus *Saccharomyces*.

Brewers buy yeast from specialty companies or cultivate their own in labs. There are dozens of strains of yeast used by brewers, each strain having different properties and effects.

Yeast is the living micro-organism, the mysterious alchemical agent, at the heart of fermentation. Yeast converts malt's fermentable sugars into alcool and carbon dioxide, among other things. In some respects, yeast is like us: it needs nutrition, and finds purpose in life by converting raw material into something new. For yeast, the nutrition required (including sugars, carbohydrates, vitamins and minerals) is also the raw material worked on.

Spices are commonly used in some of the Belgian ale styles, especially (but not only) the white (or wit or blanche) style. Coriander seed and orange (especially Curaçao) peel are often used; chamomile flowers, cumin, ginger and "aromatic" peppers are also sometimes used. Spices are finding their way into a variety of North American beers.

Buying and storing beer. The trick to buying beer, I think, goes beyond buying beer as an educated consumer. Choice is affected by shopping convenience, brand knowledge and the freshness of the beer. But it should also be affected by a sense of season, the time of day for imbibing, and the food it will accompany. Mood plays a role, as does a sense of whimsy.

Beer quality is determined many ways, but it's useful to think of two moments in time. First, at the brewery, where ingredients, brewing process and packaging are key variables, and then in the market, where method of storage and the passage of time are the key variables. Let's explore the first aspect by analyzing perceptions of cost and value.

Everyone likes a bargain, but no one should buy cheap beer. A large portion of beer sales go to what is euphemistically called the "discount" beer market. But discount from what? Unless there's price fixing, there shouldn't be a "regular" price. Beer prices should vary widely and reflect the cost of ingredients, the efficiency of the brewery, aging time, and transportation, marketing and retailing costs.

Typically, small brewers spend relatively more on labour, equipment and ingredients; large brewers spend more on marketing. In fact, marketing can form a significant portion of the cost of a mainstream brand.

With taxes on beer at 50 percent in Canada, and close to that in some of the Great Lakes states, some beer drinkers make price a key determinant in shopping.

Don't do it! Don't focus on price. Beer remains one of life's few pleasures in which you can and should ignore price and go for the best. Compared with wine or liquor, beer prices don't vary greatly. Whether the best ingredients are used or the cheapest, whether aged for twelve weeks or one, there's not much of a price spread in beer. In Canada, the most expensive beer usually costs less than three times the cheapest. In the United States, the price spread may be four to one. With wine, the multiple is about ten to one, higher for some rare wines.

For beer drinkers, this means two things. First, you can afford to drink exactly what you want, most of the time. Second, *the most costly beer is often the best bargain.* Most quality beers, made from 100 percent barley malt (or barley and wheat malt) cost less than twice the price of "discount" beer, in which more than half of the malt has been replaced by corn or rice sugars. The quality beer is therefore the better value.

If you drink moderately (a couple of bottles or pints a day, five days a week, most weeks of the year), and you start drinking when you are 18, and you live to be 90 (a reasonable assumption for moderate drinkers), you get to drink only some 36,000 bottles or pints before you die! Not half a million. Not even a hundred thousand. Just 36,000. Given this limitation, don't drink cheap. Drink the beer you want; drink the beer that provides the greatest pleasure.

Now, let's analyze the second moment when quality is determined — after beer leaves the brewery. Your goal is to buy beer that is fresh and that has been properly stored. Properly stored means at refrigerator temperature, and away from harmful fluorescent light and sunlight.

Freshness is critical to beer quality. Fresh is almost always better when it comes to beer (and most other foods), particularly for lower-alcohol beers. *Some* very high alcohol beers benefit from *some* aging.

As a food, beer has a limited shelf-life. This is especially true of good beer and low-alcohol beer. Good beer, because it's not pasteurized or too tightly filtered; low-alcohol beer, because alcohol is a natural preservative.

Here's my Four-to-Eight rule of thumb:

Four percent (alcohol by volume) beers are best consumed within eight weeks (or four "fortnights") of bottling. Eight percent beers are best consumed within eight months of bottling. Most other beers can be put on a scale between these two points, with tighter time-frames for lower alcohol beers. For example, 5 percent beers should be drunk within, say, three months of bottling; 6 percent beers within four months; and 7 percent beers within six months.

For beers with less than 4 percent alcohol — my liver and I wish there were more of them — the simple rule is, buy them only if they are very fresh, that is, less than eight weeks old.

Of course this rule implies that you know the alcohol level of a beer, and preposterously, Americans often don't. The rule also implies that you know when a beer was bottled, and sadly, we often don't, because the brewer has failed to put a clear, bottled-on date on the label. A lot of the beer sold in North America is stale. I've seen a lot of year-old 5 percent beer gathering dust in stores, waiting for a buyer. The sale of stale beer should (and usually does) alarm the brewer, but not enough, it would seem, to do something about it, that is, put a bottled-on date on the label.

What does old age do to a beer? Hop aroma fades. Malt sweetness and hop bitterness are gradually replaced by off-flavors: cabbage, cardboard (although this can come from corn adjunct), tin or iron (though a metallic aftertaste is desirable in some beers), rancid butter (bad diacetyl), or even flavors that are literally "skunky."

I said that *some* high-alcohol (that is, 8–12%) beers can benefit from

aging. Samichlaus (a Swiss lager), Thomas Hardy ale (from England), Niagara Falls' Eisbock (Ontario), Unibroue's La Fin du Monde (Quebec) and Samuel Adams' Triple Bock are some of the beers that I've seen gain in complexity with aging. I like to buy three or four bottles of these high-alcohol beers at a time, date them, store them, and open one bottle every eight or twelve months.

Some vintages, batches or even bottles of high-alcohol beer don't age well. At the first sign of the beer being past its best, I try to drink any remaining bottles quickly. Eisbock, for example, can be better — amazingly, quantum-leapingly better — after two or three years, and can be great in a so-called "vertical" tasting, that is, the simultaneous tasting of several years' versions of the same brand. I've also had eisbock that diminished from the moment it was bought.

The best indicator of freshness is not a "best before" code, but a "bottled on" date. A growing number of quality breweries are using such indicators. But even some excellent breweries don't provide them. Some brewers say there's no point in having a bottled-on (or even a best-before) date because their beer sells so quickly.

Consumers, however, know that even if rapid turnover is the usual case, there are always exceptions. And consumers themselves sometimes let beer sit around. When we find a bottle in the cellar or at the cottage, it's good to know how fresh (or stale) it is. Also, if distribution and retailing are so good that stale beer is never sold, why not prove it with a dating system?

When you bring beer home, keep it in a cool, dark place. Besides time, heat, sunlight and fluorescent light are the enemies of beer. If you're going to keep the beer for more than two weeks, keep it in a refrigerator. When possible, take beer out of the refrigerator the day before you drink it. If this sort of planning is beyond you, at least get the beer out of the fridge forty minutes before drinking, so that it will be warm enough to taste. I reduce my need for such elaborate action by keeping some of my beer in a cool, dark corner of the basement.

Buying beer in pubs and bars. The first concern for a beer drinker in choosing a pub is often the variety of beers available on tap and in bottles. I think a small pub should be able to provide draft from three or more breweries, a larger pub from as many as ten or fifteen. The trick is balance. You want competition and variety; you also want draft beer to turn over quickly. What you don't want is a "variety" of draft that all comes from the same megabrewery.

Three additional concerns for the beer drinker in a pub or bar are freshness, cleanliness of the dispensing lines and the glassware, and the honesty of the measure.

Freshness is especially important for draft beer. I like variety in a bar, but be suspicious of bars that have a huge variety of draft without the customer base to ensure quick sales. Ask your bartender or server when the keg was tapped. Other things being equal, choose the most recently tapped draft. Be suspicious of imported draft, which often contains preservatives. When you're served stale beer, tell the pub manager, and if you want to do the brewery a favor, tell the brewery. Good brewers will forego an account and remove their beer from a bar rather than have their beer sold stale.

Cleanliness. Few North American bars clean their draft lines as often as they should, which is once a week or so. Draft lines need constant cleaning. I've met bartenders who said they didn't know that beer lines ever needed cleaning! Too often, bar glasses have chlorine residue on them. This can wreck the taste of a good beer.

Honest measure. In Britain, government inspection and analysis conducted by the Campaign for Real Ale showed that 80 percent of pubs sell short-measure pints. Of course, consumers were scandalized — CAMRA called for "war" against short pints — "this costs drinkers millions of pounds a day." In Europe, measures are taken very seriously, as they should be. Trustworthy measures are fundamental to effective commerce.

Few North Americans, however, are aware of or concerned about honesty in beer measures. We should be. In California, Weights and Measures officials determined that the 16-ounce glasses made by a major supplier held only 14 ounces. In this case, pub owners took action to ensure that their customers got full measure.

In Canada, incredibly, it appears that no government agency is responsible for ensuring that pub-goers get full measure. The obvious folks — the federal government — say that a "pint" isn't even a measure. Rather it's just "jargon, used interchangeably with other terms such as mug or jar." In other words, a pint of beer needn't contain a pint. The government says that this state of affairs is "acceptable when it is commonly understood that one is not purporting to deliver a specified quantity." I wonder if it's commonly understood that a pint isn't a specified quantity. What, exactly, is a pub purporting to do when it advertises "pints" of beer?

I'm not sure how widespread the short measure problem is in the United States, but I have seen many pubs that use the term "pint" in their price list, and use non-standard glasses. Many American bars use terms that avoid measure or comparison, such as "regular" and "large."

Over the past decade, I've been served short measure in many bars. Part of the problem is that two systems of measurement, imperial and metric, co-exist, and part of the problems is that the governments in the United States and Canada don't take enforcement very seriously. Part of the problem is lack of interest (or perhaps the wrong kind of interest) on the part of pub managers. Some bar managers have no idea what a pint or a litre is. Part of the problem is that beer drinkers themselves are not demanding or knowledgeable enough.

What can draft drinkers do to protect themselves at the pub? One way to take an authentic pint glass with you into a pub, pour the pub pint into your pint, and compare. Alternatively, you can use the known quantity of a bottle to check the purported capacity of a draft glass. If you discover short measure, a good pub manager will want to know, and will change glass suppliers.

If beer weren't taxed, measures wouldn't matter so much; buying draft would be a value-for-money judgment between two contracting parties. When you are given short measure of draft in a pub, however, you're paying too much tax.

Until bars and pubs use glasses with measures, imperial or metric, marked on them, it's buyer beware.

Savoring and evaluating beer. Anyone can — and almost everyone does — enjoy beer. Thank goodness for that. Isn't it good to know that enjoyment can still be had without a string of credentials? To really appreciate beer, however, does require knowledge. Put differently, your enjoyment of beer can be increased — dramatically, I think — simply by learning. No matter how much you like beer, you can work at (if that's the right term) enjoying it more.

Essentially, savoring and evaluating consist of paying close sensory attention to several aspects of a beer, attaching words to the sensations, and placing these sense impressions within the larger context of beer style characteristics. The short-term result is an appreciation of a beer's unique qualities. Over time, the result is a deepening of your knowledge of beer, which in turn leads to a greater capacity for appreciation.

Doesn't an analytic approach to beer spoil the fun? "Do not all charms fly / At the mere touch of cold philosophy? . . . Philosophy will clip an Angel's wings, / Conquer all mysteries by rule and line" was John Keats's take on this point of view. But with all due respect to Mr. Keats, the point of view is horsefeathers.

Experience shows us that putting any sensory pleasure in a broader philosophic context, or twinning any pleasure with knowledge, will amplify the pleasure. Keats himself knew this, though he sometimes pretended otherwise. He wrote that philosophic truths are only really true when "they are proved upon our pulses." Well, sure. What we know, or want to believe as truth, must be tested in experience. Truth and experience speak to each other.

There are many sad aspects to Keats's life. One of them is that he never had the chance to sit down and think about the wonders of Great Lakes' Holy Moses or Brooklyn's Chocolate Stout, or Unibroue's Gaillarde or Wellington County's Real Ale. If he had, surely he'd agree that philosophy, now seen as warm and friendly, can create its own charms. Close examination of a beer (or a Monarch butterfly or a Bach cantata) deepens our wonder and allows us to soar with the angels (or at least the lesser orders of angels). The trick is not to use too rigid a "line and rule."

Note taking is essential for beer evaluation, and a useful tool even when you are "only" savoring beer. I've used a variety of note-taking methods, but the simplest is to note at the top of a page the brand name, style information, alcohol level, other pertinent information from the label and then a few lines each for appearance, aroma, taste, and other impressions. In a blind tasting, it can be useful and fun to add a quantitative element.

I sometimes use a twenty-point scale, with four for aroma, ten for taste, and six for overall enjoyment and fidelity to style. There are many possible variations, and you may want to devise your own rating system. For beer savoring, disregard the numeric aspect, and take qualitative and descriptive notes.

To evaluate a beer, I suggest something along the lines of the following procedure. To simply savor a beer, skip the first step.

Devise a beer grouping. A given beer is best evaluated with at least one other beer to allow comparison. The beers should be of the same style. A beer grouping can include two, three or four different labels. Given the volume of beer you have on hand, it's often best to evaluate beer with friends. It's also fun, and discussion helps you develop your beer knowledge. It adds interest if you put an import or a homebrewed beer into the grouping.

Serve the beer properly. If you don't own good beer glasses, buy some. Different beer glass styles have evolved for some of the beer styles, for example, a "sleeve" for bitter, a thin fluted glass for wheat, a tulip-shaped glass for some of the stronger Belgian beers. I've got about 40 glasses of various shapes, plus about 40 simple small sleeves (bought at the five and ten) for tastings. Good beer glasses greatly enhance beer pleasure; they add to the aesthetics, the aroma and the taste. They can help a beer to retain its head and to show off its colors.

A good start to a beer glass collection is six to eight clear sleeves or elongated tulip-shaped glasses. You need clear glass to appreciate a beer's appearance, and a shape that will trap aroma. Over time, you can add to this collection so that you have at least one suitable glass for each beer style. North American brewers often sell glasses. Many of them are attractive, but few, in comparison with Belgian or German glasses, have been designed specifically for a given beer.

Research has been done on the relationship between glass shape and appreciation. The serious beer fan can read up on this research, but anyone can perform the simple experiment of serving the same beer in two or three different glasses. You might be surprised at the difference a glass can make to aroma and taste perception, not to mention appearance. The shape of the glass, both the part that holds the liquid and the part that holds the bouquet, is important. The shape of the rim and how it directs the liquid is also important. I even think the smoothness and the density of the glass is important, at least in the tactile aspect of beer appreciation.

Use beer glasses for beer only, and wash them with plain hot water — no detergent! Milk, coffee, tea and detergent can leave residue on glass that will taint beer. Don't wipe these glasses dry. Allow them to drain and air-dry. If a beer glass gets "contaminated" (when your six-year-old pours soda or milk into it), you can "cure" the glass by washing it with warm water, then fill-ing it with warm salty water and letting it sit for ten minutes. Rinse the glass with hot water, and your glass should be "beer clean."

All the beers in your beer grouping should be served at the same temperature. If you have a cool cellar, get to know it better; learn which corners are relatively cool and which are relatively warm. If you do have a cool basement or cellar, you can easily serve beer at a temperature that enhances the flavor and aroma of the beer. The key to proper temperature is moderation. Good beer should never be refrigerator-cold.

I prefer my beers a few degrees warmer than is commonly advised. I think that most lagers should be served at 12–14° C (54–56° F) and ales at 14–16° C (57–60° F). Both suggested ranges are within the range of what is known as "cellar temperature."

Pour three or four ounces (90–120 ml) into the glass, roughly enough to get a one- or two-finger head. The head of a beer is important, both for aesthetic reasons and because the head helps prevent oxidation of the liquid. (Oxidation is one of the reasons that the last few mouthfuls of a beer drunk slowly can have a metallic bitterness.)

The glass should not be full. You want to leave room for the bouquet.

Listen to the beer. The sound a beer makes as its head collapses can provide useful information. Generally, the quieter a beer is, the better. A head that collapses quickly and noisily is often the mark of a beer with inadequate malt or hops or too much adjunct ("head-stabilizing agents," usually a type of gum, are sometimes used by breweries to try to mask this problem). It may also be the mark of the beer being stale or the glass being dirty. Knowing the distinctive sound that a given beer usually makes can help you to recognize problems like staling, improper storage, and dirty glassware when you hear more noise than usual.

Look at the beer carefully. The color of a beer in different lights is a pleasing aesthetic experience, but don't postpone for too long the next step, smelling the beer.

Bubbles in the beer and in the head itself should usually be small, often the smaller the better. Copious, large bubbles rising in the beer are often a telltale sign of artificial carbonation.

Note stability, that is, how long it takes for the head to collapse. Most beers should have some head left after 45 to 50 seconds. Many poor ones don't.

Note also whether there's any "lace," sometimes called Belgian or Brussels lace — the beautiful and intricate pattern of head residue — clinging to the sides of the glass as you drink the beer. Good lacing is often a good indicator of the quality of a beer. No lace at all can mean inadequate malt (it can also mean chlorine or other contaminant on the glass).

Smell the beer more than once. Your nose can detect one molecule of scent in a sample of a million molecules. An educated nose can identify 10,000 aromas.

Because the "aromatics" of a beer diminish rapidly,

you need to smell the beer quickly after you pour it. It's probably best to do your visual evaluation at the same time as your olfactory (aroma) evaluation. The most common odors in beer bouquets are those associated with malt (caramel, toffee, grain, fruit and many others), and hops (grass, hay, wood, forest, spice, herbs and others). Eighty percent of a beer's flavor can be detected in the aroma, so smelling is important for formal evaluation as well as for sheer pleasure. In a negative sense, faults in the aroma are almost always confirmed in the flavor. If you don't notice much aroma, let the beer warm up.

Taste the beer "front" to "back." Take a sip and think with your tongue. Using your own language, or the words in the lexicon at the end of this book, think about the initial impression that the beer makes on your tongue. Generally, sweet flavors are most noticeable at the front of the tongue, bitter flavors at the back, sour flavors at the side. Try to note flavor characteristics more than good/bad, like/dislike. But don't be afraid to use like/dislike — that's a good place to start.

Take another sip, and pay attention to the initial taste before you swallow, as well as any possible differences in flavor after you swallow (the "finish," or aftertaste). Most beers have an aftertaste that is different, sometimes quite different, from the taste. The aftertaste of a beer is one of its many pleasures, notwithstanding some of the claims made for "dry" beers. (Imagine boasting, as the large brewers have done, that your beer has no aftertaste! It's like a theologian boasting that a religion has no afterlife!) Some beers have a "middle," a change in flavor just as and after you swallow. Many pale ales, for example, have some fruit tartness in the swallow. Again, try to attach precise terms to the taste and aftertaste.

Swirl the glass to release the aroma, and smell again.

Take a third sip, swirling it in your mouth, and think about the various flavors in relation to each other. Ask yourself: Are the flavors complementary? Is the overall impression balanced? Is the change in flavor from start to finish dramatic? Subtle? Suitable? Intriguing? Before you swallow, breathe in some air: this will boost the impression made on your tongue and your nose. Your sense of taste and smell diminishes over time during a tasting, but "resting" your senses for 15 seconds will help to recharge them a little. Make notes. See if you can come up with at least three words to describe the aroma, three to describe the taste, two to describe the finish, and a phrase to distill how the beer strikes you overall.

The goal of the process is to place the beer in the context of its style, to describe its unique character, to decide how successful the beer seems to you, and to be able to articulate why.

The beer drinker's learning curve. In the 19th century, it was considered amusing to publish something called an "Inebriometer": Temperate, Steady, Tight, Corned, Drunk ("half seas over") and Dead Drunk ("Can lie on the ground without holding"). In a similar vein, the "Drunkard's Progress" was published to illustrate the path to alcoholic degradation (both are reproduced in Schivelbusch). In like but temperate spirit, I present the beer drinker's learning curve, a sketch of the beer pilgrim's progress through the trav-ales of life.

1. The formative years. Too young to drink legally, the child still learns a good deal about alcohol and food in the home. An eight-year-old, a Lego spaceship in hand, watches his father. "What's that?" he says, pointing to the strange, mousse-capped thing in Dad's hand. Amber light emanates from the glass. "It's beer. Would you like a sip?" "Yes, please. Dad, is there light in beer?"

2. First contact. The beer drinker consumes, underage and without much thought, and often without any appreciation, hundreds of litres of beer. Most of this beer is a single, heavily advertised brand, call it Brand X. He (we will focus here on the male beer drinker's learning curve) is uncomfortable when served (by a friend's father, who dresses funny and doesn't know anything) another brand of beer. It's warm and bitter. Brands other than X taste "weird." He cannot name the ingredients in beer, and believes that beer was invented by a major corporation.

3. Frat boy party drinking. At this stage of life, our hero believes that other people are impressed by, and interested in, the amount of beer he consumed the previous night. Beer "culture," such as it is, consists of a strong fidelity to X, competitive chugging, and tossing crushed beer cans, basketball-like, into a basket.

4. Something happens, consciousness arrives. A trip to Germany maybe, or a year in Britain, or living by chance with a housemate who brews beer. Maybe it's simply trying, with an open mind, one of North America's great beers, or maybe it's going out on a date with a woman who is a big wheat beer fan. Suddenly or slowly, against the background of a tympani roll and a starburst, or a tune that works its way into your mind and won't let go, the beer drinker awakens. He has been bowled over by an all-malt beer. The effect is that of a person who has had his first romantic kiss. The beer drinker cannot contain his happiness.

5. Obsession and new monogamy. X no longer satisfies; it's gassy and tasteless. X is like one of those childhood friends that one outgrows: embarrassing, gauche and crude. The beer drinker is deeply, madly in love with a new brand. In the throes of love, he says cruel things about his former companion (it wasn't love, he now realizes). The object of his affection costs a little more, but he tells himself that no price is too high for true love. "You get what you pay for," he tells his friends, "and you only live once." He tells his friends, repeatedly, about the glories of his new beer, about its profound and varied pleasures.

6. Infidelity. A few months later, the beer drinker is in a bar, and his love cannot be found (whose fault, this?). Recklessly, and without hope of satisfaction, he asks for . . . That one, that

tap handle right there ... Another brand! Awkwardly at first, without enthusiasm, he sips. It's *not at all* like his love. It is disturbingly, annoyingly dissimilar. And yet. And yet there's something there, something fetching, or (dare he think it?) more than fetching. There's something downright seductive about this new beer. What's it called again? Sure, he'll have another.

7. Promiscuity. The beer drinker has his old love and his new love *in the same evening.* Two nights later, he meets another wonderful beer. And, at his friend's house, where he finds himself one afternoon (it is the same friend with the funny-dressing, know-nothing father), he meets two more fine beers. "Is there no end to this?" he wonders. Apparently not. He buys a beer fridge and a few beer books. There is a whole world of beer out there, he discovers.

8. Ardor, proselytization, snobbery. Now a (slightly tiresome) crusader for good beer, the beer drinker owns a shelf of beer books, has joined a beer club, and haunts the beer store, looking for new brands. He will not even enter restaurants that sell only X and similar brands. "Wet air" he calls them. Like a religious zealot, he sermonizes to all and sundry. He grimaces when he sees a friend pour a good beer into a plastic tumbler. He seriously considers buying a new house within walking distance of a pub that sells Real Ale. He goes to beer tastings and plans all his holidays around beer festivals. His old friends find him a little preachy and a little stuck up.

9. Equilibrium regained. An ardent beer fan, and a curious and well-educated beer drinker, he still won't drink boring beer, even when it's free, but he is more accepting of the other beer drinkers, who, after all, live in a fallen world. Some of them grew up with lousy parenting, he reflects. Live and let live, he thinks.

Our hero may marry his girlfriend. He'll never marry a beer. When it comes to suds, he'll play the field. Quality and variety are his watchwords.

BREWERIES AND BEERS

A baedeker is a guide. Last century, Karl Baedeker (1801–1859) published a series of touring guidebooks "noted for their reliability and thoroughness." They were a success because people found them useful. I'm not sure how reliable or thorough my descriptions and comments are; I do hope you find them useful.

States and provinces are in alphabetical order, as are breweries within each jurisdiction and the brands for each brewery. For each brand, a star rating is given, and alcohol-by-volume and original gravity (OG) is noted. I've listed the ingredients, as given me by the brewer, for every brand I could. I've used the terms used by the brewer, for example, crystal or carastan, victory or biscuit malt.

Some brewers would not divulge ingredients; some brewers would not reveal a specialty malt or hop. Most brewers were very obliging. Parenthetically, I think it's important to note that brewers who won't divulge ingredients are working against the long-term good of their business and of beer culture. The more knowledgeable beer drinkers are, the more we'll see beer culture flourish. To put it negatively, treating beer ingredients as an industrial secret destructively "repositions" beer. It separates beer from its agricultural and culinary contexts.

I hope the technical information helps you to understand a little more about beer. I hope that some day soon, all brewers provide, somewhere on the packaging, the alcohol level, the original gravity, and all the ingredients used for each beer. And I hope that it won't be long before nutritional profiles are also available for the interested consumer.

The rating scheme. Herr Baedeker was the first person to use a star system to indicate "places of interest according to their historic or aesthetic importance."

I've used a five-star system to rate the beers:

★★★★★   A classic, hinting at heaven. Excellence in every technical regard, and a flair for using the art of brewing to make the beer unique, seductive, and worthy of contemplation. Arouses desire and satisfies it.

★★★★1/2   Excellent and exciting; lots to admire and think about, endless possibilities to enjoy. Technically perfect; art of the brewer apparent.

★★★★   Excellent and well-crafted, with elements of excitement, faithfully representing the beer's style or pioneering new style properties.

★★★½	Very good, very satisfying, elements of interest.
★★★	Good. Good technical properties and honestly brewed.
★★½	Fair, enjoyable, no major defects. May lack balance or distinctive character; may suffer from over-use of adjunct.
★★	Drinkable. Shows economy of ingredients, or shortcuts in brewing, or lack of distinctive character; often has identifiable defects.
★½	Drinkable only to the thirsty or undemanding; "lawnmower beer"; inadequate malt, overuse of adjunct; poor carbonation.
★	Bad. Adjunct-laden beverage with few beer characteristics; lacks malt and hop flavor.
½★	Awful. Thoroughly noxious; should not be called "beer"; warrants laboratory analysis.

In evaluating beer, I'm always impressed by the generous use of malt, by the adroit use of quality malt, and by deft hopping, which involves both choice of hop variety and timing of use in brewing. Like all beer lovers, I look for character in a beer; I look for a subtle balance between uniqueness and fit within a style. Aroma is important, as are some technical properties, especially the appearance and the sound of the head. Plain, old-fashioned enjoyment and drinkability are very important. When I find all these traits in a beer, I get excited.

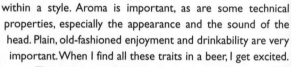

The ratings are largely a function of style. I tend to mark a beer down when it doesn't live up to its advertised style unless it seems to me that the brewer is "pushing" the style, widening its parameters. Sometimes ale is mislabeled lager, and vice versa. Brewers shouldn't do this, but I don't mark a beer down for this alone. When a beer pretends to a precise style, I judge the beer accordingly.

All ratings are based on world standards. Some readers may think I've been severe with some brands; others may think I've been too kind. I'd ask the former to remember that most brewing nations make a little excellent beer, a lot of pretty good beer, and some truly awful stuff. It's no help to the brewers (or the drinkers) of this region to rate beers by soft standards. To readers who think I've been too generous, I'd remind them that, with few exceptions, I've only included beers that are at least worth a try. Also, if you discover less in a beer than what you read here, it may be because the beer is too cold or the beer is stale. Contrariwise, I may have had a stale sample. Most, but not all, of the beers evaluated here were obtained fresh from the brewery.

Of course you'll disagree with some of the ratings. Good. *De gustibus certe disputandum est!* Think about your disagreement, and try to put it into words. This will help you develop your beer knowledge. You may find it useful to note comments and your own ratings in the margins of the guide.

The Pleasure-to-Alcohol Ratio. You'll note that for some of the beers, I've included something called the pleasure-to-alcohol ratio. It requires explanation. Although I drink a lot of beer, I try to show my liver some respect. I've always believed that with higher levels of alcohol, I should get higher rewards — more complexity and greater depth of flavor. Likewise, with lower-alcohol beers: when a beer with 4-percent alcohol by volume delivers as much flavor and depth as a 5-percent beer of similar character, I'll think more highly of the lower-alcohol beer.

Mild, which is getting harder to find in England, but which will find a place at the margins of the Real Ale scene in North America, and ordinary bitter are but two examples of beer styles that can deliver a lot of flavor with relatively low alcohol. On the other hand, brewers can achieve some forms of depth, complexity and intensity of flavor only with higher levels of alcohol. That's why some world classics are significantly higher than average in alcohol. They become classics not because of their alcohol levels, but because their rewards are commensurate with, or exceed, their alcohol levels.

I've noted the ratio for some, but not all, of the higher- and lower-alcohol beers.

The ratio connotes 10 to 10 as the norm. A ratio of 12 to 10 means that the beer is 20 percent more rewarding, in my opinion, than my subjective, benchmark expectations for a beer of that alcohol level within the given style. The ratio is a completely personal judgment. I hope that it's a useful tool for the thoughtful beer drinker.

MICHIGAN

Perhaps because its automotive industry is so famous, Michigan isn't as well known as it should be for its water wealth. This, despite being surrounded by four of the five Great Lakes. Michigan leads the United States in terms of pleasure boats and public golf courses, both of which bring to mind beer. Why, then, has Michigan so few breweries?

The first European influence on Michigan was French. Even today, cities (Detroit, or *ville d'étroit*, which means city of the straight; Sault Ste. Marie, which means Saint Mary's rapids), rivers (the St. Clair), and even cars (Sieur Antoine de la Mothe Cadillac founded the city of Detroit) bear the mark of the French on Michigan's early colonial history. British influence grew until the late 18th century; Michigan didn't become part of the United States until 1796.

Michigan's commercial beer history is relatively recent. By the 1820s, beer was being brewed on a commercial basis in Detroit. In 1836 the Detroit Brewery advertised to buy a substantial amount of barley, 20,000 bushels. The completion of the Erie Canal in 1825 made Michigan a gateway for the sale of hops to brewers further west. The state's first lager appears to have been brewed around 1848, in Detroit, by Frederick Ams, a German immigrant. By the end of the 19th century, the Stroh brewery was a substantial presence in Michigan.

Most of the state's breweries are very young, many having opened in 1995. Sadly, the oldest operating brewery, Frankenmuth (in the city of the same name founded by beer-loving Bavarian settlers in 1845), was destroyed by a tornado a month before I had hoped to visit it. The fact that local, quality brewing has only recently been revived in Michigan reflects the ages of the brewers themselves — most are in their 20s or 30s.

Retailing is competitive. Locally produced beer as well as imports can be bought in what are inelegantly known as "party stores." Single bottles can be purchased. Some of the small breweries complain about the distribution system, which is seen to be of greater benefit to large brewers than small. "It's a nightmare," one brewer said, complaining about distributors who left his brewery's beer in the heat or let it go stale in the warehouse.

There isn't yet a tremendously wide variety of beer styles being brewed in Michigan, but this will change.

● AUGUST BREWING COMPANY

Box 665
Harbor Springs, Michigan, 49740
1-800-305-0070
Year started: 1995
Tours available: phone ahead
Glassware and merchandise available

Like many other people, Pete A. Stenger developed a taste for beer through traveling. An auditor at a large accounting firm, his travels exposed him to an ever-wider variety of beer. And, like many other brewery founders, his interest in commercial brewing was an extension of his interest in homebrewing. Stenger did a lot of his homebrewing in brew-on-premise facilities in Windsor, Ontario.

August is a contract brewery with a small development facility near Harbor Springs, Michigan. Its bottled beer is brewed and packaged in the Midwest.

Part of Stenger's goal is to get Americans to see beer as part of a larger cultural tradition. He wants people to know that "beer is a natural part of family life and life with friends." Within the "spectrum of good food flavors," says Stenger, "there's always a place for beer."

Thomas Manley Amber Lager ★★★¹/₂

4.5% alc./vol.
O.G.: 1049
Ingredients: six-row and two-row pale
and caramel malts; dextrin; Nugget and
Styrian Gold hops

This enjoyable, pasteurized lager has some flavor similarities to the Munich style. Appearance: reddish mid-dark amber, with a yellowish beige head that leaves good lacing. Aroma: toffee, apricot, hint of peat, some appropriate diacetyl. Taste: given the aroma, surprisingly smoky. Starts with a butterscotch or toffee impression, with some balancing toastiness and smoky flavors. Hop astringency shows midpalate. The finish is marked by some hop taste, some acidity, and some nice six-row huskiness.

Thomas Manley Bronze Lager ★★★

4.5% alc./vol.
O.G.: 1046
Ingredients: six-row and two-row pale
and caramel malts; dextrin; Saaz and
Mt. Hood hops

Here's a beer to show that simple lagers can have body and flavor. Appearance: light to mid amber; pale beige, quiet, stable head; good lacing. Aroma: a good balance of caramel, dry graininess and hayish hops, plus hints of plum. Taste:

caramel, lightly toasted grain, and slightly acerbic plumminess (almost apricot) fading to a mild earthy-woody bitterness. Medium body, medium viscosity. Good overall profile for a simple, easy-to-drink beer.

● BIG BUCK BREWERY

550 Wisconsin South
Gaylord, Michigan, 49735
517-732-5781
Capacity: 20,000 barrels
Year started: 1995
Tours available: scheduled and on request
Glassware and merchandise available

Scott Graham, Big Buck's brewer, sees his work as part of an emerging "third wave" of brewing. The first wave was when small, local breweries dotted the map. In the second wave, national breweries came to dominate the North American beer scene. The third wave brings us back to the idea of brewing as a local business.

Graham says he is "not a beer historian nor a slave to historic beer styles." He has a marketing background, and tries to understand what will sell. "My business is not just making beer, but selling it." He also thinks that in areas such as Michigan, where the public is rediscovering beer variety, part of the brewer's job is to "help people expand their horizons." One of Graham's beer passions is making seasonal beers.

The Big Buck brewery is part of a large (almost 30,000-square-foot) facility that includes a steakhouse, a special events tent, and a striking four-storey silo built and painted to resemble a bottle of beer. The pub-restaurant features many seasonal beer styles on tap; these I found very drinkable. The brewery itself bottles one beer and may add others to its packaged lineup.

Big Buck Beer ★★★
5% alc./vol.
O.G.: 1052
Ingredients: two-row pale malt;
corn flakes; Chinook, Cluster
and Cascade hops

Appearance: straw colored; near-white, very quiet and stable head. Aroma: dry grain, light hops, paper, dry leaves. Taste: although technically an ale (ale yeast is used), this is a good take on a mainstream lager, with adjunct well done. To start, a lightly bitter grain-cereal impression. Modest malt sweetness turns dry mid-palate, with some hop taste and astringency. Finish: mild hop taste and bitterness. 18 IBUs.

BOYNE RIVER BREWING COMPANY

419 E. Main Street
Boyne City, Michigan, 49712
616-582-5588
Capacity: 1,000 barrels
Year started: 1995
Tours available: phone ahead
Glassware and merchandise available

"Laid-back ales — it's sort of our motto — and pretty well describes our brewing philosophy," says Scott Hill, the brewer at Boyne River. That, and the fact that "we like to sell the freshest draft available."

Hill and his wife, Cyndi, own and manage this tiny brewery, as well as the small, homey pub-restaurant in the same building, which was built as a barn ninety years ago. The Hills wanted to live and work in a small town, and to make beer with "no hype, no fluff. We wanted to create a pub, a family-oriented place, not a bar," says Hill.

Most of Boyne River's equipment was bought from the defunct Home Towne brewery of London, Ontario. Suitably, the brewery opened on July 1, Canada's national holiday, in 1995. About a third of the tiny brewery's production is sold on tap in the pub, a third in bottled form, and the rest on draft in other pubs.

The brewery doesn't filter its beer. The reason, Hill says, is to keep things simple and because filtration equipment takes up space. In addition to the two beers described below, Hill brews seasonals, and he plans to add a cherry wheat beer to the line of bottled beers — a natural choice, as Boyne City is in Michigan's tart-cherry-growing area.

Brown Ale ★★★1/2

4% alc./vol.
O.G.: 1052
Ingredients: two-row pale, crystal and chocolate malts; malted wheat; Chinook and Fuggles hops

Scott Hill says that in terms of style, this ale is similar to a mild. I'd agree, and a very soft, malty and drinkable ale it is, too. Appearance: dark amber with some orange; mocha-colored head. The aroma is very fresh: barley grain, roasted malt, cut grass or leaves, and with just a hint of café-mocha. Taste: initially, a strong toffee-caramel impression, with soft fruit (peaches?) evident. Hops show in a bit of astringency midpalate. In the finish, there's the taste and the unfiltered feel of hops on the tongue, with gently rising bitterness.

Lake Trout Stout ★★★¹/₂

4.5% alc./vol.
O.G.: 1050
Ingredients: two-row pale and black
malts; roasted barley, flaked barley and
malted wheat; Chinook hops

Appearance: cola color; very dark mocha-colored head. Aroma: wonderful. In
equal measures, I smell dark chocolate, roasted grain, toffee, and a balance of hop
grassiness and flowers. Taste: to start, dark grain dryness and toastiness, mocha,
fruit (plum, prune) and hop flavor. To finish, moderately bitter, with the taste of
hops and hints of toffee and walnut. This hoppy, chocolaty stout would go well
with not-too-sweet chocolate desserts.

● DUSTER'S MICRO-BREWERY

114 N. Main Street
Lawton, Michigan, 49065
616-624-3771
Capacity: 2,000 barrels
Year started: 1993
Glassware and merchandise available

"We don't try to copy anybody and we don't make any wimpy beer," Phil Balog
says firmly but amiably.

Balog and his wife, Jody, were on a ski trip in Colorado when they visited a
brewpub, got "hooked on the beer," and thought that brewing might be a good
business. Back in Michigan, Balog decided to start homebrewing, and when a
homebrew supplies store went out of business, he bought . . . well, he bought
enough brewing supplies to brew a lot of beer. As he homebrewed, he worked on
the idea of opening a small brewery.

The idea has come to fruition in a very attractive pub and brewery in the
town of Lawton in southwest Michigan. (Also on the main street of Lawton are
huge grape-juice vats; this is grape country.) The brewery is in a building that formerly housed a meat market, a bank, a drugstore and a hardware store. Attention
to detail shows in Balog's restoration. Copper and wood are the main materials
in the pub, which takes up a little more than half the floor space; the brewery
takes the rest. Aviation bric-a-brac and photographs of airplanes on the walls
reflect Balog's other job — crop dusting.

"We draw on German and English influences, but within the context of an
all-ale brewery," says Balog. He brews strictly to please his own taste, not to chase
the market. As a result, it has taken a while for the brewery to build a following.
But Balog believes that in the long run, as people discover the beers by word of
mouth, his uncompromising approach will pay off. Almost in spite of himself,
perhaps to test whether he could improve on word-of-mouth advertising, Balog
had a billboard put up on the nearby interstate highway. "A waste of money," he
concluded.

Balog says that some people see in his approach an attitude problem. However, he says — and in small print, Duster's beer labels indicate — "our ale is better than our attitude."

Classic Brown Ale ★★★

Appearance: dark brown with burgundy highlights; café-au-lait-colored, fairly quiet head. Aroma: roasted malt, with hints of grass, earth and licorice. Taste: soft toffee with earthy tones; a fair dustin' of hops shows early in flavor and bitterness. The finish is strongly grassy-hoppy.

Hop Head Red Ale ★★★★

"I'm so hoppy for you" says the label. But don't let this or the brand name scare you. This is a balanced pale ale or ESB, with hops nicely noticeable, and nicely prominent in the finish. Appearance: reddish amber; café-au-lait-colored, quiet and stable head; very good lacing. Aroma: clear, fresh hoppiness over an apricot-toffee base. Taste: starts soft, with caramel and peach-plum, and some hop taste and astringency. Hop taste and moderate hop bitterness mark the finish. Some metal and hop dust in the aftertaste.

Imperial Oatmeal Stout ★★★★

Appearance: dark cola-brown; mocha-colored, quiet and stable head; good lacing. Aroma: roasted cereal, baker's chocolate, prunes-raisins, grass, and a hint of coffee. Like thick chocolate shakes? Like hops? Here's your stout. This big-bodied stout has a big chocolate taste and is aggressively hopped. In the sweetish chocolaty start, some fruit (plums, dates) is evident, as is caramel and a hint of molasses. Then, a bit of acid, nice earthy-peaty tones, some roasty biscuit notes, and then, as if left by a hopped-up racing car, a bitter, hoppy skid mark in the mouth.

Wing-Over Ale ★★★¹/2

Appearance: mid amber; very light beige, quiet and stable head. Aroma: dry graininess and hop bitterness, caramel, hints of fruit tartness and peat. Taste: overall, soft and caramelly, offset by bitter earthiness. To start, butterscotch, apricot, and hop astringency, all nicely balanced. To finish, rising hop taste and a nice earthy-peaty bitterness. Medium body and lower-than-average viscosity make this very quaffable. Limit yourself to one pint when flying low.

● KING BREWING COMPANY

895 Oakland Avenue
Pontiac, Michigan, 48340
810-745-5900
Capacity: 2,200 barrels
Year started: 1995
Tours available: phone ahead
Glassware and merchandise available.

Scott J. King, president and brewer at King Brewing, is low-key in describing his company's aims and ambitions: "We're not reinventing beer. We're giving options to people who haven't had a lot of choice when it comes to beer.

"If people are happy with your beer, well, that's what it's all about, not whether you get so many stars in a guide. When you're working your seventy-fifth hour of the week, it can get to be a bit too much, but it is a fun business. I don't treat beer as if it's some rare commodity. It's beer. It's meant to be enjoyed. I like to make beer simple and have some fun."

King uses one yeast strain: "My experience tells me that a single yeast is safer and helps avoid the acid-wash taste." King first got interested in beer as a home-brewer at college, where he was a philosophy major. As he traveled in Colorado and Washington states, he was exposed to a variety of good beer from various independent breweries, and it was then the brewery bug bit him.

King Brewing is one of the few breweries I've seen that sells homebrewing supplies — a good idea, I think.

About 60 percent of production is bottled, 40 percent kegged. As to the future, King Brewing hopes simply to keep brewing, to celebrate the brewery's anniversaries, and to "be a local brewery serving a local market."

Crown Brown Ale ★★★★

5.5% alc./vol.
O.G.: 1052
Ingredients: two-row pale, crystal, cara-
pils and chocolate malts; Bullion hops

Appearance: dark brown with burgundy-red highlights; beige head; good lacing. I find the aroma seductive: toffee, mocha, peat, baker's chocolate, vanilla, fruit. Crown has a medium body and low-medium viscosity, making it very drinkable. Initially, what are normally undertones — peat, toastiness, mocha, a touch of vanilla — are in fact the main flavors, dominating the caramel-plum-apricot base. To finish, a dry, mildly bitter graininess, with suggestions of hops, roasted nuts and licorice root. A lovely beer, suitable for any coronation.

King's Pale Ale ★★★

5.5% alc./vol.
O.G.: 1052
Ingredients: two-row pale, crystal and
chocolate malts; Chinook, Kent
Goldings and Fuggles hops

This beer illustrates a common progression in ales: a sweet stage, a sour stage and
a bitter stage. In each stage, one flavor predominates, but the other two elements
are still apparent. Orangey mid-amber in color; pale beige, quiet and stable head.
Apricot and caramel aroma, with a hint of floral Goldings. Taste starts sweetish
with caramel and apricot. Midpalate, some sourness and tartness (not-quite-ripe
plums) cut the sweetness and hint at the bitterness to come. To finish, a grassy
bitterness (32–35 IBUs), magnified a little by lingering tartness.

Pontiac Porter ★★★¹/₂

5.5% alc./vol.
O.G.: 1058
Ingredients: two-row pale, crystal
and chocolate malts; roasted barley;
Fuggles hops

Cola-colored liquid; mocha-colored, quiet, stable head. Aroma: toffee, prunes,
tar, baker's chocolate. Medium-bodied and dryish, Pontiac starts dry and toasty,
with caramel and a hint of plum-prune. To finish, bang-on moderate bitterness,
mostly hops, some grain.

Royal Amber Ale ★★★¹/₂

5% alc./vol.
O.G.: 1048
Ingredients: two-row pale, crystal and
carapils malts; roasted barley; Bullion
and Fuggles hops

Appearance: orangey mid-amber; pale beige, quiet and stable head; good lacing.
Aroma: apricot, dried apricot, toffee, hints of peat and roasted nuts. Taste: a viscous, medium body accentuates the initial caramel and apricot impression; a nice
dry-bitter oakiness is also evident in the start. Royal Amber finishes earthy and
oaky, with some hop taste, almost tannic astringency, and a bit too much acid. A
bit fizzy. A good session beer, and the fruit-oak elements would make this one go
well with many cheeses.

● Motor City Brewing Works

470 West Canfield
Detroit, Michigan, 48201
313-832-2700
Capacity: 5,000 barrels
Year started: 1995
Tours available: phone ahead

In Central Detroit, near Wayne State University, at the back of a parking lot across the street from a popular restaurant called the Traffic Jam and Snug, in an anonymous-looking, cinder-block building, is a small brewery. Motor City Brewing Works is a vanguard brewery, Detroit's first brewery in modern times.

The origins of MCBW lie in earlier ambitions. The Traffic Jam and Snug built a small stand-alone brewery to supply beer for its own patrons. Rather late in the game, however, that is, after the brewery was built, the State of Michigan denied owner Ben Edwards a license. Eventually, a small brewery called Detroit & Mackinac leased the property, and, properly licensed, made beer until the brewer, Tom Burns, died. When D & M ceased to operate, two former Traffic Jam employees, Steve Rouse and John Linardos, started a new company with a view to using the D & M location and equipment.

Stephen Rouse (a brewer's surname, that), MCBW's brewer, says that he'd like to make "as close to a natural ale as we can achieve. It's a reaction against boring, tasteless, mainstream beer." The brewery uses only Reinheitsgebot ingredients and doesn't do any filtration. Three quarters of production is bottled; a quarter is sold on tap.

Like Rouse, partner John Linardos is in his 20s. I ask him about the young brewery's goals for the future. "Just to get the bank loan paid off," he says matter-of-factly. The youth of the two partners means that they have many years of brewing ahead of them. This fact, and the brewery's orientation to unfiltered beer, will make Motor City an interesting Brewing Works to follow over the years.

Honey Porter ★★★¹/₂

7% alc./vol.
O.G.: 1061
Ingredients: two-row pale, caramel,
chocolate, black and victory malts;
clover honey; Northern Brewer or Perle,
and Willamette hops

I'm not crazy about the honey craze sweeping the beer world, but here's an ale in which I like the clover hints. Appearance: dark cola color; mocha-colored, craggy head; no lacing. Aroma: off-dry, very roasty bitterness, hints of coffee, prune and licorice. Here's a plump porter with dry and bitter elements working nicely on a sweet and viscous base. Starts roasty, almost burnt, with balancing honey and caramel sweetness. Fruit sourness (plum, prune) shows midpalate, as does grassy hop flavor. The finish is long — a dry, bitter black malt effect, with hints of espresso bitterness and hop astringency.

Nut Brown Ale ★★★★¹/₂

6.25% alc./vol.
O.G.: 1052
Ingredients: two-row pale, crystal, black, chocolate and victory malts; Northern Brewer, Perle and Willamette hops

Appearance: very dark brown with red highlights; café-au-lait-colored, quiet, stable, craggy head. Aroma: roasted nuts (walnut, hazelnut), toffee and roasted grain, hay, vanilla and, at room temperature, hints of plum or prune — lovely. As for the taste, wow! As Newcastle gets increasingly lackluster, beer fans will welcome this great brown ale. It starts with not-too-sweet toffee, nutshell, prune and apricot. The taste of unfiltered hops shows midpalate, as does some coffee and roastiness. To finish, hop taste, bitterness and astringency (in that order), but with some lovely roastiness lingering. I found that this porterish brown improved over a five-month period: the hop powder settled out and the nutshell quality increased. Very drinkable, partly because of moderate bitterness, and partly because there's enough complexity to warrant thoughtful appreciation.

Pale Ale ★★★★

5.5% alc./vol.
O.G.: 1048
Ingredients: two-row pale and chocolate malts; Cascade and Willamette hops

Appearance: light amber or old gold; near-white, quiet and stable head; good lacing. I find the aroma very seductive: caramel, with apricot-mango, subtle hopping and some grain dryness all vying for attention. Taste: caramel and peach-apricot to start, with a touch of hop bitterness suggesting heather. A nice unfiltered finish: delicate but grassy hop taste rises, as does appropriate hop bitterness; then some peaty earthiness and a slight metallic edge. Medium-bodied; higher than average viscosity; very satisfying.

● TRAVERSE BREWING COMPANY

11550 U.S. 31
Box 158, Williamsburg, Michigan, 49690
616-264-9343
Capacity: 4,000 barrels
Year started: 1996
Tours available on demand

Like a few others who have studied English and philosophy, Jack Archiable was a longtime homebrewer. While working at a food co-op and teaching home-brewing at Northwestern Michigan College, he met his partner, John Edstrom, who was in the electronics business. The two men started to homebrew together and noticed that homebrewing "can quickly trash your kitchen."

They began to think about making beer commercially. "How hard can it be?" they'd say. Now they know, they admit ruefully.

The two would-be brewers studied at the Wild Goose Brewery in Maryland and apprenticed at a brewery in Milwaukee. They had their first beer, Manitou, brewed under contract by Arrowhead of Pennsylvania. Archiable and Edstrom continued to make plans for their own brewery. They found eight investors who were willing to put up $750,000, got a grant and a small business loan, and pur-chased a building south of Elk Rapids, not far from the eastern shore of Lake Michigan. With the help of beer consultant Alan Pugsley, they built a brewhouse, and the first Traverse-brewed beers hit the market in 1996.

"We're trying to create world-class English-style ales. And part of what we have to do is educate people as to what ale is, and perhaps especially, what it isn't," says Edstrom, explaining that in Michigan many people think of beer as a kind of bland lager.

As with other breweries with which Alan Pugsley has consulted, fermenting is done in open vessels and Ringwood yeast is used.

Plans for the future? "We hope to be Michigan's number one brewery," says Edstrom. "When people taste real beer, fresh beer, we believe that they'll be unable to drink bad beer any more." Traverse Brewing also hopes to expand its product line, to sell cask-conditioned Real Ale, and eventually, to sell its beer in other states, especially the Midwest.

In addition to the two bottled ales described below, I tried a tap version of a 6.5 percent alcohol stout. Made with flaked oats, it was medium-bodied (OG 1063), chocolaty, and had hints of burnt toast and licorice.

Manitou Amber Ale ★★★¹/2

5% alc./vol.
O.G.: 1053
Ingredients: two-row pale, crystal, cara-
pils, and black malts; roasted barley and
torrefied wheat; Perle, Cascade,
Willamette and Tettnang hops

Appearance: mid amber; beige, very quiet and stable head; excellent lacing. Aroma: caramel, grass, small Ringwood accent. Taste: caramel made lush by fine bubble carbonation, hints of tart apricot and pear. Grassy finish, with lingering tartness and fruit-seed bitterness. 32 IBUs. Can an ale have adequate complexity and still be refreshing? This one has and is, with its nice intermingling of sweet malt and tart fruit.

Old Mission Lighthouse Ale ★★★¹/2

4.5% alc./vol.
O.G.: 1045
Ingredients: two-row pale malt;
torrefied wheat; Cascade and
Hallertau hops

Appearance: gold to pale amber; pale beige, very quiet, stable head. Aroma: lovely — caramel, flowers (that's the Hallertau), grass, apricot and a hint of Ringwood woodiness. This lower-alcohol ale has great balance. Four elements play well together: caramel, tartness and tang, graininess and grain bitterness, and grassy (that's the Cascade) hop taste. To start, caramel, some apricot-plum, some grain or biscuit, and a hint of minty spice from the hops. Some tart fruit in the swallow. To finish, delicate hop bitterness and lingering fruit tartness, with a very clean, grassy, minty aftertaste. A terrific barbecue beer. Pleasure-to-alcohol ratio: 11 to 10.

NEW YORK

Until Prohibition, New York was actually called the Entire State, owing to the popularity of Porter ale among its citizens (Entire is an old name for Porter). How it came to be known as the Umpire State is another story.

At first blush, it would appear that New York has everything — the commercial frenzy of New York City, the quiet Adirondack forests, and an ample supply of sin and excess. If, until recently, it lacked any one thing, that was a variety of good, local beer. Obviously, in a state that doesn't want to lack for anything, this had to be remedied. New York is now showing every sign of becoming the great beer state it was before Prohibition.

Dutch colonists were the earliest brewers, and apparently found and used wild hops in the forests of the new colony. In the early 17th century, the West India Company, a Dutch mercantilist concern, dominated the commercial brewing scene. The Company built a brewery in New Amsterdam in the 1630s and a tavern there in 1642. In 1665 the English took control of the colony, by then a magnet for European immigrants. By the mid-1700s, New York and Philadelphia were, according to Stanley Baron, the "leading brewing centers" of the British colonies. Indeed, by 1776, it appears that there were more breweries in and around the city of New York than exist in the entire state today. Albany had a sizable brewery by 1796, and Rochester also became a brewing center in the 19th century. By 1860, New York and Pennsylvania together produced some 85 percent of the beer made in the 1,269 breweries of the United States.

From the late 1700s to the late 1800s, New York state was an important hop producer. In the 1820s, crop failures in England gave a fillip to New York production. Production peaked during the Civil War, and subsequently declined as the Pacific northwest came to dominate hop growing in North America. In the 1940s, blight virtually ended commercial hop production in New York state, but wild hops can still be found in the state's forests.

Beer retailing in New York is generally consumer-oriented. Beer drinkers and small brewers are threatened, perhaps, by a 1996 law, the "Franchise Bill," which gives distribution and retail advantages to the large brewers at the expense of small ones. Single bottles of beer may be bought, but if you want beer and wine, you will, for some reason, have to go to two different stores.

It's a fairly safe prediction to say that the number of breweries in New York state will double by the turn of the century. Excitingly, as this book goes to press, a Belgian-beer-style brewery is being built in Middlefield, New York.

● BRECKENRIDGE BREWERY

621 Main Street
Buffalo, New York, 14203
716-856-2739
Capacity: 10,000 barrels
Year started: 1995
Tours available: phone ahead, and sometimes on a walk-in basis
Glassware and merchandise available

Rick Whitehouse grew up in the western foothills of Maine, left college in 1990 to be a "ski bum in Colorado," as he puts it, and ended up doing odd jobs to pay for his lift tickets. One of those jobs was working for a Colorado-based brewery-pub chain, the Breckenridge Brewery. Whitehouse became assistant brewer at Breckenridge's Colorado location, and then was sent to Buffalo to be the head brewer of the chain's third location.

"We're a combination microbrewery and brewpub-restaurant," Whitehouse says. The brewhouse, the conditioning tanks, and the bottling area are in three different parts of the long, rectangular building. A sign proclaiming "Life is too short to drink cheap beer" hangs above the main entrance.

Will the beer renaissance help revive downtown Buffalo? The building, on the Main Street pedestrian mall, had been empty for fifty years, according to Whitehouse, when Breckenridge moved in. "The city was very happy to have us as a tenant.

"Beer drinkers in this region have not yet seen the microbrewery variety we see in other areas," says Whitehouse. "However, in just our first year here, we've seen people take an interest in beer and gain in their understanding. They used to be afraid of dark beer, but not so much now."

Given Whitehouse's earlier goal of being a "ski bum" (he does miss the mountains), I asked him what pleasures he finds in brewing. "It's a lot of work," he said, but also "a rewarding job. You get to see people drink, and sometimes really love, the product you make. I love getting the feedback." Breckenridge's main goal is "to survive," Whitehouse says. "We're the new kids on the block and we need to make ourselves better known."

Buffalo-brewed Breckenridge beers are available in many eastern seaboard states. In addition to the four packaged products listed below, Breckenridge brews a number of draft-only seasonals.

Avalanche Amber ★★★¹/2

6% alc./vol.
O.G.: 1054
Ingredients: two-row pale and caramel
malts; Chinook, Willamette, Tettnang
and Hallertau hops

Appearance: mid amber; pale beige, very quiet and stable head; excellent lacing.
Aroma: toffee, butterscotch, hay, flowers, and a hint of wood and leather. Taste:

caramel-butterscotch with some hay and earth, then a suggestion of apricot that is quickly overwhelmed by hops. Midpalate, some minty-spicy hop tartness. To finish, earthy-grassy bitterness, some ethyl detectable above the two front teeth.

India Pale Ale ★★★

6.2% alc./vol.
O.G.: 1056
Ingredients: two-row pale, caramel and munich malts; Perle, Willamette, Brambling, Fuggles and Saaz hops

This amber-colored ale has a pale beige, quiet and stable head. Aroma: dry grain, fresh hay and flowers, some caramel, all in perfect balance. Taste: caramel, hop tartness and astringency, and a suggestion of soft fruit. Clean, minty hop finish. IPA is dry hopped, and despite its 60 IBUs, seems only moderately bitter. A bit small for an IPA in terms of its malt base, but a very drinkable ale.

Mountain Wheat ★★★

5.5% alc./vol.
O.G.: 1050
Ingredients: 60% malted wheat; 40% two-row pale malt; Saaz and Hallertau hops; ale yeast

Appearance: straw to light amber; pale beige, slightly noisy but stable head; fair lacing. Aroma: dry grain, hay, caramel. Taste: caramel with sweet and tart fruit. A wee hint of grapefruit astringency in the swallow. To finish, mild hop bitterness, some hop spiciness, and a trace (not enough) of citric skin. Perhaps a true weizen yeast would bring out more wheat-beer character.

Oatmeal Stout ★★★★

4.5% alc./vol.
O.G.: 1052
Ingredients: two-row caramel, black and chocolate malts; roasted barley and rolled oat flakes; Chinook and Perle hops

Alcohol by volume is usually in synch with original gravity. For example, a 4.5 percent beer often has an original gravity of 1045. The gap between 45 and 52 in this stout tells you that you're getting lots of flavor for the (relatively low) alcohol level. Appearance: cola brown with ruby highlights; mocha-colored, very quiet and stable head with small bubbles; excellent lacing. Aroma: tar, roasted grain, almost-burnt toast, prunes. Taste: dryish, toasty biscuit and charred grain on an adequate malt base, with hints of fruit (prune? cherry?) and hay. To finish, hop bitterness and some (grassy) hop taste, lingering trace of grain and burnt toast. 45 IBUs. Oatmeal effect is small. Pleasure-to-alcohol ratio: 11 to 10. I could drink a lot of this very fine stout. Its relative dryness makes it quaffable; the hint of fruit adds interest.

● THE BROOKLYN BREWERY

79 North 11th Street
Brooklyn, New York, 11211
718-486-7422
Capacity: 15,000 barrels
Year started: 1988
Tours available on Saturdays
Glassware and merchandise available

Garrett Oliver, brewer and writer, believes that learning about beer can add to life's zest. "Some Americans have forgotten to have fun. To me, brewing and drinking beer is part of having a good time. This is especially true of quality beer. Connoisseurship isn't about snobbism, but about having fun! The more you know, the more fun you can have. Everyone has a good palate; all that's lacking, sometimes, is education."

Brooklyn Brewery started as a contract brewery, and much of its beer is still made by F. X. Matt. When I visited, the draft-only Weisse and Pale Ale were the only products brewed in-house. Brooklyn has taken some criticism for contracting out its beer making, but I think the criticism is misguided. I'm happy that people without deep pockets can design and retail beer.

Oliver says that part of his interest in brewing is in reviving beer styles that have been neglected. When I visited, he was scouring W. L. Tizard's 19th-century *The Theory and Practice of Brewing Illustrated* for information on India Pale Ale, a style Oliver thinks is due for renewed interest. "I'm a traditionalist when it comes to style, but hopefully not hidebound. Brewers denigrate themselves and their history when they mis-style or mislabel their products."

Oliver's interest in beer started with a trip to London, England. When he returned to America in 1984, decent beer was hard to find, so he started home-brewing. In 1989 he became an assistant to Mark Witty, brewer at Manhattan, the first brewpub east of the Mississippi. While Oliver developed his beer affection in England, Steve Hindy, president of the brewery, learned how to make beer when he was a journalist stationed in Kuwait.

Brooklyn beers are available in seven states, including New York, Ohio and Pennsylvania, but Oliver would like to see the brewery grow in its local market: "If we could get just one percent of this market. . . ." Interestingly, Brooklyn is also a distributor for other quality beers. A good place to spend your last day on Earth would be in the brewery's sample bottle room.

Oliver believes strongly in the need for small brewers to educate the public about beer. When I visited, the brewery, a converted matzoh bakery, was preparing for an Oktoberfest celebration. There's no point in "brewing down" to capture a wider public, Oliver says; rather, quality brewers have to educate people "up" to their beers.

Among Brooklyn's objectives are to expand the plant, and over time, to brew all its own beers.

Black Chocolate Stout ★★★★¹/2

8.25% alc./vol.
O.G.: 1087
Ingredients: two-row pale, caramel,
chocolate and black malts; wheat malt,
black barley and roasted barley; Fuggles
and Willamette hops

Imagine a club dedicated to serious drinking and "convivial fraternity," a club called the City of Lushington. Imagine a governing structure composed of a "Lord Mayor" and four "aldermen," each of whom had a portfolio of responsibility: Lunacy, Poverty, Suicide, and — the odd man out? — Juniper, the Roman god. One can imagine that the members of such a club, founded in London, England, in 1750, might drink in such a way as to give the world a new term: "lush," as in drinking to excess. By 1790, lush was the generic term for beer, or more generally, drink. Lush has another meaning: soft, luxurious, "plush." With this lovely, dense, soft, and astonishing beer, Brooklyn has made an important contribution to the world of lush. Appearance: very dark cola in color; very viscous in the pour; mocha-colored, quiet and stable head. Aroma: black malt, baker's chocolate, treacle or molasses, raisins, figs, prunes, charcoal, pitch, forest. The pitch combines with the forest to suggest pine tar. Taste: chocolate, mocha, molasses and soft, ripe fruit (peaches, figs and prunes) to start. Midpalate, there's a lovely hint of rum-butterscotch. To finish, a firm hop bitterness and roasted grain bitterness that join, but don't smother, the roasted grain, chocolate-espresso, and fruity base. With its starting gravity of 1087, this stout requires two months of conditioning, a long time for an ale. It is pasteurized and unfiltered, an unusual combination. Slightly more bitter than formerly and, I think, even better, Chocolate Stout is a need-to-have friend in the winter. It's too big to accompany most foods, but try it on its own for dessert, or with chocolate fondue. I like this beer a lot. Call me a lush.

Brown Ale ★★★★¹/2

5.5% alc./vol.
O.G.: 1062
Ingredients: two-row pale, caramel,
chocolate and biscuit malts; wheat malt;
Cascade, Willamette and Northern
Brewer hops

Reddish amber, with a café-au-lait-colored, quiet and stable head, and excellent lacing, this brown is a great show-off, technically. Aroma: fresh, very floral hop flowers and roasted grain, some huskiness and hints of toffee. Taste: roasted grain and toffee, peat, some early hop bitterness, and coffee dryness. To finish, gentle, toasty grain bitterness, hop grassiness, some roasted nuts and nutshell. Aftertaste is slightly oaky, almost tannic bitterness. Beautiful! Some folks might place this midway between a pale ale and a brown. Most folks, I think, would be captivated by this very elegant ale.

East India Pale Ale ★★★★

7.4% alc./vol.
O.G.: 1068
Ingredients: two-row pale, pipkin, halcyon, pilsner and caramel malts; wheat malt; East Kent Golding, Cascade and Willamette hops

Appearance: light amber; yellowy beige, quiet and stable head; good lacing. Aroma: fresh hops (very floral), hint of lemon skin, faint caramel — very clean and fresh. The initial taste is unusual in that a floral element is prominent. To be more exact, a soft, floral hop impression over a plum-caramel background with lemon-skin hints. The finish is a firm, almost spicy hop bitterness (half grassy, half floral), with traces of lingering caramel and an earthy aftertaste. I don't associate that hint of lemon (from the wheat) with the IPA style, but the whole package adds up to a very nice whole, a very impressive ale, suggesting perhaps a new style along the lines of "Strong Summer Ale." A bottle-conditioned version of this would be interesting.

Lager ★★★¹/2

4.5% alc./vol.
O.G.: 1050
Ingredients: two-row pale, caramel and carapils malts; Hallertau and Cascade hops

Appearance: light amber; beige, very quiet and stable head; good lacing. Aroma: lightly toasted grain, hop flowers and wildflowers and hay, grapefruit skin. Taste: initially, light tartness cutting into caramel; then, some almost husky graininess; then a tart, almost citric hop bitterness. To finish, hop bitterness more than grain bitterness, some grass, some grapefruit skin. Very refreshing. Maybe too tart for style. Pleasure to alcohol ratio: 11 to 10.

● COOPERSTOWN BREWING COMPANY

Box 206, River Street
Milford, New York, 13807
607-286-9330
Capacity: 4,000 barrels
Year started: 1995
Tours available daily
Glassware and merchandise available

The Cooperstown area is well known to sports fans for one "B." Someday perhaps it will be equally known for another.

Stan Hall, who looks after the business end of brewing at Cooperstown Brewing, says that his son Brian had been homebrewing for a decade when the two of them decided to go into business together. "We saw the beer renaissance happening, and decided that beer would be a good business," says Stan. Brian, who looks after the brewing end, adds, "I've got a wife who'd been carrying my sorry ass for as long as I can remember, and I decided that I needed a job of my own."

Stan Hall sees the term "brewing philosophy" in my notes, and volunteers, "Fresh and local. We have a fresh beer philosophy and that means that we go no further than a truck can go in a day." Cooperstown brews only one packaged brand, and I ask Brian Hall how he arrived at Old Slugger. "Pale ale is for me the most drinkable kind of beer on a day-to-day basis. So we wanted a pale ale." "But we wanted a big beer," adds Stan. Brian Hall notes that the old in Old Slugger is a deliberate reference to Britain's "old" style, of which Old Peculier is perhaps the best-known example in America.

The brewery is in a former creamery, the Weatherly Creamery and Cheese factory. As with other Peter Austin-designed breweries, Ringwood yeast is used, beer ferments in open vessels, and a hop percolator is employed. The Halls try to fill the bottles as much as possible to reduce the volume of oxygen in contact with the beer. Two-thirds of production is bottled.

In coming years, the brewery would like to double or triple production to take full advantage of its bottling line. Currently Old Slugger is available in parts of New York state, Pennsylvania, New England and New Jersey. Old Slugger may some day be available in a Real Ale format.

In addition to Old Slugger, Cooperstown brews Nine Man Ale, a summer seasonal made with honey; and a winter porter called Benchwarmer.

Old Slugger ★★★★
5.5% alc./vol.
O.G.: 1054
Ingredients: two-row pale, crystal, cara-
malt and chocolate malts; torrefied
wheat; Cascade, Mount Hood and
Fuggles hops

Old Slugger, eh? The cap shows the stitching on a baseball. Just another gimmick beer, one might be tempted to think. Well, Old Slugger is no gimmick; it's a fine, slightly strong pale ale, with some ESB qualities. Were this beer available at my local Triple-A ballpark, I'd go more often. Appearance: orangey mid-amber; beige, very quiet, fairly stable head; excellent lacing. Aroma: a very nice balance of caramel, peat, fruit (apricot, dried apricot, plum) forest and hay, plus a wee trace of Ringwood yeast. Taste: caramel and fruit (apricot and plum) with toffee and woody-earthy notes. I like the finish: half bitter (hay and some grass: a very pure hop taste) and half dry (yeasty, woody).

The moderate bitterness and delicate but detectable fruitiness would make this a fine accompaniment to many meats (steaks, roasts, ribs, burgers) as well as sweetish baked vegetables (squash, turnip, carrots). Drink this one at proper ale temperature (15–16° C or 56–58° F). At cooler temperatures, you'll miss the fruit and the lovely peaty notes.

● DryTown Brewery

3 Round House Road
Oneonta, New York, 13820
607-431-2337
Capacity: 2,500 barrels
Year started: 1995
Tours available Sundays and by appointment
Glassware and merchandise available

Located midway between New York City and Lake Ontario, on the northern edge of the Catskills, DryTown has a street address that alludes to the railyards surrounding the brewery. People who tend to lose things will be interested to know that the brewery building itself was "lost during production," according to the brewery's newsletter.

It was a trip to Germany in the early 1990s and the sight of a small brewery in a private residence that got Harold Leitenberger, owner of a carburetor repair business, interested in beer. With two partners, he founded DryTown. His son-in-law Mark Bishop, who was on that trip to Germany, is now DryTown's brewer.

Bishop was a residential contractor before he started brewing. "Brewing was definitely something new when I started, that's for sure. But when you really study it, and understand the equipment, you can learn quickly."

DryTown is an all-ale, one-yeast brewery. Almost all beer is bottled; a very small portion is kegged. DryTown beers are available in parts of New Jersey and Connecticut as well as New York state. DryTown also does some contract brewing for stores and pubs.

DryTown is "trying to produce a good product that people will enjoy and come back to," Bishop says. "Our system is consistent, and the beers are too." DryTown's main objective for the future is to expand its marketing and sales.

Catskill Amber ★★★

5.3% alc./vol.
O.G.: 1054
Ingredients: two-row pale, munich and
caramel malts; Mount Hood hops

Light amber with an orangey hue; pale yellowy-beige, quiet head; good lacing.
Aroma: caramel, light toffee, apricot, hint of hay. Taste: slightly sweet caramel-
butterscotch, apricot, touch of diacetyl. Threads of plum tartness midpalate. To
finish, modest, slightly grassy, slightly hayish bitterness. Very drinkable.

Susquehanna Gold ★★★½

5.2% alc./vol.
O.G.: 1053
Ingredients: two-row pale, caramel and
carapils malts; Cascade and Kent
Golding hops

Gold to light amber in color, and with a very pale beige, quiet and stable head,
Susquehanna Gold has an aroma of caramel, butterscotch, apricot, and a trace of
hay. Good lacing. Taste: caramel, butterscotch, plums and apricot, with a nice
hint of woody or peaty dryness. Finish is mild, almost grassy hop bitterness, some
fruit tartness, and lingering butterscotch. This easy-to-drink, butterscotchy pale
ale would be good with lentil soups, naan or Persian breads, and julienne or
Caesar salads.

Upstate Amber ★★

5.3% alc./vol.
O.G.: 1054
Ingredients: two-row and six-row pale,
munich, caramel and carapils malts;
Willamette and Hallertau hops

Light to mid amber, with a pale beige, quiet, stable head. Good lacing. Aroma:
butterscotch, huskiness, earth, some buttery-leathery diacetyl. Taste: toffee-
butterscotch and peaty-earthy tones initially; a nice flash of plum tartness midpalate; firm, grassy hop taste and earthy dryness to finish. Leather and earth in
aftertaste. I like most of the elements except the diacetyl, but they don't seem to
add up to a balanced whole.

● F.X. MATT BREWING COMPANY

811 Edwards Street
Utica, New York, 13502
www: Saranac.com
315-732-3181 (for tours, phone 732-0022)
Capacity: 300,000 barrels
Tours available Monday to Saturday, and Sundays in the summer
Glassware and merchandise available

Founded in 1888 by a German immigrant, Francis Xavier Matt, and managed by three subsequent generations of descendants, F. X. Matt is a significant regional brewery and a useful addition, I think, to the beer scene of the Great Lakes area. It is America's second-oldest family-owned continuously running brewery, coming only after Yuengling of Pennsylvania. The current chairman is F. X. Matt II; his brother Nicholas is president. They are grandsons of the founder.

Jim Kuhr, Matt's head brewer, was born in Ohio and grew up in Michigan. His first exposure to brewing was at a large brewery best known for its cheap beer. "When I started brewing," he says, "I wouldn't even say that I liked beer. It was actually a college job. When I came to Matt, with its range of beers and flavors, well, it was here that I really learned to like beer.

"Instead of trying to make an extreme version of a style, we try to make a balanced, drinkable version that is still true to style. We try to make the best beer we can," Kuhr says.

Like other mid-size breweries, Matt was facing challenges, if not difficulties, in the 1980s. Ninety percent of sales came from two undistinguished brands, Utica Club and Matts Premium. Matt launched a new line of quality beers, the Saranac line, of which the inaugural product was Adirondack Amber, first brewed in 1985. The new beers were well received. "A turning point," Kuhr recalls, "was the gold medal we received at the Great American Beer Festival in 1991." The first beer that Kuhr designed himself (although he emphasizes that product development is very much a team effort) was the brewery's Pale Ale.

Kuhr enjoys working in a largish brewery: "You have to juggle a lot of things. It's a challenge, as well, working for the Matts, who are a very proud brewing family."

Nicholas Matt, president of the brewery, says that over the past "hundred and eight years, our family-owned brewery has seen many changes and new products. However, our brewing philosophy has remained unchanged: we brew high-quality beers with only the best ingredients."

At 300,000 barrels per year, F. X. Matt is the twelfth-largest brewery in the United States. About 20 to 30 percent of its beer is sold in draft format, and this draft portion is growing. Matt uses two house yeasts, and has a full-time microbiologist on staff. The company also contract brews for such demanding customers as Brooklyn and Dock Street. Beyond New York state, Matt beers are available in Michigan, Ohio, Pennsylvania and Vermont.

Saranac Adirondack Amber ★★★1/2

5.4% alc./vol.
O.G.: 1052
Ingredients: two-row pale and caramel
malts; Cascade, Hallertau and Mount
Hood hops

Appearance: light amber; pale beige, quiet and stable head; excellent lacing.
Aroma: grass and flowers over caramel and lightly toasted grain. Simple and
fetching. Many beers start with caramel and early hop astringency. This lager has
that, but this initial impression is also helped by just enough graininess and peat
to intrigue the palate — that and a hint of apricot. Whereas most amber lagers
"bend" from the start to the finish, this one throws on the brakes and pulls hard
on the steering wheel. For the finish, you're suddenly on a new road: firm, grassy,
almost metallic Cascade hoppiness. A beer to redefine America's lager habits.

Saranac Chocolate Amber ★★★1/2

5.7% alc./vol.
O.G.: 1058
Ingredients: two-row pale, caramel,
munich and chocolate malts; wheat;
Northern Brewer, Hallertau-
Hersbrucker and other hops

As you might guess from the name, the style is problematic. My eyes and nose
tell me this is a porter; my tongue (initially, at least) tells me this is a pale ale or
a Scottish ale. In fact, this beer is a lager. Appearance: very dark amber; beige,
creamy, quiet, stable head; good lacing. Aroma: a balance of roasted barley and
hay and flowers, with hints of chocolate, coffee and raisins. Here's a fine dark
lager in which malt firmness, graininess, fruit and hops are all in balance. To
start, the taste is caramel, with a hint of fruity sweetness and mocha. Then some
grain and hop dryness show, and finally, some roastiness or burnt toast, as well
as some mild hop earthiness and bitterness. I taste very little chocolate. A drinkable beer, perhaps a bit small for the alcohol level.

Saranac Black and Tan ★★★

5.4% alc./vol.
O.G.: 1054
Ingredients: two-row pale, caramel,
chocolate and black malts; East
Kent Golding, Hallertau and
Willamette hops

This black and tan is a true blend of lager and stout. Appearance: walnut- or cola-
colored with red highlights; beige, fairly quiet and stable head with small bub-

bles; good lacing. Aroma: dry, roasted grain, toast and hay. Taste: a very drink-able, if unexciting black and tan. Grainy and dryish, with almost-burnt toast, some mocha and toffee to start, and modest, slightly earthy hop bitterness to fin-ish. Hint of coffee bitterness in aftertaste.

Saranac Black Forest ★★★¹/₂

5.2% alc./vol.
O.G.: 1052
Ingredients: include two-row pale and
caramel malts

Dark lagers are, I think, a challenge for the brewer. Too many taste like what I call painted beers: color for color's sake, or even worse, "soya sauce beers." This lager is neither. Matt calls this a "Bavarian Black Beer"; I'm not sure what to make of it. It has good technical properties, it has a decent profile, and it's thought provoking. But — and here I'm reminded of a very, very nice girl I knew in high school — I don't know how much of this beer I could drink. Appearance: chestnut with burgundy highlights; café-au-lait-colored, quiet and very stable head; good lacing. Aroma: toast, dry roasted grain, hay, flowers, hint of plum or pear. Taste: roasty-grainy (almost-burnt toast), light toffee, some plum-prune character, enough early hop bitterness to diminish malt sweetness. The finish dries and bitters a little, with hay, and acerbic, earthy bitterness. Appropriate acidity in the aftertaste.

Saranac Golden Pilsener ★★★★

5.3% alc./vol.
O.G.: 1048
Ingredients: malts; wheat and roasted
barley; Cascade, Cluster and Tettnang
hops

Draw your own confusions with this one. Matt makes better beer than copy for labels. This beer is both a "pilsener" and, according to the label, "American Wheat." Golden describes the color; but in terms of style, this is no pilsner. The first time I tried this beer, I rated it (as a pilsner) at two stars. What style is it? It's really a hybrid, a new style that might best be termed American wheat lager, the style for which I've given the above rating. The head attests to the wheat: white, very creamy, stable and quiet, leaving good lacing. Aroma: fresh hops, some cereal or biscuit, a tiny hint of flowers, and enough wheat to produce a faint lemony suggestion. Taste: grainy-bready with clean, clear, fresh hop taste. Then, a bit of caramel, some lemon without the sourness, and in the finish, half-grain, half-hop bitterness, and then (only when the beer is fresh) a subdued grapefruit-skin effect. When the beer is stale, the aftertaste is woody.

Saranac Maple Porter ★★¹/₂

Ingredients: include two-row pale,
caramel and chocolate malts; Fuggles
and East Kent Golding hops

Appearance: dark amber with red highlights; quiet, stable, café-au-lait colored
head; good lacing. Aroma: maple sugar, coffee, toffee, hint of hay or flowers.
Taste: slightly sweet toffee, brown sugar, roasted grain, mocha and fruit hints. To
finish, hop and grain bitterness and grassy taste. Not entirely successful. Not as
roasty or as big as a porter, and the maple somehow gets lost in the shuffle.

Saranac Mountain Berry Ale ★★

4.7% alc./vol.
O.G.: 1046
Ingredients: include caramel and chocolate malts; wheat, blueberry honey and
raspberry and blackberry extracts; hops

This mid amber, almost orangey beer has a cream-colored moussey head. Very
faint aroma, with no discernible fruit, some grass or heather, roasted malt, maybe
a hint of fructose or cider. Taste: unremarkable. Hard to tease out the fruit, which
is not identified other than "a variety of mountain berries" — what are mountain
berries? — and the honey from the malt. Some of the sour-bitterness has a slightly ciderish quality.

Saranac Pale Ale ★★★★

5.7% alc./vol.
O.G.: 1054
Ingredients: two-row pale, victory and
other malts; wheat; East Kent Golding
and Cascade or Fuggles hops

I often like complexity, but here's a pale ale that wins applause for its simple but
satisfying profile. Appearance: mid amber; very pale beige, very quiet and stable
head; excellent lacing. Aroma: simple, attractive and balanced — caramel, lightly toasted grain, hay, flowers, hint of oak. Taste: not huge, but balanced and stylistically true. To start, a lovely tension between the malt (caramel and grain, with
a hint of huskiness) and the hops (a balance of grass, hay and forest or flowers).
This ale dries a little in the finish, and a pure hop taste rises but does not overwhelm the lingering malt. (Sometimes — it seems to depend on whether
Cascade or Fuggles are used — I find a truly wonderful hop character in this
beer.) An ideal accompaniment to oily meats (duck, goose, ribs) and roasted vegetables.

Saranac Wild Berry Wheat ★

4.8% alc./vol.
O.G.: 1043

I get dizzy just reading the label: "berries" and "honey" and "hefe weizen." Fruit beer? Mead? Unfiltered wheat? Appearance: pale to mid amber, some haze; pale beige head, very quiet and stable; good lacing. Aroma: raspberry essence. Taste: sweet and soda-like, a mélange of mead, fruit extract, and stale hop bitterness. I'm reminded of Stephen Leacock's man who jumped on his horse and "rode off in all directions."

Saranac Winter Wassail ★★★

Appearance: amber; light beige, very quiet and stable head; good lacing. I like the aroma of this "cinnamon spiced ale" — allspice, cinnamon, toffee and orange skin — like a mulled ale. Taste: tongue-warming spiciness on a toffeeish, mildly bittered base. In the finish, wood-hay bitterness, some astringency, lingering spice.

● LAKE TITUS BREWERY

HCR #1, Box 58B
Malone, New York, 12953
Capacity: 400 barrels
Year started: 1993
Tours available on demand
Glassware available

Eight or nine miles south of Malone, just outside the northern boundary of the Adirondack Park, is a tiny addition to the brewery world. The term "cottage brewery" came to mind as I visited this microbrewery in a small, cottagelike building in the sylvan splendour of upper-state New York.

Fred Ruvola was living on a barge in Holland in the early 1970s when he fell in love with Dutch beer. Amstel Gold and Grolsch Special are two of the brands he remembers with affection. "I never liked beer until I went to Holland," he says.

When he returned to the United States he became a "fanatical" homebrewer, at it "morning and night, two or even three times per week." In 1993, he opened Lake Titus Brewery.

The brewery uses malt extract, and caps bottles by hand. Ruvola's partner, Jerry Ida, says that northern New York state is "bottle country," as it's difficult for new brewers to sell draft to bars.

Ruvola's goal is simply "to make a living at it. We try to brew as well as we can, make the best-tasting beer possible, and hopefully, we'll make a living. We started this business underfinanced. Now we're trying to grow, trying to survive."

Amber Ale ★★★

5.25% alc./vol.
O.G.: 1050
Ingredients: malt extract and crystal
malt; Northern Brewer and
Cascade hops

Reddish mid-dark amber, with a café-au-lait-colored, quiet, stable head. Excellent lacing. Aroma: tart fruit, toffee, and cherry-plum phenols (medicinal). Taste: caramel-toffee, plums and prunes, lots of malt. Nice touch of fruit tartness midpalate. Firm hoppy finish: hop taste, hop bitterness and some hop powder. A homebrew-phenol quality comes from using malt extract, as opposed to grain.

Pale Ale ★★★

5.25% alc./vol.
O.G.: 1050
Ingredients: malt extract and crystal
malt; Northern Brewer and
Cascade hops

Appearance: russet-amber; beige, quiet, stable head; good lacing. Aroma: toffee, cherry phenols. Taste: toffee, cherry-plum phenol, then some fruit sourness. Finishes with clean hop taste; tart-acerbic aftertaste. Good small bubble carbonation. Enjoyable, fruity, phenolic and full-bodied.

Porter ★★¹/₂

5.25% alc./vol.
O.G.: 1050
Ingredients: malt extract, crystal and
black malts; Northern Brewer and
Cascade hops

Dark cola-brown in color with burgundy highlights, and with a mocha-colored, quiet and stable head, this porter has an aroma of fruit (cherries and prunes), hop flowers (unusual in a porter) and roasted grain. Taste: toffee, cherry-prune fruitiness, coffee and burnt toast. Finish is firm, with slightly raw hop bitterness and roasted grain. A hophead's porter?

● MIDDLE AGES BREWING COMPANY

120 Wilkinson Street
Syracuse, New York, 13204
Phone: 315-476-4250
Capacity: 6,400 barrels
Year started: 1995
Tours available Saturdays
Glassware and merchandise available

Mary and Marc Rubenstein, president and head brewer, respectively, of the Middle Ages Brewing Company, seem to have followed Teddy Roosevelt's advice: "Do what you can, with what you have, where you are."

Marc worked in his dad's scrapyard as a kid, and found that he was good at fixing things. Later he developed a passion for homebrewing. Mary, a medical technologist, found that she was a capable business manager. With these talents — what they had, where they were — they built Syracuse's first brewery in 33 years. It's in an old Sealtest ice-cream factory, just outside the downtown core.

"We wanted a business we could work in together," says Mary. Marc went to work with Alan Pugsley at Kennebunkport Brewing, and he and Mary both apprenticed at Shipyard Brewing. They visited 25 microbreweries, talked with over 50 brewers, and took business courses. In 1995, about 600 years after the end of the Middle Ages, the brewery opened.

As president, Mary Rubenstein is 51 percent owner. "That keeps the feminine touch," she says. As head brewer, Marc gets to do, well, almost everything. His experience "fixing things" comes in handy. Middle Ages uses Ringwood yeast, and fermentation is done in open vessels. A hop percolator is employed late in the brewing process.

The name? You might have guessed. Marc is a keen Monty Python fan, and with the Holy Grail film in mind, and his fortieth birthday occurring the year the brewery opened, Middle Ages seemed apropos. And, says Mary, the beers are "our interpretation of ales that were brewed during the Middle Ages." The brewery uses no computers to control the brewing cycles, and all of the work is done by hand. Rousing the wort by hand, the Rubensteins have been told, can help the brewer to "become one with the yeast."

Beast Bitter ★★★

5.3% alc./vol.
O.G.: 1052
Ingredients: two-row pale and crystal malts; torrefied wheat; Cluster, Cascade and Fuggles hops

Appearance: orangey mid-amber, with a pale beige, craggy head (quiet and stable); good lacing. Aroma: Ringwood stamp, hops, toffee, forest, earth, apricot. Taste: initially, a mix of mild bitterness and vaguely apricot fruitiness, with some toffee. Midpalate, peat dryness and bitterness. To finish, hop flavor and lingering earthiness. Beast may be hopped a wee bit too aggressively for the malt base. While overall bitterness is fine at 45 IBUs, I'd like to see more toffee and fruit in the initial impression.

Grail Ale ★★★

4.9% alc./vol.
O.G.: 1050
Ingredients: two-row pale, crystal, cara-
pils and chocolate malts; torrefied
wheat; Northern Brewer, Cascade and
Tettnang hops

I don't know what Sir Percival or Joseph of Arimathea would have thought of this pale ale, but I like it. Russet-amber below, and up top, a stable beige head. Grail Ale has a unique aroma: tangy-earthy with a hint of citrus. The Ringwood yeast used by the brewery helps to produce a taste that starts peaty and malty, then shows a grainy middle, and finishes with enough hops and sourness to make you want another. Lush mouthfeel. Compare Grail Ale with Magic Hat's (Vermont) and MacAuslan's (Quebec) ales, also brewed with Ringwood yeast.

Wizard's Winter Ale ★★★¹/2

O.G.: 1060
6% alc./vol.
Ingredients: two-row pale, crystal and
chocolate malts; torrefied wheat;
Northern Brewer, Fuggles and
Cascade hops

I can just imagine Merlin having bad luck keeping the fire going some damp winter evening. "Well, I'll just conjure up a strong ale," he'd say. "That'll warm the old bones." Hold this one up to the weak winter light: a lovely orange-tinged amber with a cream-colored wizard's cap. Very quiet head, good lacing. Wizard's has a great nose: apricot, creme caramel, roasted grain and cereal, heather, peat and Fuggles hops — all of this in a balanced package. Taste: soft on the palate, with a dry, toasty maltiness to start. In the swallow, some plums, a hint of orange zest, and caramel. In the finish, the fruit fades to a firm, purely hop bitterness (45 IBUs), with a very green, almost astringent quality. Overall, there's just enough malt and adequate attenuation to work well with the distinctive Ringwood stamp and aggressive hopping.

White Knight Light Ale ★★★¹/₂

4% alc./vol.
O.G.: 1043
Ingredients: two-row pale and carapils malts; torrefied wheat; Fuggles and Cascade hops

In chess, knights move indirectly. So too with this ale. Your eyes and nose make you think you know what's coming, but your tongue finds out there's more. A reasonably big ale for a "light." Appearance: yellow gold; near-white, craggy, fairly quiet and stable head. Aroma: hops, apricot, and roasted grain, all in balance over an earthy, yeasty background. Taste: an initial hop bitterness takes on some fruit sweetness and a peat-wood bitterness midpalate. White Knight has a fairly long, hop-bitter finish with traces of caramel and fruit. Pleasure-to-alcohol ratio: 11 to 10.

● MOUNTAIN VALLEY BREW PUB

122 Orange Avenue
Suffern, New York, 10901
914-357-0101
Capacity: 6,000 barrels
Year started: 1992
Tours by request
Glassware and merchandise available

"Very few people did it back then," Jay Misson says. "It was hard to get information on it." He's talking about homebrewing, which he's done since he was sixteen years old. Misson apprenticed at a small brewery in New Jersey in the late 1980s, and in 1990–91 he worked for a brewer in Germany.

Mountain Valley, a brewery-restaurant, focuses on "traditional European styles," Misson says. "We emphasize balance, and use only imported European malts." The small size of the brewery makes consistency a challenge, but "we try to stress quality. Hopefully, any small variations are within the context of good quality."

The brewery hosts seasonal beer festivals and uses beer in many of the dishes it serves at the restaurant. In addition to the beers described below, Mountain Valley brews seasonals such as a stout, a summer raspberry wheat, and a Christmas ale.

Ruffian Copper Ale ★★¹/₂

4.8% alc./vol.
O.G.: 1050
Ingredients: two-row pale, munich, caramel and chocolate malts; East Kent Golding hops

Appearance: mid amber with an orangey hue; beige, quiet and stable head. Aroma: toffee; some apricot, hay and peat. Taste: toffee, sour-citric fruitiness (grapefruit) that isn't suggested in the aroma, some metal. Copper bitters and dries in the finish to suggest hay and wood. Aftertaste: grapefruit skin. Overall, this is fruity, slightly sour, slightly out-of-balance. I bought this ale at a store, not the brewery. It may have been stale.

Ruffian Pale Ale ★★★¹/2
4.2% alc./vol.
O.G.: 1047
Ingredients: two-row pale, sour and
crystal malts; Saaz hops

Appearance: yellow straw or pale gold in color, a touch hazy; very pale beige, quiet and stable head; good lacing. Aroma: caramel (hints of toffee), hay, flowers. Taste: slightly acerbic, very clean, lightly toasted malt offset by a citric undertone. This pale ale finishes with clean, grass-hay bitterness and a partly dry, partly tart aftertaste. Very refreshing.

Ruffian Porter ★★★★
5.8% alc./vol.
O.G.: 1056
Ingredients: two-row, munich, caramel,
chocolate and black malts; Northern
Brewer and East Kent Golding hops

Appearance: chestnut to cola brown, red highlights; café-au-lait-colored, quiet and stable head; good lacing. Aroma: dry roasted grain, mocha, hay. Taste: mmm-mmm. A blend of fruit (prunes, cherries, peaches), toffee and mocha. The finish is similar, but fades to an off-dry, bitter, roasted malt flavor. I'm very impressed by the combination of semi-dryness and salient fruitiness. A great dessert beer, I think. How about this with blueberry crumble or a raspberry tart?

Ruffian Oktoberfest ★★¹/2
5.2% alc./vol.
O.G.: 1054
Ingredients: include munich and pils
malt, Hallertau-Hersbrucker and
Spalt hops

Orangey mid-amber in color, with a yellow-beige quiet head and good lacing. Aroma: dry grain, butterscotch, hay, trace of apricot. Taste: caramel-butterscotch, peat and plums; then an inappropriate, earthy astringency and stale hop taste. Finishes with woody hop bitterness and fruity-metallic tartness that don't integrate well. Maltiness and density appropriate to style; fruity astringency not. Seasonal.

NEPTUNE BREWERY

448 West 16th Street
Manhattan, New York, 10011
www: neptunebeer.com
212-229-2129
Capacity: 3,000 barrels
Year started: 1995
Tours available by arrangement
Glassware and merchandise available

On the sixth floor of a building in Manhattan's meat-packing district, Chelsea, is a sign on a door that speaks of two businesses within: a "bridal" company (etymology: "bride ale," or the ale-drinking that follows a wedding), and a "brewery," Neptune Brewery. Nice combination.

Craig Montano, Neptune's land-based brewer, says the mission of the brewery is "to make unique, hand-crafted, quality products that are different from both the majors and other micros."

While rents and taxes are high in Manhattan, "we can deliver fresh draft to the local market," Montano points out. Neptune is doing some Real Ale for pubs in Manhattan, and takes the time to educate publicans and the public about the virtues of cask-conditioned beer. Neptune beers are also available in Pennsylvania and New Jersey.

Roughly half of production is bottled, half kegged. Neptune uses one yeast, an American ale yeast.

Paul Levitt, founder and president of the brewery, developed some of his appreciation for beer as a homebrewer, and apprenticed for a time at Ontario's Niagara Falls brewery. "Our beers are of a very high quality. We don't use any adjunct," says Levitt.

Neptune is ambitious. "We would like to grow, to be a regional brewery in the New York, New Jersey, Pennsylvania region," says Levitt, "like Sierra Nevada or Anchor, two well-run, mature businesses I respect."

Black Sea Stout ★★★★

4.8% alc./vol.
O.G.: 1052
Ingredients: two-row pale, caramel, chocolate and black malts; roasted barley; Tettnang and Willamette hops

Appearance: cola-colored with red highlights; mocha-colored, quiet and stable head; good lacing. Aroma: almost-burnt grain, toast, coffee, and hints of toffee, prune, apricot and pitch. This fine, dryish stout is balanced and easy to drink. Every sailor should be entitled to a daily supply. It starts with a swaggering burnt-toast and dry grainy taste, complemented by toffee and subtle suggestions of dark fruit. It finishes with hop and tobacco bitterness and a hint of licorice root (35 IBUs). Aftertaste: a wee bit of coffee acidity. Slightly less than medium body; less than medium viscosity; good overall balance. Would go with many aperitifs including caviar — Russian caviar, of course.

Neptune U ★★★¹/₂

This ale may be reformulated as a nut brown. The version I had was an unfiltered brown ale. Appearance: mid amber with a beige, quiet head; good lacing. Aroma: caramel-toffee, apricot, a hint of hay and flowers. Taste: butterscotch, apricot, okay diacetyl, and a hint of biscuit. Midpalate, toffee and peat. The finish bitters and dries nicely, with a soft, hayish hop flavor as well as some dry grain.

66 ★★★

4.6% alc./vol.
O.G.: 1048
Ingredients: two-row pale and caramel
malts; a tad of dextrin and malted
wheat; Cascade hops

Appearance: old gold; yellow-beige, fairly quiet, stable head; good lacing. Aroma: butterscotch, some diacetyl, peach-apricot, hay. Taste: a peachy, buttery ale. To start, sweet caramel and butterscotch; peaches and plums turn tart midpalate. In the finish, butterscotch and diacetyl linger, as does fruit tartness and earthy hop bitterness. When not fresh, leather-diacetyl mars this beer. 28 IBUs.

● NORTH COUNTRY BREWERY

131 Excelsior Ave.
Saratoga Springs, New York, 12866
518-581-0492
Capacity: 50,000 barrels
Year started: 1996
Tours available: phone ahead
Glassware and merchandise available

Eastward ho! Like Breckenridge in Buffalo, North Country is an eastern extension of a west-based brewery. When beer fan and homebrewer Bob Craven read that Oregon's Nor'Wester brewery was looking to expand in the east, he made a home video extolling the virtues of Saratoga Springs and sent it to Nor'Wester's head office. It must have been a good video. The Nor'Wester folks immediately flew east to meet Craven, and within a year had built a $6.5-million brewery. By December 1996, North Country was brewing beer with Craven as general manager.

North Country's brewer, Brian Bush, grew up in Colorado and spent six years in the Navy as a medic. "I'd always had an interest in beer," he says. "When

I turned eighteen I tried a lot of imported beer. I especially loved German beers."
Then wine called. Bush worked for a doctor in California whose brother was a
wine maker. He decided to study fermentation at U.C. Davis and graduated with
a degree in Fermentation Science in 1986. "I worked in Sonoma County at a
vineyard, and I began to think that the future would be brighter in beer."

Bush's first brewing job was in Anheuser-Busch's St. Louis pilot brewery. "I
worked there for six months," he says, "and then I was transferred to [Anheuser-
Busch's plant in] Baldwinsville, New York." In 1996 he was recruited by
Nor'Wester to brew at Saratoga Springs.

As head brewer of a new brewery, Bush says, "We're trying to achieve beers
of a very high quality, that are distinctive, balanced and very drinkable."

Bush's hopes for the future are to increase production and to brew some new
styles, including, perhaps, a fruit beer.

Maple Amber ★★★¹/₂

5% alc./vol.
O.G.: 1044
Ingredients: two-row pale and munich
malts; torrefied wheat and maple syrup
(about 2%); Willamette and
Tettnang hops

"No man manages his affairs as well as a tree does," G. B. Shaw opined. Perhaps
that's why — out of sheer jealousy — we tap trees to make maple syrup and
maple beer. Here's an ale that respects the taste of maple. Appearance: light to
mid amber; very pale beige, quiet, stable head; good lacing. Aroma: caramel,
maple syrup, wee hint of grass. Taste: true maple syrup taste; hint of plum in the
middle; hops are evident in wood and floral suggestions in the finish. Nice iron-
tin hints in aftertaste. Maple Amber would go well with baked ham and ham-
and-cheese crepes.

Whiteface Pale Ale ★★★★

5.2% alc./vol.
O.G.: 1048
Ingredients: two-row pale, crystal and
munich malts; wheat malt; Target,
Willamette, Mt. Hood and
Tettnang hops

Old gold below, up top a pale beige, very quiet and stable head. Very good lacing. Aroma: balanced and enticing — caramel, flowers and plums, with hints of
grain and forest. Taste: caramel and grain give way to a mild, plummy tart-
bitterness and gentle spiciness. To finish, firm earthy bitterness, with traces of
grass and flowers. A wee bit overcarbonated. Medium body, medium viscosity. A
great addition to the pale ales of the region; notably bitter (40 IBUs) but very

well balanced. A German ale yeast is used. Whiteface is big and bitter enough to make a fine accompaniment to sweet and spicy Mexican, Malaysian or Indonesian food.

Fat Bear Stout ★★★

4.9% alc./vol.
O.G.: 1046
Ingredients: two-row pale and crystal
malts; roasted barley; Willamette,
Chinook and Target hops

This cola-brown stout has a café-au-lait-colored, quiet and stable head. Very small bubbles. Fair lacing. Aroma: caramel, creme brûlée, roasted grain, some forest or hay. Taste: dry, almost-burnt toast to start, with noticeable plum (sweet-tart), and hints of toffee and tar. Finish is bitter (40 IBUs) and lightly acidic, with burnt grain, coffee and plum traces. Some hay-grass in aftertaste. Not fat, despite the name, but dryish, lightly fruity, and quaffable. Low viscosity.

● WOODSTOCK BREWING COMPANY

20 Saint James Street
Kingston, New York, 12401
914-331-2810
Capacity: 10,000 barrels
Year started: 1991
Tours available: call for a schedule
Glassware and merchandise available

Like Kingston, Ontario, this Kingston was once a capital, in this case, of New York state. Kingston and the Hudson Valley have been home to several breweries over the years, some 22 of them between New York City and Albany. When Woodstock Brewing opened in 1991, it had been 50 years since the last of these breweries closed. I hope the good folks of Kingston celebrated the birth of Woodstock and the reappearance of local suds — it must have been akin to waking from a long sleep.

Nat Collins, brewer and owner of Woodstock, has a cosmopolitan background. Born in Spokane and educated in Mexico, Florida and New York, Collins has taught disturbed teenagers, and owned and managed a variety of food-related businesses and construction and real estate development companies. He was also, for 27 years, a homebrewer. Why open his own brewery?

"A good question," he says. "I work really hard. I guess it's because I really like it when people say that they like my beer. I'll tell you a story, a true story: There's a guy, a customer, who tells me: 'Now that I drink your beer, I can't drink alone any more. My wife insists that she go drinking with me!'" Collins smiles, his satisfaction evident. "Brewing is a great trade. Brewers are a friendly lot. But I guess I opened the brewery because I like beer."

Collins sees himself as part of a brewing tradition. Kingston has had many historic breweries; "We're just the latest."

Nancy Baker, general manager at the brewery, says that about a third of production is bottled. Woodstock beer is available out of state in New Jersey, but the "four local counties" are the brewery's natural market. "One of our goals is to stay a micro, never to get too big," she says.

In coming years, Collins would like to consolidate what he's built. "I've been buying all these instruments. Now I want to fine-tune the orchestra and enjoy the music."

Big Indian Porter ★★★★

5.8% alc./vol.
O.G.: 1061
Ingredients: two-row pale, crystal, chocolate and black malts; Cluster, Hallertau and Mt. Hood hops

Appearance: cola brown with red highlights; café-au-lait-colored, quiet and stable head; excellent lacing. Aroma: roasted nuts, nutshell, toffee, burnt toast, plums and prunes. Taste: almost-burnt toast, toffee that merges into soft fruit, coffee, and a tiny trace of licorice. The finish is firm: dry, roasty grain bitterness, some grassy hop bitterness, and nicely lingering coffee (or mocha?). 42 IBUs. I like this soft but not too soft, full-bodied but not corpulent, roasty, near-dry porter. It's sexy.

Hudson Lager ★★★¹/₂

5.2% alc./vol.
O.G.: 1051
Ingredients: two-row pale and munich malts; Hallertau and Tettnang hops

Appearance: old gold; yellowish pale beige, quiet, stable head; good lacing. Aroma: dry grain, caramel, fresh bread or dough, fresh hay. Taste: caramel and grain bitterness, hint of non-fruit tartness. In the finish, a good grain-hop balance in the rising but modest (20 IBUs) bitterness. Nice hay effect. Wee bit fizzy. The topsail sloop on the label makes me think that this would be a fine lager to have on board a sailboat on a lazy Hudson afternoon.

Ichabod Crane ★★★★

O.G.: 1098
10% alc./vol.
Ingredients: two-row pale, munich,
caramel and vienna malts; sugar pump-
kins, cinnamon, cloves and nutmeg;
Hallertau, Cluster and Tettnang hops

Washington Irving, who invented the character Ichabod Crane, penned the aphorism "those who drink beer will think beer." With pumpkin as an ingredient, Ichabod is an unusual and exciting winter lager. Is drinking this what mom meant when she said "Eat your vegetables"? Appearance: reddish dark amber, with a beige, quiet and stable head, and excellent lacing. The aroma is fetching — nutmeg and allspice (light, but enough to predominate), caramel-toffee, hints of pumpkin, smoke and peat. Taste: mmm-mmm, a real contribution to the winter seasonals of the region. To start, toffee and a spice complex (nutmeg, cloves, cinnamon) and apricot hints, all in a soft but very firm malt base. The taste darkens midpalate to a peaty-smoky ethyl and bitter pumpkin skin. The finish bitters slowly and nicely with oaky-earthy-spicy elements. The toffee takes on bitter pumpkin-skin tones, and hops produce a minty flavor that combines with some ethyl freezing. The spice is restrained and well married with the overall profile. The bitterness of this lovely fireside beer distinguishes it from barley wines, and makes it go well with sweet winter desserts such as shortbread, figgy duff, and treacle cookies. Ichabod might age well over a six-to-twelve-month period.

St. James Ale ★★★¹/₂

5.5% alc./vol.
O.G.: 1057
Ingredients: two-row pale, crystal and
carapils malts; Cluster, Hallertau and
Mt. Hood hops

Appearance: light amber; near-white, quiet, stable head; excellent lacing. Aroma: light and delicate, a balance of caramel, grain and plums, with a hint of dough. Taste: mildly tart butterscotch, apricot-plum, some grain. Finish is clean, mildly grassy, slightly acerbic at the edges, with a hint of huskiness. 28–30 IBUs. This highly drinkable pale ale is noteworthy for its lovely combination of tartness, caramel and graininess. A deft use of Hallertau, not commonly used in pale ales.

OHIO

Ohio's beer roots go back to the early 1800s. In Cincinnati, the Davis Embree brewery was operating in 1810; other, undocumented breweries may have been operating a little earlier. In 1816, a certain David Thomas wrote that attached to the Embree brewery was a "treadle-mill . . . It is turned by horses and grinds a hundred and twenty bushels of malt a day." In Cleveland, commercial brewing started between 1820 and 1840. The city was baptized, so to speak, by a Baptist: "Elijah F. Willey, a Baptist clergyman, put in operation on the Walworth run near Willey Street a Brewery, so the introduction among us of this wicked beverage cannot be laid at the door of the immigrant Teuton" (both quotations are taken from Stanley Baron).

A glimpse of Ohio's beer history can be seen on the wall of the bar at the Great Lakes Brewing Company in Cleveland — brewery names that still resonate for local beer lovers: Oppmann Brewing Company, Cleveland and Sandusky, Schmidt and Hoffmann . . . At one point, there were over 25 breweries in Cleveland alone. In the late 19th century, Cincinnati had 36 breweries and consumed more beer per capita than any other American city.

While Ohio is a much younger state than New York and Pennsylvania, it is the site of some of the earliest documented lager brewing in America. According to Stanley Baron, a new brewery "for the production of lager, named Fortmann and Company, was announced in 1844, located in the Over the Rhine section of Cincinnati. Interestingly, this part of Cincinnati, near the old Miami and Erie Canal, is now undergoing a good deal of renewal.

With the possible exception of the Hudepohl brewery, this thread of brewing history was broken as various local and regional breweries succumbed to Prohibition. Of course, as the birth state of the Women's Christian Temperance Union, Ohio merits special mention in any history of drinking in North America.

Two things strike me with regard to Ohio's current brewing scene. There are a modest number of breweries (about half a dozen that bottle beer), and the overall quality of the beer is very good.

Retailing is fairly competitive, and one can buy single bottles of beer. Ohio's particular beer inanity is that brewers cannot brew any beer with more than 6 percent alcohol by weight (about 7.5% by volume). You'd think a state with a winter like Ohio's would make it mandatory for every brewery to brew a good winter warmer.

I'm not sure why Ohio thinks it useful to prevent its citizens from drinking Ohio-made barley wines and strong lagers, while allowing them to buy wine, liquor and strong imported beers. An employee of the Ohio Liquor Commission told me that "it's the regulation." When I said that I was interested in knowing the purpose of the regulation, the employee replied: "I just told you. It's the rule, it's the law, it's the regulation."

● COLUMBUS BREWING COMPANY

535 Short Street
Columbus, Ohio, 43215
614-224-3626
Capacity: 3,500 barrels
Year started: 1989
Tours available: phone ahead
Glassware and merchandise available

Columbus is James Thurber country. Like Walter Mitty, some Columbus folk have big dreams; unlike Walter Mitty, some realize their dreams. The new Columbus Brewing building was under construction, but already brewing when I visited. Previously, the brewery had been in rather cramped (900-square-foot) quarters. The new building will have a pub-restaurant on premises.

Brewer Ben Pridgeon says that his goal is "to produce the highest quality beers I can in given circumstances. I try to produce beers that, when you've taken the first swig, beg you to finish them."

In 1983, Pridgeon, who was a musician, became a "diehard" Samuel Smith Pale Ale and Tadcaster Porter fan. "That's an expensive habit for a poor musician, so I started homebrewing." In 1989 the Columbus brewery was founded, and soon Scott Francis, the founder and original brewer at Columbus, who also had taught Pridgeon how to homebrew, was asking him to help with the brewing. In 1993, Pridgeon became the head brewer of Columbus; a year later he took a course at the Siebel brewing school.

"Running a brewery is a bit like running any small plant, except — and this is what makes it exciting — the fact that your product exists at the whim of a living organism: yeast." Pridgeon calls himself a "hophead," but he explains that for him this simply means an interest in the taste and the effect of hops.

Located on the edge of the city's Brewery District, Columbus is very much a local brewery. Ninety percent of its beer is sold in the home county. Pridgeon says that the on-premise pub will serve Real Ale.

Pale Ale ★★★★

5% alc./vol.
O.G.: 1050
Ingredients: two-row and crystal malts;
Cascade and Columbus hops

Appearance: orangey amber; orangey beige, very quiet and stable head. Aroma: caramel, peach-apricot, cut hay, flowers. Here's an ale that has a distinct front, middle and finish, and with excellent balance at each stage. Initially, a soft, apricot-nectarine-caramel impression, nicely offset by a touch of peat and biscuit. Then hop bitterness creeps in, as does superb hop taste, ranging from grass to flowers. Finally, hop bitterness and taste, grain bitterness and astringency, with a lingering iron-metallic touch at the back of the tongue. 38 IBUs. This ale will be superb in a Real Ale format.

Nut Brown ★★★★
5% alc./vol.
O.G.: 1050
Ingredients: two-row pale, crystal and
chocolate malts; roasted barley;
Northern Brewer, Columbus and
Cascade hops

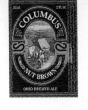

Appearance: dark brown with red-burgundy highlights; beige head. Aroma: roasted cereal, hazelnuts, mocha, flowers and forest. This is an American — that is to say, slightly hoppy — take on the English nut brown style: Columbus hops would seem to cascade in Columbus. Taste: caramel undercut by a plummy tartness as well as a nutty, peaty and roasted grain flavor (some of this is the result of the London Ale yeast employed). Finishes with hop taste, hop bitterness (40 IBUs), and a dry, earthy tone somewhere between peat, tobacco and roasted nuts. Very enjoyable: medium bodied, medium viscosity, hoppy, and very well balanced.

● CROOKED RIVER BREWING COMPANY

1101 Center Street
Cleveland, Ohio, 44113
216-771-2337
www.crookedriver.com
Capacity: 18,000 barrels
Year started: 1994
Tours available: phone ahead
Glassware and merchandise available

Nothing bent about this brewery's philosophy: "Just great beer" is the company's slogan.

Located in the Flats region of central Cleveland, and surrounded by docks, warehouses, rusting bridges and railway tracks, Crooked River is dedicated to "making Cleveland a brewing capital once again." So says brewer Mark Ward. "We try to cover a variety of styles, everything from Bavarian lagers to English ales."

Head brewer and president Stephan Danckers met partner Stuart Sheridan at college in Indiana. Danckers went on to study brewing at the University of California at Davis and, on a Fulbright scholarship, at the Faculty of Brewing at Weihenstephan in Munich, Germany.

Sheridan says that while the company is serious about making good beer, "we also believe that beer should be fun. . . . We make some beer that is dead-on in terms of style, and others that aren't." In terms of market, "we're a local brewery as much as a microbrewery."

Crooked River emphasizes freshness as a virtue in beer (as indeed it is). In addition to its line-up of permanent brands, the brewery makes seasonals that include a pumpkin beer, a doppelbock, and a Christmas ale.

Bicentennial Wheat ★★★¹/₂

4.95% alc./vol.
O.G.: 1048
Ingredients: two-row pale malt;
50% malted wheat; Mt.
Hood hops

Appearance: yellow straw, bit of orange haze; near-white, quiet and stable head; fair lacing. Aroma: cloves, banana, yeast, fresh bread, lemon skin and toffee. Taste: to start, yeast, bananas and lemon-grapefruit on a light caramel base. Cloves (or nutmeg) are apparent in the middle. To finish, modest hop bitterness, some citric sourness, and some nice earthy-woody notes. Brewed to celebrate Cleveland's 200th birthday, this lovely hefeweizen would be great with warm salads, bean salads, multigrain breads, and red-pepper-and-cheese pizza.

Black Forest Lager ★★★★

5% alc./vol.
O.G.: 1054
Ingredients: two-row pale, vienna,
munich and caramel malts; Mt. Hood,
Hallertau and Saaz hops

This medium-bodied, medium viscosity beer has enough hop bitterness to make it a good "session" beer, so long as you like full flavor in every sip of your session, as I do. Amber colored, with a yellowish beige, fairly quiet and stable head; excellent lacing. Aroma: faint caramel, cut grass and flowers, some yeasty-breadiness. Malty, almost butterscotchy to start, but not cloying or oversweet. Black Forest shows some roastiness midpalate, and in the finish, a touch of hop astringency, a very nice Hallertau-Saaz flavor, and gentle hop bitterness.

Cool Mule Porter ★★★¹/₂

5.05% alc./vol.
O.G.: 1057
Ingredients: two-row pale, caramel,
munich, chocolate, black, and special
roast malts; Cascade hops

Appearance: very dark cola-brown; mocha-colored, creamy, fairly quiet and stable head; good lacing. Aroma: dry, roasty malt, coffee, licorice, burnt toast, figs. Taste: dry, mildly bitter roastiness on a toffeeish and fruity (peach, prune) base. Some hop astringency midpalate. In the finish, hop and earth bitterness, and hints of bitter chocolate, coffee, and burnt toast. High viscosity and slightly high carbonation diminish the flavor.

Lighthouse Gold ★★★

4.6% alc./vol.
O.G.: 1046
Ingredients: two-row pale and caramel
malts; Perle, Cascade and Mt. Hood hops

Appearance: gold to light amber; pale beige, fairly quiet and stable head; little lacing. Aroma: strong caramel, dried apricot, hints of grape, peat and grass. Taste starts with caramel and apricot and a hint of plum tartness. In the finish, a nice peaty earthiness lingers, as does the hop taste and some tart acidity. A bit fizzy.

Settlers Ale ★★★¹/₂

5.57% alc./vol.
O.G.: 1061
Ingredients: two-row pale, vienna and
caramel malts; Perle, Cascade and
Goldings hops

Appearance: orangey mid-amber; pale yellow-beige, quiet and stable head; excellent lacing. Aroma: mmm mmm — a balance of fruit (apricot, plum, hint of melon), caramel, toasted grain, and hints of earthiness. Taste: slightly sweet butterscotch start, then a slightly tart, astringent offset suggesting plums. Finishes with dry cereal, grain bitterness, hop bitterness. High viscosity (too high?) accentuates the caramel. This ale would go well with hamburgers, Lebanese sandwiches, Reuben sandwiches, and with or in Scotch broth.

● THE GREAT LAKES BREWING COMPANY

2516 Market St.
Cleveland, Ohio, 44113
216-771-4044
Capacity: 14,000 barrels
Year started: 1988
Tours available: phone ahead
Glassware and merchandise available

"Basically, we're trying to make the best beer we can," explains brewer Andy Tveekrem. "We try to take a classic beer style and do the best we can with it." However, Tveekrem says, "it may be more full flavored than other beers in the style — I hate wimpy beer!"

Located in Cleveland's central market area, Great Lakes Brewing is Ohio's oldest microbrewery of those currently in operation. The 1860 building in which the brewery is located has a charming mahogany bar (the oldest in Cleveland), a restaurant, and a leafy patio looking onto Market Street.

Seasonal beers, which include a wheat, an Irish ale and a winter warmer, are not packaged, but can be bought and brought home if you bring your own container — ask the brewery for details.

Great Lakes has won many medals, including gold medals from the Beverage Testing Institute of Chicago and the Great American Beer Festival. In 1994, Great Lakes was named "Microbrewery of the Year" by the Beverage Testing Institute.

This award-winning brewery doesn't "scrimp on costs," says Tveekrem. "We're very driven by customer satisfaction."

Burning River Pale Ale ★★★

5.8% alc./vol.
O.G.: 1056
Ingredients: two-row pale, crystal,
and biscuit malts; Galena and
Cascade hops

"Hophead" is an American term for a brewer or beer drinker whose philosophy is akin to "Heavy on the hops!" I've always liked and been intrigued by the effects of *humulus lupulus*, both in the way it marries its bitterness to the malts in the taste of beer, and in the way it can lend a distinctive noble character to the aroma. I like a number of highly hopped beers, and often find the hopping levels of many North American beers too low. Sadly, more and more Dutch and German lagers, particularly brewed-for-export lagers, also seem to have reduced levels of bittering and aromatic hops of late. Many mainstream lagers now have bitterness levels below the threshold of detectability, that is, 10 to 12 International Bitterness Units. And so, predictably, a revolt occurs and we get the term "hophead." What then do we make of a pale ale with 73 IBUs? Brewer Andy Tveekrem describes Burning River, named for the notorious Cuyahoga River fire of 1969, as a "massively hoppy pale ale." And indeed it is.

Appearance: mid amber with a touch of orange; yellowish beige, quiet and stable head. Aroma: mild caramel and grassy hops, which together, perhaps, suggest tart fruit; plus a hint of spice (allspice?). Taste: initially, caramel and apricot-plum gift wrapped in hops. Hop grassiness and bitterness (almost like chicory) grow. Finish is strong (but very leafy) hop bitterness, as well as some astringency and tartness. Medium-plus viscosity and low carbonation give this ale the mouthfeel (but not the flavor) of a British ESB, like Fuller's. Two contradictory impressions result from the high level of hopping in Burning River: a "green," almost minty coolness, and a "red" level of bitterness that resembles suggests heat. Might this ale be ideal as the main course at a hopheads' banquet?

Dortmunder Gold ★★★★

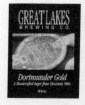

5.4% alc./vol.
O.G.: 1056
Ingredients: two-row pale, caravienne
and carapils malts; Hallertau and
Cascade hops

Here's a welcome addition to the lagers of North America. Not quite as firm or sharp-edged as, say, DUB Export, Great Lakes' take on the Dortmunder style is softer and grainier — and it's one terrific beer. Appearance: light amber to old gold in color, with a pale beige, quiet and stable head. Aroma: lovely balance between sun-on-grain and light caramel-butterscotch, with soft hayish notes and a hint of oak. Taste: caramel, with grain and hop bitterness to start, Dortmunder dries in the finish and shows some woodiness as well as a tiny tart edge. In Hell, there's a room in which mediocre megabrewers are given this lovely lager — just once — and then, for the rest of eternity, they're allowed to drink only the product they made and sold on Earth.

Edmund Fitzgerald Porter ★★★★¹/₂

5.9% alc./vol.
O.G.: 1060
Ingredients: two-row pale, crystal and chocolate malts; roasted barley; Northern Brewer, British Columbia Kent and Cascade hops

Appearance: dark cola-brown, burgundy-red highlights; café-au-lait-colored, quiet and stable head; good lacing. Aroma: roasted barley and burnt toast are prominent; beneath the surface, there's coffee, licorice, toffee and dates. Taste: A real achievement! With a medium body and medium viscosity, intense, dryish, dark grain flavors, and just a bit wider spectrum of flavor than Catamount's porter has, EF has a beautiful balance of grain and hop bitterness. The initial impression is of near-dryness, but is in fact closer to bittersweet, thanks in part to aggressive but skillful hopping. To be more specific: coffee and burnt toast to start, with a soft underside of plum, prune or even nectarine, although this is not a very fruity porter, overall. In the finish, earthy-grainy bitterness lingers, with hints of espresso, burnt toast, licorice root, walnut shell, and grass or chicory. How about this for dinner, and Cheval Blanc's Titanic (from Quebec) for dessert? Both go down easy.

Eliot Ness ★★★★¹/₂

O.G.: 1060
Ingredients: two-row pale, munich, caravienne, and caramunich malts; malted wheat; Hallertau hops

The Vienna style is often referred to, seldom seen. I'm not sure anyone can rigorously define the parameters of the style, at least in contemporary terms, but I sure like this pretender. Named for the "Cleveland Safety Director" who frequented the bar now in the pub at the Great Lakes brewery, Ness is a very reddish mid to dark amber with a yellow-beige quiet and stable head. Excellent lacing. Aroma:

caramel-toffee, bit of roastiness and demerara, detectable Hallertau, and maybe some apricot or peach. Is the taste balanced? Well, maybe. Perhaps it's a curious and attractive friction between big, viscous maltiness, dark, grainy dryness, an adequate hop bitterness. Initially, roasty and grainy and, intriguingly, with Hallertau flavor evident right from the start. Midpalate: darker grain flavors increasing bitterness and astringency and acid (almost fruit). Maltiness diminishes in the finish leaving a very clean hop bitterness. Overall: terrific.

Holy Moses ★★★★¹/₂

5% alc./vol.
O.G.: 1054
Ingredients: two-row pilsner malt;
unmalted wheat, malted wheat, raw
oats, dextrin, coriander, orange peel,
and chamomile flower; Hallertau hops

Not terribly big, but delicate and subtle, here's a significant contribution to the wheat beer style. This beer has less wheat as a percentage of fermentables than many other wheat beers, which contributes to its unique character, and allows the chamomile to show. Appearance: straw-gold, with a white, moussey, quiet and stable, small-bubble head; excellent lacing. Aroma: a light complex of spiciness (coriander seed, plus two spices that aren't actually in the ingredients: white pepper and cumin seed) over a sun-on-lemon-skin, chamomile and yeast background. Taste: soft caramel perfectly balanced by grapefruit skin and, at warmer temperatures, orange skin and a gentle spiciness with white pepper and coriander being the most prominent. Finish is dry, slightly acerbic graininess and yeastiness, with further hints of grapefruit, orange and chamomile. The eleventh commandment: don't drink beer too cold. Holy Moses won't reveal its secrets until it's almost at room temperature.

● HOSTER BREWING COMPANY

550 South High St.
Columbus, Ohio, 43215
614-228-6066
Capacity: 5,000 barrels
Year started: 1989
Tours: Sundays and by arrangement
Merchandise and glassware available

Hoster's (pronounced HOSS-ters) is a brewery and brewpub in the heart of Columbus's reviving Brewery District.

Victor Ecimovich III, Hoster's brewer, grew up within a stein's throw of the Siebel Institute in Chicago, and later attended this brewing school. His grandfather was brewmaster in Chicago's Peter Hand brewery.

"Our commitment is to grow beyond the brewpub," he says. To this end, Hoster's has installed a modern German brewhouse and a good bottling machine. The brewery uses 22-ounce screened-enamel bottles: "A lot of people do judge books by their cover, and we wanted a bottle that shows we're making a premium product."

Before Ecimovich arrived in 1994, the brewery made lagers only. Now, "we cover the style spectrum fairly well in the sense of having something for everyone's palate. I like to make and to drink all types of beers." Hoster's uses several yeasts. Ecimovich says that to "make beer properly, you need style-specific yeast." In addition to the beers described below, Hoster's makes an amber lager and several seasonal beers.

Hoster's goal is "to maintain the quality as we expand sales," Ecimovich says. On the horizon, but not firmed up as yet, is a dedicated brewery separate from the brewpub with a bottling line for 12-ounce bottles.

Eagle Dark Lager ★★★¹/₂

6% alc./vol.
O.G.: 1060
Ingredients: two-row pilsner, vienna, munich, caramel, chocolate, toasted and black malts; roasted barley and malted wheat; Northern Brewer, Saaz and other aromatic hops

Many of the darker lagers in North America are what I call "painted" beers: darker malts have been used for no reason other than to color the beer, and thus to signal, apparently, that the brand is chic, not mainstream. Not so Eagle Dark. I think this lager shows very well how the dry toastiness of the darker malts can be used to balance hop bitterness. Appearance: dark reddish amber; beige, fairly quiet and stable head; good lacing. Aroma: dry and biscuity, roasted cereal, and hints of baker's chocolate, toffee and earth. Taste: Eagle starts soft but dry, with toasted grain and toffee flavors, and a wee hint of prunes. Burnt toast middle (burnt toast made from good bread). For the finish, the dryness evolves to medium-plus bitterness, with roasted grain, hops, and earthy-espresso flavors.

Gold Top ★★¹/₂

5.2% alc./vol.
O.G.: 1048
Ingredients: two-row pilsner, vienna, munich and caramel malts; Saaz, Tettnang and Liberty hops

Appearance: old gold; near-white craggy and stable head; good lacing. Aroma: dry grain with a floral hint. Taste: sweet and cerealish start; an astringent and bitter finish that seems a little out of whack.

Rev. Purley Pale Ale ★★★¹/₂

5.4% alc./vol.
O.G.: 1050
Ingredients: two-row pale and caramel
malts; 11% malted wheat; Fuggles,
Goldings, Cascade and Centennial hops

Appearance: orangey mid-amber; yellowy pale beige head; fairly quiet and stable.
Aroma: sweet, orange zesty, with a bit of caramel and hay. Taste: sweetish caramel
offset by some tartness (almost orangey) and nice peaty tones. The Reverend finishes earthy-bitter, with some hop astringency and a pure grassy-floral taste. I like
this unusual, slightly tart ale. I don't taste the "dryness" mentioned on the bottle,
but I wouldn't hold that against a man of the cloth.

● HUDEPOHL-SCHOENLING BREWING COMPANY

1625 Central Parkway
Cincinnati, Ohio, 45214
513-241-4344
Capacity: 500,000 barrels
Year started: merger effected in 1986
Tours: not available

There are a number of pressures on mid-sized breweries. In some ways they are
caught between the nimble microbreweries, which can cater to small niches in the
market, and the megabreweries, which have greater economies of scale.
Hudepohl-Schoenling, it seems to me, is responding to these pressures in an intelligent way. It's producing products that range from mainstream to Reinheitsgebot;
it contract brews for other breweries; and it tries to maintain and promote local
brands. All of this amounts to what the company calls "survivorship."

Hudepohl-Schoenling is the result of a 1986 merger between the (at that
time) 101-year-old Hudepohl Brewing Company and the 55-year-old
Schoenling Brewing Company. In 1885, Louis Hudepohl and George Kotte
bought the Koeler Brewery and founded the Hudepohl and Kotte Brewing
Company. Hudepohl became sole owner in 1900, and by the time of his death
in 1902, the company was brewing 40,000 barrels of beer a year. Like Yuengling
in Pennsylvania, Hudepohl survived Prohibition by brewing "near beer." The
Schoenling Brewery opened its doors in 1933, after Prohibition had run its
course.

The idea of the merger was to combine Hudepohl's local strengths with
Schoenling's wider markets. As John Piening, Hudepohl-Schoenling's brewmaster, says, "Regional breweries are on the endangered list. We have to work hard
to survive."

In 1997 the Boston Beer Company, America's tenth-largest brewery, announced that it would buy Hudepohl-Schoenling. H-S had already brewed several beers, including Old Fezziwig and Boston Lager, for the Boston Beer Company, which until this acquisition had been a contract brewery only. Boston Beer will continue to brew H-S beers. I believe this acquisition will benefit the Great Lakes beer scene.

Hudy Bold ★★

4.6% alc./vol.
O.G.: 1044
Ingredients: six-row pale malt; corn syrup or grits; Cluster, Cascade and Hallertau hops

Appearance: straw-yellow; near-white head; bit noisy. Aroma: dry grain, faint hops, faint paper. Taste: sweet graininess to start, then sweetish maize and some hop bitterness. Cardboard effect in aftertaste.

Little Kings Cream Ale ★★★

5.5% alc./vol.
High-gravity brewed;
O.G. equivalent to 1053
Ingredients: six-row pale malt; corn syrup or grits, dextrose; Hallertau and Cluster hops

Appearance: yellow-straw; near-white, slightly noisy head; good lacing. Aroma: dry cereal grain, moderate sweetness, hints of paper and white bread. Taste: light caramel dominated by a grainy, slightly tart bitterness. Fizzy. Finishes with hop bitterness, maizy sweetness and some earthiness. Little Kings is a warm-fermented lager. The success of this cream ale is due in part to its biscuity graininess.

Morlein's Cincinnati Bock ★★★¹/₂

Ingredients: Reinheitsgebot

Appearance: reddish dark amber; beige, quiet and stable head; good lacing. Aroma: toffee, toasted grain, nectarine. An unusual (and likable) characteristic of this bock is that peaty-smoky bitterness shows right at the start, on a firm toffee base. A tiny hint of nectarine or apricot in the midpalate changes in the finish to earthy bitterness and some fruit sourness.

Morlein's Cincinnati Select Lager ★★★¹/₂

O.G.: 1049

Ingredients: two-row pale and
caramel malts; Cluster, Saaz and
Hallertau hops

Here's a simple, enjoyable beer that shows what happens when "mainstream" taste meets honest Reinheitsgebot ingredients. This rounded, slightly grainy lager is the kind of beer that should give mainstream a good name. Appearance yellow-golden; near-white, very quiet and stable head; good lacing. Aroma: cereal, caramel, flowers, grass-hay — simple and pleasing. Taste: to start, malt sweetness balanced by cereal dryness. Midpalate, a bit of astringency (almost tannic), greenness, and perhaps a hint of apricot. Finishes with slight hop bitterness (15 IBUs) and grain dryness. Medium body and viscosity make this a highly drinkable beer.

● LIFT BRIDGE BREWING

1119 Lake Avenue
Ashtabula, Ohio, 44004
216-964-6200
Capacity: 1,200 barrels
Year started: 1994
Tours available: phone ahead
Glassware and merchandise available

Once an important terminal on the Underground Railway, Ashtabula, Ohio, is where Dan Madden found his freedom. Madden grew up near Lake Erie. After attending law school in Columbus, he decided that he'd like to raise his family in a small town on the Erie shoreline.

Madden's a brewer, sailor and lawyer who wants to do more brewing and sailing and less lawyering. He seems to be getting his way. The Lift Bridge brewery, in which he is the brewer and jack-of-all-trades, is located not far from Ashtabula's lift bridge and yacht basin. The lift bridge was built to remind motorists that they'd rather be sailing.

Madden says that Lift Bridge aims "to produce a high quality product from natural ingredients. Our motto is quality, not quantity." The brewery does "not use corn, rice, or other inexpensive adjuncts, which increase profits while compromising quality."

Lift Bridge bottles about two-thirds of its production; the rest is sold on tap.

Beer is a food, Madden says. He believes that some of the larger breweries push beer as an alcoholic product, and aim their marketing efforts at younger drinkers. Lift Bridge aims to tap into the growing interest in beer, and to remind people, Madden says, that "Europe isn't the only place that can make great traditional beers."

Amber Lager ★★★¹/₂

4.4% alc./vol.
O.G.: 1048
Ingredients: two-row pale,
caramel, munich, and carapils
malts; flaked barley; Perle hops

Appearance: amber, with a pale beige, very quiet and stable head; good lacing. Aroma: butterscotch, hay, (good) diacetyl, leather. I like this buttery, slightly viscous lager. It starts with butterscotch balanced by a hayish hop bitterness, with touches of apricot, grain and peat. The finish is grain bitterness, hop bitterness (earthy, not grassy) and a hint of smoke. This profile — malty with some peaty and smoky elements — makes me think of a low-alcohol oktoberfest.

Eisbock ★★★★

6.9% alc./vol.
O.G.: 1072
Ingredients: two-row pale, munich,
caramel, carapils, chocolate and black
malts; flaked barley; Perle and
Hersbrucker hops

Not quite as huge or complex as Niagara Falls' Eisbock, this is still a great beer — very soft, thanks to the eis process. The yeast is a Bavarian lager yeast. Appearance: mid amber tinged with orange; beige, fairly quiet and stable head. Aroma: demerara, butterscotch-toffee, peach-plum-date, hints of peat, roasted grain, diacetyl and oak. Flavor: butterscotchy with peach or nectarine notes to start, Eisbock has some sassy, grassy hop taste midpalate, as well as a touch of tartness and grain bitterness. The finish dries nicely, with firm hop bitterness (oak, hay), and in the aftertaste, sherry warming and metallic bitterness at the back of the tongue.

Extra Special Bitter ★★★★

6.6% alc./vol.
O.G.: 1070
Ingredients: two-row pale, caramel and
carapils malts; flaked barley; Northern
Brewer and Willamette hops

Appearance: reddish mid-amber; beige, quiet head. Aroma: caramel and plums, roasted grain, peat, floral hops. Taste: soft and sweetish toffee, offset nicely by some plummy and peaty notes. In the swallow, some fruit astringency and grain roastiness. This lovely ale finishes with a grassy but svelte hop taste, moderate hop bitterness and flaked barley dryness. I like the touch of iron in the aftertaste.

High viscosity, medium body. This ESB would go well with stroganoff or any medium-sweet fruit dessert, such as pears poached in beer.

India Pale Ale ★★★¹/₂

5.3% alc./vol.
O.G.: 1052
Ingredients: two-row pale, caramel and carapils malts; flaked barley; Northern Brewer and Cascade hops

Appearance: amber; pale beige head; good lacing. Lovely aroma: lightly roasted grain, peat, nectarine and toffee with some high alpha and some floral hop character. Taste: butterscotch and apricot with some plummy astringency and a hint of peat. Finishes with hop-flavored bitterness, iron, and a pleasing hint of oak. This rounded and satisfying ale is like an IPA in its hop character, but lacks ethyl complexity and is perhaps too soft and butterscotchy for the IPA style.

Oatmeal Stout ★★★★¹/₂

5% alc./vol.
O.G.: 1055
Ingredients: two-row pale, carapils, chocolate and black malts; flaked oats and roasted barley; Galena and Fuggles hops

Here's a great dessert beer (the brewer says it makes a fine ice-cream float). It would also be a magnificent "drawing room" ale. Sip. Converse. Sip. Appearance: dark cola-brown with red highlights; mocha-colored, quiet, stable head. The aroma is lovely: prune-fig-raisin, mocha, roasted grain, forest, and earth. The taste starts soft and very slightly sweet, with suggestions of café-mocha, biscuit-cereal, and plum-prune-raisin (very little sourness). Viscosity disappears nicely midpalate. Finishes with medium hop bitterness, some grain bitterness, and a lovely fading taste of dry, highly roasted malt, as well as some grassy hop taste. A balanced beer, nice movement front-to-back, and very big, I think, for a gravity of 1055. Pleasure-to-alcohol ratio: 13 to 10.

Oktoberfest ★★★★

4.9% alc./vol.
O.G.: 1052
Ingredients: two-row pale, munich,
caramel and black malts; wheat;
Northern Brewer hops

An oktoberfest with some bock characteristics. Appearance: reddish, mid to dark amber; with a café-au-lait-colored, quiet and stable head; good lacing. Aroma: toffee, brown sugar, okay diacetyl, roasted grain, nuts, hay, sherry — very nice, very bock-like. Taste: the aroma doesn't prepare you for the moderately aggressive hopping that makes this firmly malty ale very drinkable. Starts with toffee and dark fruit (raisins, figs, plums, prunes). A touch of smoke and peat mid-palate. Finishes with a lovely fade of soft earthy bitterness and lingering dark fruit; slight metallic edge.

Winter Gale Ale ★★★¹/₂

6.9% alc./vol.
O.G.: 1068
Ingredients: two-row pale, crystal and
carapils malts; flaked barley; Galena,
Perle and Cascade hops

Appearance: orangey mid-amber; orangey beige, quiet and stable head; good lacing. Aroma: butterscotch, apricot, dried apricot, some hay. Taste: soft and butterscotchy with some early grassy bitterness and fruit astringency. A long grassy-hop finish with nice floral elements. Not quite as complex as one might expect from a 7 percent ale (I wonder what some chocolate malt might do), this very drinkable, unfiltered winter warmer is worth seeking out.

ONTARIO

Ontario is the biggest beer province in Canada: it has more breweries, more brewpubs, more brands of beer than any other province. Its beer scene reflects British roots and the influences of later waves of immigrants from Germany, the United States and other countries. In the 18th and 19th centuries, Ontario was very British, and British influence was reinforced by the immigration to Canada of "Loyalists," Americans who remained loyal to Britain and the Crown during the War of Independence, and who fled to Canada (and Britain and the Caribbean) to escape American "republicanism." In one year alone, 1784, as many as 5,000 Loyalists settled in Ontario. In the 19th century, Ontario had scores of British-style breweries, producing a variety of ale, porter and stout.

In 1805 a group of Mennonites from Pennsylvania bought a tract of land in the Grand River Valley (present-day Kitchener-Waterloo). The village of Berlin was founded, and a large German-speaking community developed. In this part of Ontario, German-style breweries were operating by the mid-1800s. During the American Civil War, Ontario became an important exporter of barley and hops to American brewers.

Prohibition (1916–27) decimated brewing activity in the province, and when it ended, heavy-handed government controls were introduced, the kind of controls that discourage local brewers more than national brewers. Local brewers were also bullied by the large brewers. This bullying can be seen in a comment by E. P. Taylor, owner of the Carling brewery, when he wrote the premier of Ontario to say, "I told [the small brewer] that if the matter was not settled this week, our company would have to engage in a price war to regain our position and either put our competitors out of business or make them so groggy that they will behave."

By the 1970s, three large breweries, Carling O'Keefe, Labatt and Molson, dominated brewing and had a stranglehold on retailing. Fewer breweries, fewer styles, more adjunct . . . it seemed that Ontarians had fallen into a trance, and forgotten good beer. And then, in 1984, Jim Brickman opened the Brick Brewery in Waterloo. Upper Canada Brewing and the Wellington County Brewery opened shortly thereafter.

Suddenly, real choice and good quality were once again available. Although some folks thought that interest in beer was a passing fad, another dozen breweries opened. More good beer and more styles became available. Beer festivals were held. Interest in good beer wasn't a fad, of course; it was a show of loyalty to the province's past, to the good beer tradition that had been interrupted, but not forgotten.

Most beer is sold in the Beer Store. The LCBO (Liquor Control Board of Ontario), the provincial liquor monopoly, sells imports and some Canadian beer. Because small new breweries cannot afford Beer Store fees, a third tier of tiny "cottage" breweries is developing in the province. These breweries sell draft beer directly to pubs, and packaged beer at the brewery.

BRICK BREWING COMPANY

181 King Street South
Waterloo, Ontario, N2J 1P7
519-576-9100
Capacity: 120,000 hectolitres
Year started: 1984
Tours: by arrangement
Glassware and merchandise available

The plant is a handsomely restored, Victorian building. A brick building, of course. The location is Kitchener-Waterloo, two connected cities whose original names, Berlin and Waterloo, allude to two great brewing nations. Kitchener-Waterloo is the site of the largest Oktoberfest in the world outside Germany. And indeed, beer roots here owe much to the area's large German population.

Brick is Ontario's oldest microbrewer, and the first Ontario microbrewery to be listed on the Toronto Stock Exchange. For its first 12 years, Brick brewed lager only. In 1994 Brick brewed its first ale, Red Cap, and in 1996 it bought the trademarks of the Conners Brewery, a respected Ontario microbrewery known best for its ales. In 1997, Brick acquired Algonquin Brewing, a largish Ontario brewer that had been started in 1987 by Carling O'Keefe alumni. Brick also brews under license for Henninger Brau of Frankfurt, Germany, and makes Old Vienna for Molson for export to the United States. Molson has a minority stake in Brick.

"We like to see ourselves in two lights," says founder Jim Brickman, "as a local brewery, and as a brewery that comes up with new ideas — a specialty brewery, if you like."

Brickman seems neither pro- nor anti-growth, but rather opportunity-oriented in the best sense of the word. "Forget all the medals," he says (Brick has won many). "Forget the nice packaging. The question for us is: Can we make an excellent beer? If we can, if we can brew a really excellent beer, we'll do it, by ourselves or in an alliance."

Brewmaster Bill Barnes joined Brick in 1994, initially to brew Red Cap, and meet the challenge of introducing an ale yeast strain into what had been a lager brewery. At the age of 25, Barnes joined the Peller Brewing Company of Hamilton. He spent many years brewing for Carling, and now, in his seventies, he's back to brewing for a small brewery.

An obvious question for a brewer who has worked in both large and small plants: Are there advantages to working in a small plant? "Sure," Barnes says, "from the brewhouse right through to packaging, you can read it all at a glance. Here I can walk from end to end in five minutes. In a larger brewery, it can take thirty. . . . I enjoy the work. It's just three days a week, but of course your mind is on the brewing seven days a week."

Brickman, too, enjoys the business. "I love it," he says. "Look at all the different breweries in all the different countries. The brewing fraternity is a great one."

Amber Dry ★★¹/₂

5.5% alc./vol.
O.G.: 1050
Ingredients: two-row pale and carastan
malts; corn; Hallertau and Yakima
Cluster hops

Mid amber, with a pale beige, slightly noisy head. Aroma: hints of toffee, grain and hay. Taste: not so much dry as moderately bitter: caramel-toffee offset by earthy bitterness; metallic edge in the finish. Slightly astringent mouthfeel, hint of ethyl. Pleasure-to-alcohol ratio: 8 to 10.

Anniversary Bock ★★★★¹/₂

7% alc./vol.
O.G.: 1067
Ingredients: two-row pale, carastan and black malts;
roasted barley; Hallertau and Yakima Cluster hops

This bock varies a little year to year. The 1994–95 tenth anniversary edition was higher in alcohol, virtually a double bock, and definitely a five-star beer. In other years, in the 7 percent range, it varies in terms of the play of its darker flavors. The 1996–97 version was overwhelmed by hops, a real disappointment. In its better years, it is a standout among North American bocks. Appearance: reddish, very dark amber; café-au-lait-colored, quiet and stable head. Aroma: chocolate, fruit (plum, dried apricot, fig, date, raisin), toffee, sherry-phenolic, molasses, vanilla. Taste: initially, all of the flavors associated with these aromas, especially toffee, figs and dates. Then, a long, slow finish, with grain and hop bitterness, traces of vanilla, something akin to espresso, earthiness, and a small, perfectly appropriate metallic edge. Pleasure-to-alcohol ratio (at 7% alc./vol.): 12 to 10.

Henninger Kaiser Pilsner ★★★★

5% alc./vol.
O.G.: 1047
Ingredients: two-row pale
malt; Hallertau and Yakima
Cluster hops

This splendid, brewed-under-license lager is worth seeking. Kaiser Pils is a good example of the soft, malty German pilsner style. Delicate, subtle, and very smooth, Kaiser Pilsner shows what can be done using good quality pale malt and simple, judicious hopping. Appearance: straw-gold; near-white, quiet, stable head; good lacing. Aroma: white bread, dry grain, grass and flowers. Taste: lightly astringent, mildly bitter, softly malty palate. Caramel and graininess are offset by some early hop bitterness, and a touch of grapefruit skin astringency. Grassy bitterness to finish (26–30 IBUs). Very good carbonation.

Premium Lager ★★★★

5% alc./vol.
O.G. 1047
Ingredients: two-row pale malt;
Hallertau and Yakima Cluster hops

I've long liked this clean, Reinheitsgebot lager. It's a brand that shows that "clean" needn't be a dirty word. Unlike many "clean" beers, this lager provides great rewards. Appearance: straw-gold; near-white head; good lacing. Aroma: grain, white bread, hay, Hallertau (sun on grass), and hints of flowers. Taste: a mix of dry grain and caramel with some huskiness to start. Drying a little in the finish, the bitterness (24–28 IBUs) evolves from grassy to earthy to slightly metallic — just right for the style. A fine, food-friendly beverage.

Red Baron ★★

5% alc./vol.
O.G.: 1047
Ingredients: two-row pale malt;
corn; Hallertau and Yakima
Cluster hops

Appearance: straw-colored with a white, slightly noisy head; little lacing. Aroma: dry grain and paper. Taste: grainy, with some caramel and paper to start; mild earthy bitterness to finish. A bit too much adjunct for the malt, I think, but drinkability is helped by the use of good-quality hops, which shows, even with the modest level of hopping.

Red Cap ★★¹/2

5% alc./vol.
O.G.: 1047
Ingredients: two-row pale malt; corn;
Yakima Cluster, Hallertau and
Bullion hops

The beer cemetery, alas, has headstones for many old friends. What do you do when a dead brand comes back to life? Pour a glass, I guess. In 1994, Red Cap came back. Old-timers will remember Carling Red Cap, which in its day was a very big label, one of the best-selling beers on the market. At least theoretically, Brick's Red Cap is identical to the beer sold by Carling in the 1960s. Red Cap's an interesting beer to illustrate the role of adjunct. With less than 10 percent corn adjunct, Red Cap has more malt flavor than many mainstream ales, which may have three or four times as much corn, making them sweet and maizy. Corn is detectable in Red Cap at cellar temperature (sweetness and paper), in part, perhaps, because of low hopping (13–17 IBUs), but I enjoy this drinkable ale. The red jockey's cap connects this ale with former Carling brewery baron, E. P. Taylor, who owned many racehorses, including Northern Dancer.

Waterloo Dark ★★¹/2

5.5% alc./vol.
O.G.: 1050
Ingredients: two-row pale and
carastan malts; corn; hops

Dark red-brown in color, with a café-au-lait-colored, slightly noisy head. Attractive aroma of caramel, vanilla, roasted grain, sugar, cut grass. Taste: sweet toffee, licorice, some coffee, apricot, and burnt toast. While corn flavor doesn't show, adjunct sweetness does. A stronger malt base would help to carry the various flavors.

Algonquin Country Lager ★★

5% alc./vol.

This golden lager has a near-white, noisy, quickly collapsing head. Aroma: sweet, maizy, papery. Low hopping and too much adjunct give this beer a sweet, cardboardy profile. Some nice husky touches.

Formosa Springs Bavarian Bock ★★¹/2

6% alc./vol.

This Algonquin brand is mid amber, with a tinge of orange, and has a beige, slightly noisy head. No lacing. Aroma: toffee, peat, wood, plum and raisin, corn and paper. Taste: butterscotch-toffee, fruit (cherry? apricot?), and grain huskiness. Some roasted malt and paper midpalate. Finishes with earthy hop bitterness, cardboard and metal. The flavors don't quite complement one another. Slightly fizzy.

Royal Amber Lager ★★★¹/2

5% alc./vol.

Appearance: amber colored with a pale beige, quiet and stable head; good lacing. Aroma: caramel, grain, hint of apricot, traces of okay diacetyl and hay. Another Algonquin brand, Royal Amber starts with caramel, butterscotch, some okay diacetyl, and some apricot-plum. To finish, a mild hay bitterness. Very drinkable, a bit overcarbonated. With its caramel, butterscotch and mild fruitiness, this is an ale-like lager. Wheat malt is used, but is evident only in lacing.

Special Reserve Dark Ale ★★★

5% alc./vol.

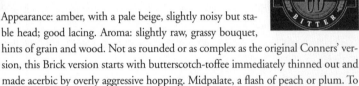

Appearance: russet-tinged amber, with a beige, slightly
noisy head (collapses in about 30 seconds). Aroma: caramel,
fruit (plum, apricot, berries), wood, paper, hint of hay. Algonquin brand. Taste:
sweet, slightly maizy caramel, some plum or apricot, offset by some earthy-
papery bitterness. When fresh, a touch of fruit tartness shows in the swallow.
Finishes with lingering malt, paper or wood, and a hint of peat. When fresh,
this ale shows its fruit nicely; when stale, paper-cardboard is prominent.

Conners Best Bitter ★★★

5% alc./vol.

Appearance: amber, with a pale beige, slightly noisy but stable head; good lacing. Aroma: slightly raw, grassy bouquet,
hints of grain and wood. Not as rounded or as complex as the original Conners' version, this Brick version starts with butterscotch-toffee immediately thinned out and
made acerbic by overly aggressive hopping. Midpalate, a flash of peach or plum. To
finish, firm bitterness, slightly too grassy and metallic. Acidic-metallic aftertaste.

Conners Dark Ale ★★

5% alc./vol.

A disappointment for fans of the old Conners brand.
Appearance: russet to dark amber, with a pale beige, quiet and stable head; very
good lacing. Aroma: grainy, with hints of toffee, lactic acid and grass. Taste: dominated by an out-of-balance grassy acidity, the result, I would guess, of an unsuit-
able, high-alpha hop strain overwhelming a tenuous malt base. Too fizzy.

● COPPERHEAD BREWING COMPANY

174 Colonnade Road South
Nepean, Ontario, K2E 7J5
613-226-8340
www:Copperhead-Brewing.com
Capacity: 6,000 hectolitres
Year started: 1992
Tours: on demand
Glassware and merchandise available.

Brian Nixon, owner and brewer at the Copperhead Brewing Company, says,
"We're specialty brewers. We're trying to create Canadian-style beers, not just

import European styles. We take pride in waving the flag, and think that Canadian beer should be better known."

Located in the Ottawa suburb of Nepean, Copperhead sells about 98 percent of its beer on draft in area pubs and restaurants. The rest is sold in plastic 500-ml bottles at the brewery.

Nixon believes that almost half of the people who drink his beer are women. "We try to make beers that are neither too strong nor too light in profile, flavorful but drinkable, not just for special occasions, but for everyday drinking." Nixon thinks that breweries should try to educate beer drinkers, but also be able to give them a beer that will please them regardless of where they are on the learning curve.

Copperhead is looking at the United States as a possible market. "Ontario's beer retail system is oppressive," Nixon says, "but what doesn't kill you, makes you stronger. Small breweries have to learn to work together. I believe that in the future, they will have to form alliances, especially territorial alliances. Rather than finding my own distributor, I'd rather find a brewer who would like to look after my beer on a reciprocal basis."

The brewery's plans are to grow slowly, perhaps to the 20,000-hectolitre level, and to improve its retailing.

Redds ★★

4.8% alc./vol.
O.G.: 1050
Ingredients: two-row pale, carastan,
munich, roasted and chocolate malts;
Northern Brewer and Hallertau hops

Appearance: reddish, mid to dark amber; café-au-lait-colored, fairly quiet and stable head; good lacing. Aroma: dry, lightly roasted grain, paper. Taste: caramel, some paper, hint of toast. Hops on a slightly inadequate malt base give the impression of earthy-bitter thinness. 16 IBUs.

White ★★★

4.8% alc./vol.
O.G.: 1050
Ingredients: two-row malt; malted
wheat, rolled oats, orange peel and
spices; two types of hops

Gold in color, with a white, quiet and stable head; fair lacing. Aroma: grapefruit skin, lemon skin, caramel. Here's a straight-ahead and drinkable wheat. To start, caramel, grapefruit tartness and hop bitterness, all in balance. In the finish, the caramel disappears, the mouthfeel becomes more acerbic and a balanced bitter tartness remains. 21 IBUs. White's yeasty half-sister, Hefeweizen, available in Ottawa-area pubs, is even better.

CREEMORE SPRINGS BREWERY

Box 369, 139 Mill Street
Creemore, Ontario, L0M 1G0
705-466-2531
www:barint.on.ca/creemore
Capacity: 25,000 hectolitres
Year started: 1987
Tours available: often on a walk-in basis, or phone ahead
Glassware and merchandise available

"The fox knows many things, but the hedgehog knows one big thing." The remark, attributed to Archiochus, a pre-Socratic philosopher, may well have been meant to describe different approaches to brewing. I think of Creemore Springs Brewery as the hedgehog of Ontario brewing. It makes one brand (and one seasonal), and it tries as hard as it can not to grow.

Located in an old hardware store on the main street of the village of Creemore, near Georgian Bay, in a broad valley that contains the Noisy and the Mad Rivers, Creemore Springs appears to be a quiet, sane brewery.

Creemore's goal is no different than it used to be, says brewer Gordon Fuller: "It's to make a delicious beer, a beer that represents its style well, and at the same time is very drinkable."

The brewery brings water by tanker truck from a spring west of the village. "We don't treat the water at all," says Fuller.

Brewery founder John Wiggins is modest about the brewery's success and cautious about the future. "We've been through the honeymoon, and this period is ending. It behooves us not to be cocky. We need to be flexible and not to make too many long-term plans. We do some soul-searching. We're not complacent. We try to get an idea of where we are and measure ourselves against the competition."

Wiggins says that there will be a shakeout in the brewing industry. He says that currently there are no plans to expand, but he is interested in leveraging the brewery's expertise. Associations, partnerships and consulting are some of the possibilities. "Our plans are the same, only different," he says with a laugh.

"My job is rewarding," Wiggins says, partly because of "the people I work with. Also, it's a fickle business, so it's great to have a product that people seem to like."

Creemore Springs Premium Lager ★★★ 1/2

5% alc./vol.
O.G.: 1048
Ingredients: two-row pale, carastan and
carapils malts; Saaz and Hallertau-
Tradition and/or Hallertau-Hallertau
and/or Tettnang hops

Appearance: old gold, with a pale beige, quiet and stable head; excellent lacing.
Aroma: fresh bread, dry grain, Saaz (grass, flowers, hint of pepper), hint of fresh-

cut wood — clean and enticing. This stunningly well-made lager is softly malty, with just enough graininess and hop elements to beguile the senses. To start, a soft maltiness with toffee and grainy threads, offset by some early, delicate, almost woody hop bitterness. The finish is a dryish, very mild bitterness (22 IBUs), with the taste of grain and the quiet but clear taste of hops (grass, hay) apparent. Part of the glory of this classic is its relative bigness for its overall gentleness, an impression aided by perfect small-bubble carbonation. A German-derived lager yeast is used. The beer is loosely filtered. Available in 500-ml bottles, Premium is a different beer — greener, wortier — on tap. Premium has the Saaz-respectful hop taste of a Czech pilsner as well as the viscosity and low bitterness of the Vienna style. Very food-friendly, Premium is perfect on summer picnics, and malty enough to be a fine winter lager. Must be drunk fresh. The fragile beauty of this beer suffers under the harsh fluorescent light used in Beer Stores.

Urbock ★★★★

6% alc./vol.
O.G.: 1062
Ingredients: two-row pale, carastan,
carapils and black malts; Saaz hops

Appearance: mid to dark amber, russet tinge; beige, very quiet and stable head, very small bubbles; good lacing. Aroma: unusual for a bock in that Saaz is the first impression. In addition to the delicately floral Saaz, there's lightly toasted grain or fresh-baked bread, and hints of toffee and peat. Taste: a very soft toffee-caramel, with an apricot-plum flash as you swallow. Malt sweetness fades to a black malt bitterness in the finish. 31 IBUs. It's hard, I think, to make a good small bock. Bigness can mask flaws; smallness makes craftsmanship (or the lack of it) evident. This seasonal offering is a fine small bock, a welcome addition to the region's winter lagers.

● THE ELORA BREWERY

55 Mill Street
Elora, Ontario, N0B 1S0
519-846-2965
Capacity: 750 hectolitres
Year started: 1993
Tours available by arrangement
Brewery-related clothing available

Consider this thought from Ben Jonson: "In small proportions we just beauties see / And in short measures life may perfect be."

With a capacity of 750 hectolitres a year, the Elora brewery is, Jonson would say, a beauty of small proportion. Less poetically, it is one of the smallest commercial, non-brewpub breweries in North America. It occupies a space little bigger than a double garage. Unlike a double garage, this space has soul: a 19th-century limestone building that originally retailed grain from the mill across the street, and then became a bakery.

The Elora Brewery is the latest fruit of a very old tree, Taylor and Bate, a significant name in Canadian brewing history. Crozier Taylor, whose ancestors were principals in Taylor and Bate from its beginnings in St. Catharines in 1834, lives in Elora and is president and major shareholder of the brewery. The full name of the brewery — "the Elora Brewery Limited, operating as Taylor and Bate Brewery" — reflects this heritage.

Brewer Charles MacLean says that brewing at Elora "is a real art," given the brewery's size. "We like to have unique beers" within traditional styles, says MacLean. All of the controls are manual, which keeps him busy. "It's a lot more labor-intensive than most breweries."

"Best beer by a dam site" is the brewery's slogan. By a dam site it is, and by a mill site too. For across the street, Mill Street, and beside the dam, stands the Elora Mill. This imposing stone building, one of the few five-storey gristmills in existence, was a working mill for more than a hundred years. Now it is an upscale hotel, catering to tourists.

You can have a pint of Elora beer at the Mill and watch the Grand River roar down the limestone canyon. There are caves in the walls of the gorge, and whirlpools and rapids mark the course of the river. Native people believed that their spirits lived between the walls of this canyon. Just 15 metres away, in the middle of the river, stands the "Tooth of Time," a tooth-like rock formation. Interestingly, the Mill still provides electricity for some of the town, including the Elora Brewery.

I asked Crozier Taylor what he was hoping to achieve. "I'd like to return the product to the general public with as fine a reputation as it had hundreds of years ago," he said. "My objective personally is to reestablish the family brewery."

Grand Porter ★★★¹/₂

5.5% alc./vol.
O.G.: 1055
Ingredients: two-row pale, crystal,
chocolate and black malts; flaked barley;
Northern Brewer, Kent Golding, and
Fuggles hops

Appearance: very dark brown with red highlights; café-au-lait-colored, quiet, stable head; good lacing. Aroma: chocolate or mocha, grain and hay — simple and fetching. Taste: chocolate and roasted grain with sweet and dry elements; hint of nutshell. Some coffee in the swallow. Mildly grassy, almost minty, hop finish, with lingering mocha. Low to medium viscosity and low to medium body are bang-on for style.

Pale Ale ★★★¹/₂

5.5% alc./vol.
O.G.: 1056
Ingredients: two-row pale and crystal
malts; East Kent Golding and
Northern Brewer hops

This amber-colored beer is a straightforward, medium-bodied pale ale. It varies a little batch to batch in bitterness and roundedness. The simplicity of the formulation, I think, allows Goldings to show clearly. Quiet, stable head, and excellent lacing. Aroma: heather, caramel and fresh Goldings. Taste: caramel and some grain overtaken by hop grassiness. Finish is clean, with grassy hop taste, moderate bitterness, touch of hop spiciness. Occasionally, when hopping is lower, a hint of plums or currants is evident.

● GLATT BROTHERS BREWING COMPANY

151 Thompson Road
London, Ontario, N5Z 2Y7
519-668-6203
www.glattbros.on.ca
Capacity: 3,000 hectolitres
Year started: 1993
Tours available: phone ahead
Brewery-related clothing available

In the beer world, London, Ontario, is perhaps best known for the presence of Labatt. Could tiny Glatt supplant Labatt in London?

Not with the current retail constraints in place, says John Glatt, brewer and, with his brother Paul, partner in Glatt Brothers Brewing. "The Beer Store fees are unmanageable for a small operation," he says. The fees "constrain the retail market, but they are a reality, so we're trying to carve out a niche. American micros, given their retail scene, can get small brands on the shelf. We can't."

Glatt beers are available at the brewery in half-litre ceramic swing-cap bottles, and some brands are available at some local LCBOs. "If the retail system doesn't improve, the consumer will suffer," says John Glatt. "Ontarians won't have access to their own beers!"

Glatt brews a long line of beers. John Glatt says that the brewery is "trying to produce as wide a range as possible, including some of the things we consider important, Chilli beer and a framboise, for example. These specialties don't sell by the boatload, but they do help people remember our name."

The brewery relies on word-of-mouth advertising: "It's cheaper, and, in the long run, more effective." London is a university town, and like brewers in other university towns, Glatt finds the local students "conservative" with regard to

beer: "You'd think that students would be interested in trying new brands, but they are constantly bombarded by advertising from the big brewers."

The brewery would like to extend its retail sales in coming years to include, perhaps, Detroit and the Quebec market.

Avalanche ESB ★★★

4% alc./vol.
O.G.: 1044
Ingredients: include two-row pale and munich malts; flaked barley

At 4 percent alcohol, this is an ordinary bitter rather than an ESB. Appearance: mid amber; pale beige, quiet and stable head; good lacing. Aroma: butterscotch-toffee, hints of hay and wood. Taste: toffee and peat to start; a not-quite-metallic, not-quite-sour acerbic character midpalate; and acerbic, woody bitterness in the finish.

Barley Wine ★★★★

9% alc./vol.
O.G.: 1094
Ingredients: include two-row pale malt; roasted barley

Here's a simple, fruity barley wine in the best English tradition. This unfiltered ale shows some benefits of bottle conditioning; you might want to put a bottle away for a year. Appearance: russet to deep amber; café-au-lait-colored, quiet and stable head; excellent lacing. Aroma: toffee, caramel and rich ripe fruit (apricot, plums, berries), plus a hint of peat. Taste: to start, toffee, molasses, lush fruit (apricot, prune, cherry), and vanilla. Very dense, but viscosity is only medium: wonderful. To finish, the fruit and molasses dry, leaving a peaty, almost tobacco taste, a brandied-fruit and vanilla effect on the roof of the mouth, and an ethyl freeze above the canines.

Green Chilli ★★★

3.3% alc./vol.
O.G.: 1038
Ingredients: include two-row pale malt; flaked barley and chili peppers

Gold to light amber in color, with a near-white, quiet and stable head. Aroma: lightly toasted grain, fresh chili peppers. This low-alcohol, big-taste beer is marked by a pure chili taste on a caramel wood background. Medium hot. I very much like the freshness and purity of the chili flavor; the woody, almost cottony sensation in the finish points to the difficulty of getting hops to work in specialty beers. I think this hot beer would go well with hot foods such as tamales, stuffed chilies, spicy chicken wings. The label alludes to "digital fire brewing." Does this mean that the brewer sticks his fingers in the fire?

Double Roast Dark Espresso Ale ★★★¹/₂

5% alc./vol.
O.G.: 1055
Ingredients: include two-row pale,
munich and crystal malts; flaked barley
and an espresso decoction.

Appearance: dark amber, with a café-au-lait-colored, quiet and stable head. Aroma: mocha, coffee, chocolate, toffee. Taste: mocha, chocolate, roasted grain, finishing with coffee bitterness and some grain and hop bitterness. A bit too sweet and intensely mocha-ish for me, but a must-try for the mocha lover.

Framboise Strong Ale ★★

5.9% alc./vol.
O.G.: 1060
Ingredients: include two-row pale malt
and 20% raspberry juice

Cranberry red to amber in color, with a pale pink, quiet and stable head; little lacing. Aroma: raspberry juice, hint of hay. Taste: moderately sweet raspberry juice, coolerish or sodalike, with some mild, earthy hop bitterness. Carbonation a little harsh.

Harvest Ale ★★★★¹/₂

4.7% alc./vol.
O.G.: 1052
Ingredients: include two-row
pale malt

This is, to the best of my knowledge, the first "organic" commercial beer in Canada, or at least the first in recent times. I found the beer disappointing, but applaud Glatt for the initiative. Undoubtedly, this will be better in years to come. Straw-colored with a near-white, fairly quiet head, Harvest has an aroma of dry, toasted grain and wet paper. Taste: dry, acerbic, grainy and papery. In this light-bodied ale, the acerbic character combines poorly with the bitter, cardboard element.

Kölsch ★★★

4.7% alc./vol.
O.G.: 1052
Ingredients: include two-row pale and
munich malts; wheat

Appearance: light to mid amber; pale beige, fairly quiet head; no lacing. Aroma: light caramel, light grain, flowers — very nice. Taste: caramel with a peat offset, and peach-cherry-apricot sweetness. Finishes with a light hop bitterness, some grain bitterness, and some out-of-style sourness. Too sweet and fruity for the Kölsch style, but enjoyable.

Mulligan's ★★¹/2

4.5% alc./vol.
O.G.: 1045
Ingredients: include two-row pale malt;
flaked and roast barley

Light to mid amber; pale beige, quiet, stable head; fair lacing. Aroma: caramel and toasty grain in balance, plus paper, wood and hay. Taste: pleasant, unremarkable. Dry, lightly toasted graininess, some caramel, hint of tart plums. Woody-papery bitterness to finish.

Pale Ale ★★★¹/2

4.8% alc./vol.
O.G.: 1055
Ingredients: include two-row pale,
munich and crystal malts; flaked barley

Appearance: mid amber; beige, slightly noisy head; some lace. Aroma: butterscotch-toffee, apricot-melon, some hay. Taste: butterscotch-toffee, apricot sweetness, plum tartness, a bit of peat. To finish, a delicate hop bitterness, some hayish hop taste, a touch of earth. Pleasure-to-alcohol ratio: 11 to 10. Would make a fine cask-conditioned ale.

Ruby Porter ★★★

4.2% alc./vol.
O.G.: 1055
Ingredients: include two-row pale,
crystal and munich malts; roasted barley

Two phrases on the label of this beer regarding the porter style are puzzling: first, "The benefits of barley was [sic] common knowledge and was added liberally to this ale," and second, "nearly a lost beer style." One might get a strange idea of brewing from the first phrase; from the second, one might not realize that scores of porters are being brewed in North America. Appearance: dark amber, red highlights; quiet, stable, café-au-lait-colored head; good lacing. Aroma: roasty-grainy, toffee, hay, toast, plums or prunes. Coffee and fruit predominate the initial taste of this flavorful, low-viscosity porter. Note the relatively low alcohol for a starting gravity of 1055. Taste: fruit (plum-cherry, prune-raisin), coffee, toffee and some dry graininess. Finishes with a hop and grain bitterness, with hints of grass and wood.

Oktoberfester ★★★

4.4% alc./vol.
O.G.: 1046
Ingredients: include two-row pale and
munich malts; flaked barley

Light to mid amber in color, this seasonal has a beige, fairly quiet and stable head. Aroma: caramel, hints of apricot and flowers. Taste: caramel, plum, hint of apricot, and a nice peaty offset. In the finish, mild hop bitterness with a smoky, peaty character. Some viscosity helps this low-alcohol oktoberfest feel like a medium-bodied beer. Not big enough for style.

Wayback ★★★

4.4% alc./vol.
O.G.: 1042
Ingredients: include two-row pale malt;
flaked barley

Appearance: old gold; near white, fairly quiet and stable head; little lace. Aroma: lightly toasted grain, faint hay and flowers. Taste: balance of caramel and dry grain, finishing with hop dryness and peat-earth bitterness. This ordinary bitter is slightly fizzy.

● HART BREWERIES LTD.

175 Industrial Ave.
Carleton Place, Ontario, K7C 3V7
613-253-4278
www:HartCanada.com/
Capacity: 15,000 hectolitres
Tours: on Sundays, and other days by arrangement
Glassware and merchandise available

Starting with some of the brewing hardware of the old Ottawa Valley Brewing company, Hart Breweries opened its doors in 1991. The brewery is located in the charming town of Carleton Place, just west of Ottawa.

Blessed with an on-site artesian well, Hart doesn't need to dechlorinate its water. Open fermentation makes a visit to the brewery worthwhile, if only to see the thick mousse atop the fermenting ale. Hart uses a hop percolator, as well as the distinctive Ringwood yeast, which by now has developed a house profile.

Although several partners are involved in the business end of things, Hart is very much a family brewery. Founder of the brewery, and an amiable host for many of the brewery's tours is Lorne Hart. Hart believes that "small brewers should produce high-quality beers that are distinctly different." Hart also thinks it important to understand and be sensitive to a local market, in this case, the Ottawa Valley. Linda Hart, Lorne's wife, looks after the front office. Son Keith, who is head brewer, served some of his apprenticeship at the McAuslan brewery in Montreal.

Keith Hart says that it's important for Hart to be "dedicated to consistency and to minimizing variation." Part of what makes Hart beers unique, according to Keith, is the brewery's use of hops. "I really love hops. And I think that because beer drinkers are becoming more educated, they're learning to appreciate hop flavors."

Some Hart beers are available in a Real Ale format in the Ottawa and Toronto regions.

Amber ★★★¹/2

5% alc./vol.
O.G.: 1052
Ingredients: two-row pale, carastan, and
chocolate malts; torrefied wheat;
Cascade, Willamette, Tettnang and
Mt. Hood hops

Appearance: orangey mid-amber, with a very pale beige, very quiet and fairly stable head. Good lacing. Aroma: subdued hop impression, with a hint of sunlight on orange. More subtle and rounded than formerly, Hart's flagship brand is an ale that stands on its own and goes well with sweet and dark meats — a tart ale with heart. It starts caramelly and lightly tart, and then a clean, astringent hoppy flavor shows with enough caramel for support. To finish, a hop taste, some apricot sweetness and sourness, and just a hint of heather.

Cream Ale ★★★

4.5% alc./vol.
O.G.: 1050
Ingredients: two-row pale, carastan and
pilsner malts; torrefied wheat; Cascade,
Willamette and Saaz hops

Appearance: straw-gold; near-white, craggy head. Aroma: Saaz hops are evident in the delicate floral aroma, and nicely complement the green grassiness of the bittering hops: very appealing on a summer day. To start, Cream Ale tastes clean, a bit green, with some caramel and firm fruit. It finishes with hop flavor, modest bitterness, a touch of lingering caramel and some sweetness. All told, a quaffable and enjoyable beer with character.

Dragon's Breath ★★★★

4.5% alc./vol.
O.G.: 1047
Ingredients: two-row pale, carastan and
chocolate malts; torrefied wheat;
Cascade, Willamette and Mt.
Hood hops

Brewed for the Kingston Brewing Company, a fine brewpub in downtown Kingston Ontario, Dragon's Breath is a distinctive, highly drinkable ale, a real contribution to the evolving ale styles of the region. Appearance: light amber; good lacing. In the aroma one finds the first sign that this is a distinctive beer — the hops speak clearly. Malt is detectable, but only beneath the grassiness of the hops, which predominate. Taste: initially, lightly malty with some grain and hop bitterness that is more gentle (35 IBUs) than the aroma might lead you to imagine. Hop astringency and bitterness show in the finish, as does a lightly grainy, very slightly peaty taste. Pleasure-to-alcohol ratio: 12 to 10.

Festive Brown ★★★★

6% alc./vol.
O.G.: 1060
Ingredients: two-row pale, carastan, and
chocolate malts; torrefied wheat and
roasted barley; Northern Brewer,
Cascade, and Saaz hops

Launched in late 1994 as a seasonal beer, Festive Brown is, in terms of style, akin to but slightly hoppier than a north England brown ale. The aroma is inviting: apricot-plum, sun on oranges, hops, peat and toffee. Sometimes I think I detect cinnamon. Flavor starts with soft toffee and apricot notes as well as a hint of sourness. Some darker malt and grain flavors show in the middle. The finish has a delicate, slowly rising hop bitterness with a hint of peat and roasted malt. A nice balance of edges and roundedness. Festive is the first beer completely designed by brewer Keith Hart, who called the design process his "first real challenge in brewing." At the table, Festive is well suited to darker flavors: curry, bratwurst, steak and kidney pie, and roast vegetables. In Real Ale format, Festive is even finer.

Finnigan's Irish Red ★★

5% alc./vol.
O.G.: 1050
Ingredients: two-row pale, carastan,
carapils and chocolate malts; flaked
maize and torrefied wheat; Willamette,
Tettnang and Cascade hops

Appearance: mid amber hinting at orange; pale beige, craggy head. Good lacing.
Aroma: woody-yeasty, toffee, with a hint of fruit. Soft and malty to start, with
caramel turning to toffee. Apricot and some grain dryness show midpalate.
Finishes with hop bitterness and some paper.

Hardy Stout ★★★¹/₂

5.5% alc./vol.
O.G.: 1055
Ingredients: two-row pale, carastan and
chocolate malts; roasted barley, torrefied
wheat and flaked maize; Tettnang,
Hallertau and Mt. Hood hops

This walnut-colored stout is medium bodied and of average to high viscosity.
Torrefied (roasted) wheat helps produce a creamy head. Although this beer is
only moderately bitter (45 IBUs), grain bitterness (roasted barley) reinforces an
impression of a relatively dry and bitter stout. Hopping is aggressive, but well-
married to the malts. Initially, an impression of roasted grain (and nuts?), dry
toast, and perhaps a hint of fruit. The finish is relatively dry (not astringent),
with hints of chocolate, coffee and licorice. Ideal with oysters.

Valley Gold ★★¹/₂

5% alc./vol.
O.G.: 1052
Ingredients: two-row pale, pilsner, cara-
pils and crystal malts; torrefied wheat;
Hallertau, Tettnang and Mt. Hood hops

Appearance: yellow-gold; near-white, moussey head. Aroma: sweet, papery, faintly hoppy. Taste: sweet and caramelly, some hops in the swallow, tart and earthy
to finish.

● KAWARTHA LAKES BREWING COMPANY

687 Rye Street
Peterborough, Ontario, K9J 6X1
705-741-1819
Capacity: 2,500 hectolitres
Year started: 1996
Tours available Sundays
Merchandise available

Peterborough is an attractive, red-brick city on the Trent-Severn Waterway, the canal system that links Lake Ontario with Georgian Bay. In 1996, Kawartha Lakes Brewing opened, becoming Peterborough's first brewery since the Calcutt Brewing and Malting closed in 1922.

According to president Andrew Cousins, Kawartha Lakes Brewing has its origins in a longstanding friendship and in homebrewing: "Jon and I were home-brewers, but very serious ones. We milled our own grain. I was going to Trent University, and we were brewing a batch of beer when I proposed doing a feasibility study for a new brewery."

Jon Conquer, the brewer at Kawartha, may be one of the few brewers in Canada who combines an academic background in biology with several years' experience as a city cop. His explanation of KLB's roots: "Andrew and I went to high school together and we lived not far apart. He had family in England and he'd come back from trips to England talking about the beer. I remember reading about the opening of the Creemore Springs brewery. I went to Trent to study biology and fell in love with Peterborough. I became a police officer for eight years, but when I started brewing professionally, it took me back to my academic roots."

Kawartha Lakes started as a draft-only brewery. It introduced packaged beer in 1997 in large, 473-ml (16 American ounce) bottles, which are sold in eight-packs. Packaged beer is sold only at the brewery. KLB draft is available in Toronto, Kingston, Ottawa and Peterborough. Retailing at the Beer Store is "not a possibility," says Cousins. "It's not affordable. It's not a fair system."

Sales have outpaced predictions. Handling strong growth can be a real problem, according to Cousins. "You have to plan. Growth is great, but I'm fearful of rapid growth. Growing too fast can cost money. Our challenge is to get to our planned point — four to five hundred hectolitres per month — and hold it there."

Kawartha Lakes is one of the few breweries in North America that ferments in open vessels using a yeast other than Ringwood. KLB uses Young's London Ale yeast for all its beers.

As to the future, Conquer says that Kawartha will "concentrate on good beer and good service. That's where we started and that's where we're going."

Cream Ale ★★★¹/₂

4.7% alc./vol.
O.G.: 1047
Ingredients: two-row pale and carastan
malts; about 5% wheat malt; East Kent
Golding hops

Here's a lightly fruity, slightly tart, effervescent pale ale: a great ale for a picnic.
Pale amber below; up top, a near-white, moussey, very quiet and stable head.
Excellent lacing. Aroma: a fine balance of caramel, grain and very floral hops.
Taste: caramel and some (fine) diacetyl, mild tart fruitiness (plums mostly, some
hard fruit), hint of grain. Finishes with soft hop bitterness: a balance of flowers,
grass and hay (26 IBUs). A bit overcarbonated. Pleasure-to-alcohol ratio: 10 to 10.

Nut Brown Ale ★★★★¹/₂

4.5% alc./vol.
O.G.: 1049
Ingredients: two-row pale, carastan,
munich, chocolate and honey malts;
wheat malt; Perle and East Kent
Golding hops

"I design beers in my head. Sometimes I luck out," says brewer Jonathon
Conquer. I'll say. This is a lovely ale — highly drinkable, with a range of nut
brown and mild flavors. Chestnut-mahogany in color. Head is café-au-lait, fairly quiet and stable. Excellent lacing. Aroma: soft, roasty tones over a toffee base.
Some floral-forest hints. Taste: initially, a balance of toffee, roastiness (that's the
chocolate malt) and fruit (apricot, plum), with some nice grainy dryness. I like
the sweet-bitter balance (sweet dominates a little), and the subdued hints of fruit
sourness. Finish is gentle, fairly pure hop bitterness (20 IBUs) over a hinting-at-
grain base. Soft yet firm, with a pleasure-to-alcohol ratio of 12 to 10, this flavorful ale is a very welcome addition to Ontario's lower-alcohol ale scene.

Premium Pale Ale ★★★★

5.2% alc./vol.
O.G.: 1052
Ingredients: two-row pale and carastan
malts; about 1% wheat malt;
Northdown, Fuggles and East Kent
Golding hops

Appearance: mid amber; beige, quiet, stable head. Very fine bubbles. Aroma: subdued caramel, some apricot, grain and hay, trace of flowers. At room
temperature, some fine diacetyl. Taste: caramel-toffee and apricot-plum; an
earthy-grassy bitterness kicks in early and firmly (37 IBUs). Grass bitterness in

the finish, with hints of toffee, grain and fruit tartness lingering in the medium-plus viscosity. Like the Peterborough town clock depicted on the label, this Pale Ale is meant to be noticed. Premium's clean, grassy bitterness would make it ideal as an accompaniment to sweetish meats (pork roast, steak, duck) and vegetables (corn on the cob, sweet potato).

Raspberry Wheat ★★★¹/₂
4.5% alc./vol.
O.G.: 1047
Ingredients: two-row pale, carastan and
one other malt; 50% wheat malt and
raspberry extract; Perle hops

Russet-amber in color, with a near-white, quiet and stable head, RW has a great collar of wheaty lace. Aroma: raspberry juice, hints of caramel and grass. Taste: raspberry and soft malt flavors quickly offset and thinned out by a floral, plum-my tartness. Finish is mildly woody, mildly metallic, mildly acidic tart-bitterness. Honest raspberry flavor. On tap this ale is sweeter, and I like to mix it (one to ten) with stout or lager. It would make a good float, and could be used in making a fruit crumble.

● LAKES OF MUSKOKA COTTAGE BREWERY

13 Taylor Road
Bracebridge, Ontario, P1L 1S0
705-646-1266
Capacity: 4,000 hectolitres
Year started: 1996
Tours available Sundays; call ahead
Brewery-related clothing available

Gary McMullen was born in 1967, Canada's centennial year, and grew up in Huntsville, in the Muskoka Lakes region of Ontario. Muskoka is southern Ontario's cottage country: three large and several small lakes nestle among granite hills, the southern reaches of the Canadian Shield. "The beer we're brewing is like the Muskoka Lakes: unique and clean," McMullen says.

The brewery's single product is a cream ale. The uniqueness McMullen refers to is in the profile and the style. "When I first started to formulate a North American cream ale style, I wasn't happy. I decided to look across the Atlantic for further inspiration." The result, he says, is a darker, hoppier cream ale.

McMullen says that the brewery's goal is to establish itself as a "niche brewery" with a focus on quality. "There's a lot of change in the market these days," McMullen says, and one way to protect the business against fickle markets is to "build a strongly loyal following. The challenge is to educate local consumers that beer can be fresh and local."

The brewery's main market is the Toronto region, and it is looking "very cautiously" at selling beer in Northern Ontario. So far, Muskoka Cream is available only at the brewery and the LCBO, as well as on tap at various pubs. Goals for the future are "modest growth, to grow with changes in the market."

Muskoka Cream ★★★★

5% alc./vol.
O.G.: 1050
Ingredients: two-row pale and carastan malts; malted wheat; two types of hops

Here's a welcome addition to the world of pale ale. Appearance: light amber; pale beige, quiet and stable head. Aroma: apricots, dried apricots, plums; caramel or toffee; traces of hay and flowers; plus a wee trace of okay diacetyl-leather. Initially, Muskoka Cream tastes of caramel and fruit (apricot and plum), with hops leaving two impressions: grassiness, and fruity, almost metallic tartness. Midpalate, there's a delightful flash of toffee. The finish is long, with grassy, earthy hop bitterness as well as grain dryness. 28 IBUs. A great, food-flexible beer.

● NIAGARA FALLS BREWING COMPANY

6863 Lundy's Lane
Niagara Falls, Ontario, L2G 1V7
905-374-1166
Capacity: 16,000 hectolitres
Year started: 1989
Tours available by appointment
Glassware and merchandise available

One of the bloodiest battles that ever occurred between Canada and the United States took place in Lundy's Lane toward the end of the War of 1812–14. Almost 1,400 men were killed or wounded. Neither side won, but following the battle, the Americans retreated to Fort Erie. Lundy's Lane in Niagara Falls is now home to one of North America's great, innovative breweries: Niagara Falls Brewing.

Founded in 1989, the brewery was the first in North America to make an eisbock (since 1989) and, to my knowledge, the first to brew a maple-wheat beer and an apple ale. Think of the those folks who, for excitement, go over Niagara Falls in a barrel. Niagara Falls Brewing is similarly daring, but with a better chance, I believe, of survival. Its ambitions are oriented to quality and interest, rather than just market share. "We try to produce unique products. We're not afraid to experiment," says Claude Corriveau, general manager and brewer at Niagara.

Niagara Falls would like to "elevate the image of beer, to go beyond its current public perception and to put it on the same level as wine," Corriveau says. Beer hasn't yet developed "the kind of mystique that wine has, but perhaps it should." Corriveau should know: he has a background in wine, as do other partners in the brewery.

As to the future, Niagara would like to maintain its reputation for "unique, high-quality products." Other goals are to brew at capacity (the brewhouse was expanded in 1996) and to pursue the American market. Niagara Falls beers are available in parts of the United States. Corriveau would like to see a full 40 percent of production sold south of the border.

If Niagara Falls products had been available in 1814, I reckon the Americans might have put their weapons down and joined their Canadian neighbors for a beer.

Apple Ale ★★★¹/₂

6.5% alc./vol.
O.G.: 1062
Ingredients: two-row pale malt; wheat malt; apple concentrate from three apple varieties; Northern Brewer and Nugget hops

Not a cider, but North America's first apple beer, and very apple-ish it is, redolent of Granny Smith and McIntosh. Appearance: yellow-gold, wee tinge of green; near-white, very quiet and stable head; very good lacing. Aroma: fresh apple cider, dominated by Granny Smith; wee hints of caramel and hay. Taste: apple cider partly offset by caramel and malt, hints of spiciness (almost ginger, almost cayenne, but very subdued), and hay. The finish is half apple tartness and half hop bitterness. Aftertaste: yeasty-earthy mild bitterness with some warming ethyl and spice. A successful marriage, I think, of fruit and grain. Excellent low carbonation. 20 IBUs. Try this one with weiner schnitzel, warm apple pie, or fruit-and-brandy desserts.

Brock's Extra Stout ★★★★¹/₂

5.8% alc./vol.
O.G.: 1057
Ingredients: two-row pale, carastan, (malted) roasted barley, and chocolate malts; (unmalted) roasted barley; Nugget, Hallertau, and Northern Brewer hops

Perhaps because an ancestor of mine helped to carry General Isaac Brock off the Queenston Heights battlefield (where Brock was mortally wounded in the War of 1812), I've always had an interest in stout. I mean history. Here's a stout that is worthy of the Canadian hero; it's even bigger and better than it used to be. Appearance: dark cola; mocha-colored, craggy, quiet and stable head; good lacing. Aroma: toffee, pitch, burnt toast, plum-prune-fig (sour-sweet), licorice, hint of coffee. Taste: low carbonation helps produce a thick, creamy initial impression. To start, toffee, burnt toast, licorice, bitter chocolate and coffee. There's a blush of sourness (cherry or prune) midpalate. Brock's finishes with a wonderful dry bitterness (35 IBUs): burnt toast, roasted grain and tobacco. In the aftertaste, I find a wee bit of lingering coffee-like acidity. Medium-plus viscosity, big bodied.

Eisbock ★★★★★

8% alc./vol.
O.G.: 1060
Ingredients: two-row pale, carastan and ground roasted malts, one undisclosed barley malt; Hallertau hops

Eisbock is a potent form of bock beer. Icewine is a familiar concept to wine drinkers: you allow grapes to freeze on the vine, then press the frozen berries for their sweet, acidic and highly concentrated juice, which is then fermented into an exotic (and expensive) wine. Eisbock (ice bock) beer is made by freezing the wort (at temperatures as low as -15° C) and extracting the ice, which is water rather than alcohol. A beer of only medium-high original gravity, in this case 1060, thus gains in strength and character. The unique fortifying process results in a malty, velvety smooth, complex lager. Appearance: amber; very pale beige, quiet, stable head; excellent lacing. The seductive aroma is perfectly balanced: fruit (cherry, apricot, plum, hint of dates), toffee, grain, peat, forest and hay. Taste: soft, well-married flavors that present themselves in new combinations of emphasis throughout the profile. To start, apricot and toffee nicely offset by peat and a hint of tobacco. In the finish, just the right amount of peaty nutshell bitterness to complement, but not overwhelm, the still-firm malt base. Ethyl evident but soft. Very soft overall, very rounded and gentle for an eight percent beer. Pleasure-to-alcohol ratio: 13 to 10. Part of this is due to the gorgeous, delicate small bubble carbonation: liquid velvet on the tongue. Sold in 750-ml bottles, this is the perfect beer to call for after a good dinner, alone or with pastries.

Gritstone Premium Ale ★★★★

5.5% alc./vol.
O.G.: 1056
Ingredients: two-row pale, carastan, and ground roasted malts; Hallertau hops

An old friend, this flavorful ale. I could (and have) spent whole evenings, whole nights, with this pleasing but characterful companion. Appearance: amber, with a pale beige, stable head; very good lacing. Aroma: a bit hoppier, I think, than formerly — butterscotch-toffee, apricot, plum and peach, hints of oak, peat, hay, flowers and maybe a soupçon of vanilla. Flavor starts soft and fruity (apricot and nectarine, which is appropriate given the brewery's location in soft-fruit country) with caramel, a hint of smoke and toasted grain. Perfectly suitable, slightly higher-than-average viscosity carries lots of flavor in the middle and the end. Fruit sourness, peat, and roasted grain are apparent in the finish, as is counterbalancing hop dryness and bitterness. A bit of astringent fruitiness in the aftertaste. 18 IBUs. Wonderful in bottled format, sometimes even better on tap.

Kriek ★★★★

6.5% alc./vol.
O.G.: 1060
Ingredients: two-row pale malt; wheat malt; sour cherry concentrate; Northern Brewer and Nugget hops

When Kriek was first launched in 1994, I thought of it as a promising start: better than many of the soda- or cooler-like fruit beers coming out, but still, not Liefmans. Which is unfair. I shouldn't expect a North American brewer to duplicate one of the best of the Belgian krieks, the mildly sour cherry beer style. Still, I think North American cherry and berry beers need some, usually more, sourness. They need a very firm malt base and a cunning use of hops (some of the Belgian brewers use stale hops). This kriek has gained in firmness and complexity over the years. Essentially a sour cherry version of Old Jack, with cherries added just before fermentation, Kriek is amber-tangerine in color, with a pinkish beige, stable head that is sometimes fizzy; good lacing. Aroma: fruit (cherry, hints of apricot, plum and pear), caramel, grain, toffee, peat, hay, flowers. Taste: lightly sweet malt firmness with some peat. In the swallow, a lightly tart, mildly sour cherry flavor and some early hop bitterness. The finish is mildly sour; sourness moves out to the edges of the tongue; hop bitterness lingers at the back of the tongue. Good carbonation. A bit thin for a 6.5 percent beer. Drink fresh. An excellent and unusual dessert beer.

Maple Wheat ★★★★

8.5% alc./vol.
O.G.: 1074
Ingredients: two-row pale and ground roasted malts; 15% wheat malt; maple syrup; Northern Brewer and Nugget hops

Here's the best maple beer I know of in North America. Judicious use of wheat for mostly technical properties and the right amount of residual sugar result in a real New World contribution to beer style. Gold or light amber in color, with a pale beige, very quiet and stable head; excellent lacing. The aroma is very refined and balanced for the style: fresh bread, maple sap, maple syrup, and (hard to accomplish, this) a minute whiff of hay and flowers. As always, the taste is a function of age and temperature. Despite the alcohol level, I think this one's best when fresh, although there's no bottled-on date to help. Maple flavors ferment out over time. The initial impression is of big, very true maple flavor and of superb soft carbonation. Depending on the vintage and the temperature, other flavors that show are caramel, mango-plum and smoke. The finish tends to smoky bitterness and some earth, with lots of lingering malt and maple. Pleasure-to-alcohol ratio: 10 to 10. Like half and halfs? Try mixing this ale with a stout.

Old Jack Bitter Strong Ale ★★★¹/₂

7.2% alc./vol.
O.G.: 1062
Ingredients: two-row pale, carastan, and
ground roasted malts; Nugget and
Northern Brewer hops

There's a wonderful moment of suspension when you sit in a pub, waiting for your friend to show. You order your beer, your mind clears, and your thoughts start to roam. That appears to be the state of mind of the fellow on the label of Old Jack. Appearance: light to mid amber; pale beige, quiet and stable head; excellent lacing. Aroma: rich butterscotch and toffee, apricot and peach, peat and hay — very enticing. Taste: soft toffee, lush mouthfeel, hints of apricot and peach. Some fruit tartness midpalate. Finishes with threads of smoke and peat in the still highly malty taste, with roasted grain, gentle grass bitterness (28 IBUs) and oaky-earthy tones. Style? A suave barleywine, I think, with the ethyl discreetly hidden under the sweetish, malty cloak. Pleasure-to-alcohol ratio: 9 to 10. A great cooking beer, Old Jack is happy in stews and soups.

Trapper Cold Filtered Draft ★★¹/₂

5% alc./vol.
O.G.: 1051
Ingredients: two-row pale
malt; 15% corn; Nugget and
Hallertau hops

Appearance: light gold; near-white head, some noise; good lacing. Aroma: sweetish caramel and grain, some diacetyl, paper or popcorn hints. Taste: caramel, nectarine or plum, some maizy sweetness. Finish: modest, slightly woody bitterness.

SLEEMAN BREWING AND MALTING COMPANY

551 Clair Road West
Guelph, Ontario, N1H 6H9
519-822-1834
Capacity: 400,000 hectolitres
in Guelph; 200,000 hectolitres in
western Canada
Year started: 1987
Tours available by arrangement
Glassware and merchandise available

The second (chronologically) of Guelph's two breweries, Sleeman Brewing is emerging as a national brewer. There are many barriers to the free flow of beer from province to province, but Canadian beer drinkers should be grateful to Sleeman for its efforts to overcome these barriers. When Sleeman broke into the Quebec market, despite opposition from Molson and Labatt, it became, to the best of my knowledge, the first Canadian brewer from outside Quebec to sell its beer there for many decades. "We're determined to be there, come hell or high water. We won't let Molson or Labatt stop us," John Sleeman told me in 1994. He didn't, and as a result, Quebec beer drinkers can now drink beer from other parts of their own country.

In 1996, Sleeman merged with the Okanagan Spring brewery of British Columbia, giving Sleeman a near-national presence. Sleeman is said to be looking for a Quebec-based brewery to acquire.

Sleeman markets itself as a revival of the old Silver Creek brewery in which president John Sleeman's grandfather, great-grandfather and great-great-grandfather were involved. John Sleeman's grandfather was caught smuggling beer into Detroit in the 1930s. Two generations later, grandson John is selling his ale legally in the United States.

Despite the company name, Sleeman does no malting. Head brewer Al Brash says that Sleeman is "trying to make the truest beer we can. Whatever the category, we do what we have to make the best beer. We don't compromise for cost considerations. John Sleeman doesn't even know what hops cost. He doesn't care."

In addition to its own beer, Sleeman brews under license for Interbrew (Stella Artois) and Watney's (Red Barrel and Cream Stout). Brash points out that such contract brewing helps Sleeman not only to use its capacity, but also to better analyze and improve its brewing operations with the feedback, or "report cards," it receives from the other breweries.

Sleeman beers are available in most of Canada, as well as Michigan and Pennsylvania.

Cream Ale ★★¹/₂

5% alc./vol.
O.G: 1048
Ingredients: two-row pale and carastan
malts; corn grits and syrup (30%);
Fuggles and Goldings hops

This pasteurized Cream Ale is all ale. Appearance: copper; very pale beige, fairly quiet head. The aroma — caramel, husky grain, paper and hay — suggest the Canadian ale style. Taste: caramel with some early earth bitterness, some huskiness, some corn sweetness (but no cardboard). To finish, an earthy-woody bitterness; some astringency. A bit too fizzy, but adequate bittering and almost adequate malt make this a fine summer ale. Replacing half the adjunct with malt would make this a classic Canadian-ale-style beer.

Dark ★★★★

5% alc./vol.
O.G.: 1049
Ingredients: two-row pale and carastan
malts; Fuggles and Goldings hops

I very much like Dark, Sleeman's only all-malt beer. It suggests elements of the pale ale style, the brown ale style, and, I think, despite its alcohol, mild. The play between sweet and bitter is just right, and accentuated by peat and a touch of tartness. Appearance: amber, with a beige, very quiet and stable head; excellent lacing. Aroma: caramel-toffee with perfumy floral hops, hints of plum and peat. Taste: toffee and peat, with some early hop flavor. In the swallow, a tart plummy astringency. Finish is a nice mix of dark grain roastiness and mild but fresh hops. 22 IBUs.

Silver Creek Lager ★★¹/₂

5% alc./vol.
O.G.: 1046
Ingredients: two-row pale malt; corn
grits and syrup; Hallertau and Saaz hops

Appearance: straw to gold, with a near-white, slightly noisy head; good lacing. Aroma: dry grain, trace of hay. Taste: sweetish, mildly husky flavor, caramel and corn. Finish is mild, slightly woody bitterness. Pasteurized. 19 IBUs. Not as malty or hoppy, and more highly carbonated than formerly.

TRAFALGAR BREWING COMPANY

760 Pacific Road, Unit 9
Oakville, Ontario, L6L 6M5

¿C'est What? Coffee Porter ★★★

5.5% alc./vol.
O.G.: 1060
Ingredients: two-row pale, munich,
carastan, chocolate and black malts;
rolled oats and two types of ground
coffee; hops include Northern Brewer

Coffee lovers, rejoice! You know it's sometimes tough to fit java into a busy beer day, but this porter, brewed for the ¿C'est What? brewpub on Front Street in Toronto, should help you to better manage your imbibing time. Appearance: coffee colored, with a stable, café-au-lait-colored head. Aroma: bang-on — coffee beans, roasted malt, roasted barley, molasses. Taste: varies with temperature and batch. I like this one cool — fridge temperature plus about ten minutes' warming time. This makes for a dark refresher in the same way iced coffee can refresh. Overall, the impression is one of espresso and roasty porter, with some chocolate hints. In its bottled format, Coffee Porter is available in just one or two Toronto LCBOs.

UPPER CANADA BREWING COMPANY

2 Atlantic Avenue
Toronto, Ontario, M6K 1X8
416-534-9281
Capacity: 100,000 hectolitres
Year started: 1985
Tours available by arrangement
Glassware and merchandise available

Upper Canada Brewing, founded in 1985, is one of the original three breweries of the modern craft beer renaissance in Ontario.

Richard Rench, UC's brewmaster, brewed for Bass at Burton-on-Trent for about 13 years. His background is in yeast biochemistry. "Brewing is fun," he says. He very much likes the responsibility that goes with responding to the "unpredictable" work in a smaller brewery. "I like the decision-making that goes with the job."

Upper Canada's mission is to "make beers that taste good, look good and that are representative of their style, plus, to give the customer good bang for the buck," Rench says. Upper Canada was the first North American brewery to export to Germany, a country that then allowed the import of Reinheitsgebot beers only.

Upper Canada currently brews a half-dozen year-round brands and another half-dozen specialties. Rench would like to extend the specialty line to make "more weird and wacky" brews. About 70 percent of production is bottled; 30 percent kegged. "We may get up to twenty brands that we can brew on a seasonal or specialty basis, while staying with six or seven permanent brands." The brewery currently uses a single yeast, a German lager yeast. "If you know your malts and hops, you can do a lot with a single yeast," Rench says.

Rench says that, compared with the early years of the beer renaissance, "beer drinkers are now more selective, and a little more receptive, a little more willing to try."

In 1996, Upper Canada went public with a $25-million share offering. In coming years, Upper Canada would like to increase its exports to the American market. A brewery purchase in the United States is also contemplated. Frank Heaps, who founded the brewery, resigned as chairman in 1996, but remains a director and equity holder.

Colonial Stout ★★★

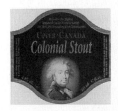

4.8% alc./vol.
O.G.: 1048
Ingredients: two-row pale, carastan and
black malts; Challenger and Cascade
hops; lager yeast

It's possible to make full-flavored, big-bodied ales that are still low in alcohol. In Britain, mild and brown ale are good examples of flavorful, low-alcohol beer styles. In the Great Lakes region, I like Breckenridge's lower-alcohol stout. Upper Canada's 4.8 percent stout is a fair attempt at a small stout, but needs a bit higher starting gravity, I think, and doesn't show the benefits that an ale yeast would bring. Some lacing in the glass, but not enough. Colonial fails the "head test" as stouts should not: almost no head after one minute. Faint, but attractive aroma, with black malt, and some hops detectable. Taste: dominated by black malt, some grass. A good balance between hop bitterness and black malt bitterness; not enough malt firmness. Thin in body and mouthfeel. 40 IBUs. Pleasure-to-alcohol ratio: 9 to 10.

Dark Ale ★★★¹/₂

5% alc./vol.
O.G.: 1048
Ingredients: two-row pale, carastan,
crystal and black malts; Challenger
hops; lager yeast

Appearance: mid to dark amber; beige, quiet and stable head; fair lacing. Aroma: toffee, peat, leather, hint of hay. Taste: slightly smoky toffee, some butterscotch and diacetyl, hints of mocha and early hop grassiness. Finishes with a mild hop taste, hop and grain bitterness, some toasty-roastiness. 25 IBUs.

Lager ★★¹/₂

5% alc./vol.
O.G.: 1045
Ingredients: two-row pale malt;
Hallertau Northern Brewer and
Hallertau-Hersbrucker hops

Appearance: gold to light amber; near-white, slightly noisy head; fair lacing. Aroma: lightly toasted grain, gueuzy caramel, flowers. I think two things work against this brand: a sort of gueuzy-butterscotch form of diacetyl (evident against the plain pale malt background), and low hopping. Taste: butterscotch, leathery-gueuzy diacetyl, some graininess, some lactic tartness. In the finish, butter, hops, and lactic-earthy bitterness (22 IBUs). Medium body, medium-plus viscosity.

Light Lager ★★★

4% alc./vol.
O.G.: 1037
Ingredients: two-row pale malt;
Hallertau Northern Brewer and
Hallertau-Hersbrucker hops

Appearance: golden, with a near-white, quiet and stable head; some lace. Aroma: caramel, gueuze-butterscotch (diacetyl), faint hay. A wee bit too much diacetyl, but other than that, a flavorful, lower-alcohol lager. Initially, a gueuzy caramel offset by sweet and sour fruit, with an astringent grainy background. Hint of grapefruit skin midpalate. To finish, hop and grain bitterness, a touch of earthiness, and lingering citric tartness. Pleasure-to-alcohol ratio: 10 to 10.

Rebellion Ale ★★★

5.2% alc./vol.
O.G.: 1049
Ingredients: two-row pale, carastan and
black malts; Cluster and Cascade hops;
lager yeast

Appearance: mid amber; beige, fairly quiet and stable head; good lacing. Aroma: toffee, peat, earth, gueuze-lactose-leather, hint of flowers. Taste: toffee, butterscotch, some early hop taste and bitterness. To finish, a grassy-earthy hop bitterness (29 IBUs), some plummy tartness, with residual toffee-flavored viscosity.

Rebellion Lager ★★★¹/₂

6% alc./vol.
O.G.: 1057
Ingredients: two-row pale malt;
Hallertau Northern Brewer and
Hallertau-Hersbrucker hops

Appearance: gold; near-white, slightly noisy head; good lacing. Aroma: toffee, butterscotch, gueuze, hay. Taste: light toffee offset by peat and some early hop bitterness. Is there a hint of apricot or plum? Finishes with two complementary forms of bitterness: mildly grassy and earthy. Relatively long conditioning subdues the gueuzy character, and adds subtlety and balance. The butterscotchy character of this lager would make it go well with buttered lobster. You can also use Rebellion to make a sweet beer sauce for crème brûlée. 28 IBUs. Pleasure-to-alcohol ratio: 9 to 10.

True Bock ★★★¹/₂

6.5% alc./vol.
O.G.: 1062
Ingredients: two-row pale, carastan and
black malts; Hallertau-Northern Brewer,
and Hallertau-Hersbrucker hops

I like this bock, in part because of its three months' conditioning. It changes a little year to year; sometimes it's got some dark flavors, sometimes it's a little lighter in palate and body. Appearance: medium to dark amber with a touch of orange; beige, quiet and fairly stable head with small bubbles. Aroma: plum-apricot-mandarin, butterscotch, some heather or grass. The taste is fruity. Plum, nectarine, maybe even a hint of cherry, as well as some caramel, give way to a bit of sourness and black malt peatiness. The beer "darkens" as it finishes. A soft but durable bitterness shows (30 IBUs), as does some fruit and metal. This bock has enough complexity to engage the tongue and the brain. I like it with bratwurst; I also like to sip this one on a February day when the snow melts and I see that the sun is a bit higher in the sky than it used to be.

Wheat ★★¹/₂

4.3% alc./vol.
O.G.: 1041
Ingredients: two-row pale malt;
malted wheat (roughly 50% of
each); Hallertau-Northern Brewer
hops; lager yeast

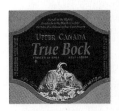

A relatively small wheat beer, perhaps because of the yeast, more or less in the Weizen style, but with no banana esters. Yellow-straw in color, with a white, slightly noisy head; fair lacing. Aroma: grain and lemon skin, some butterscotch, some hay. Taste: slight lemon tang on a dry grain and caramel base. Finish is a pleasant mix of tartness and bitterness. When Wheat is less than fresh, the head disappears quickly and the dry grain and lemon flavors diminish.

Winter Brew ★★★¹/2

7.4% alc./vol.
O.G.: 1072
Ingredients: two-row pale, caras-
tan, crystal and black malts;
Challenger, Cascade and
Hallertau-Hersbrucker hops

God gave us memory so that we might have roses in December. So said J. M. Barrie, the Scottish author of *Peter Pan*. Aye, and malt that we might have a solar souvenir in January. Here's a unique beer that celebrates winter, and that shows how strong lagers can achieve the softness and complexity — and even some of the fruitiness — one associates with winter ales. It's dressed for winter: russet-amber below, with a creamy beige cap. Aroma: brown sugar and caramel, with a distinct vanilla undertone; leafiness makes noble hopping evident. A very lush mouthfeel accentuates the soft, butterscotchy start. Then some surprising (for a lager) fruit undertones start to show: banana, plum, apple and pear. In the finish, hop bitterness with a metallic (iron?) and woody (oak?) edge, some ethyl, and fruit still showing in a hint of sourness.

Woody's Wild Ale ★★¹/2

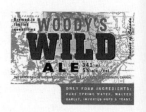

5% alc./vol.
O.G.: 1046
Ingredients: two-row pale and crystal
malts; Challenger and Willamette hops;
lager yeast

Amber colored, with a pale beige; quiet and stable head. Aroma: light toffee, hints of plum and peat. Taste: butterscotch-caramel, with some plum tartness and some diacetyl. The slightly acerbic mouthfeel heightens the woody bitterness of the finish. The label says "only four ingredients," and names them. I can understand that. I wish I could understand the freshness code. The label says "brewed in limited quantities": aren't all beers?

WELLINGTON COUNTY BREWERY

950 Woodlawn Road
Guelph, Ontario, N1K 1B8
519-837-2337
www:sentex.net/wellington
Capacity: 8,000 hectolitres
Year started: 1985
Tours by appointment
Glassware and merchandise available

Wellington County holds a special place in the affections of North American ale lovers. In its beers one can see a great deal of respect for the British ale tradition as well as a New World willingness to adapt. It is Ontario's second-oldest microbrewery, and the first modern brewery in North America to make cask-conditioned Real Ale.

Real Ale, says brewery owner Philip Gosling, was "the brewery's dream, right from the start. We wanted to make and sell Real Ale." He recalls with a smile, "We thought that every pub in Canada would want it. Well, we soon found out otherwise!"

Very few Ontario drinkers understood the concept of Real Ale in the mid-1980s. (Even today, I meet brewers who have never drunk Real Ale and who don't understand the term.) Gosling recalls the difficulties in getting publicans to handle the delicate beverage properly. Today, the Real Ale scene in the Guelph-Toronto area, small though it is, is the best in eastern Canada. Beer lovers who have discovered the joys of Real Ale can thank Wellington County for its pioneering efforts.

Mike Stirrup started at the brewery in 1987 as a "caustic washing and general joe-boy." He can remember a precise point at which he became keenly interested in beer. He was in Strasbourg with his father and brother. When they tried a strong lager called Jubilator, they were impressed enough ("it really stood out") to take a cab to the brewery and to ask for a tour. This was the start of what became a vocation. Stirrup worked under two brewers at Wellington before he was given the reins in 1992.

Stirrup says that the brewery's philosophy is simple: "quality before quantity. We use very traditional methods; it's a hand-operated brewery."

Stirrup is well aware of the reputation Wellington has built up over the years. While he's proud of formulating two new beers, Honey Lager and Iron Duke Porter, he is most proud of maintaining the brewery's reputation.

Arkell Best Bitter ★★★★

4% alc./vol.
O.G.: 1040
Ingredients: two-row pale,
crystal and chocolate malts;
Fuggles, Goldings, and Styrian
Golding hops

Appearance: light amber with a copper tinge; near-white head; good lacing. Aroma: caramel-toffee, peat, apricot-plum, some hay and flowers. Who says low-alcohol beer can't have full flavor? Here's an ale that shows a deft brewing hand, a good example of how a good brewer can accomplish great things in a low-alcohol beer. A wonderful initial impression: toasted grain, nutshell, hints of apricot and peat on an adequately firm caramel base. Slight hint of almonds, slight astringency, slight nectarine sourness. Peaty and floral touches are adroit and evident from start to finish. Pleasure-to-alcohol ratio: 13 to 10. This is a five-star beer at its peak in a Real Ale format. I think it worth repeating something I've said before to dieters and those who want to reduce their alcohol consumption: Stop drinking that "Lite"; pour it down the drain. Rush out and buy this brilliant bitter. Great with traditional British fare: Cornish pasties, fish and chips, ploughman's lunch, shepherd's pie.

County Ale ★★★★

5% alc./vol.
O.G.: 1052
Ingredients: two-row pale, crystal and
chocolate malts; Magnum, Goldings
and Styrian Golding hops

Complex, robust, and full of character, here's a pale ale to savor. County Ale is big but well mannered. It introduces itself diplomatically with an aroma of light toffee, some roasty graininess, some roasted nuts (filberts? chestnuts?), and a bit of Goldings-induced peatiness — all in all, beautiful and bewitching. Taste: to start, a soft, malty-toffee flavor nicely offset by roasted grain and just a whisper of soft fruit. The finish is a perfectly modulated hop bitterness and grain bitterness, with the latter suggesting nutshell (32 IBUs). The aftertaste nicely distills the start and finish. Medium viscosity. The movement from front to aftertaste and the complexity and balance at each stage makes this one of my favorite ales. County Ale has been available in Real Ale format for about a decade. In this format, the virtues of cask conditioning are dramatically evident. With soft, minute-bubble carbonation (carbonation as God meant it to be) and a slightly "greener" flavor than in the bottle, Real Ale County Ale can be heavenly.

Honey Lager ★★¹/₂

5.2% alc./vol.
O.G.: 1048
Ingredients: two-row pale and carastan
malts; clover honey; Magnum and
Mount Hood hops; ale yeast

Appearance: gold-copper; near-white, fairly quiet and stable head; good lacing.
Aroma: caramel and butterscotch, hints of honey and confectioner's sugar combined nicely with floral hops. I'm not crazy about honey beers: if you like honey, drink mead, I say. In honey beers you tend to have cloying, glycol sweetness, or classically trained hops trying to dance with a partner who knows only line-dancing. This "lager" (an ale yeast is used) avoids the first problem, and doesn't do too badly with the second. Taste: some early hop bitterness complements (and doesn't muddy) the honey-malt sweetness. The honey taste is true, not glycol sweetness. Almost a ginger effect midpalate. Finishes with a woody-earthy bitterness, suggesting, perhaps, the challenge of getting hops to dance with honey.

Iron Duke ★★★★

6.5% alc./vol.
O.G.: 1065
Ingredients: two-row pale, crystal and
black malts; Northern Brewer, Goldings
and Styrian Golding hops

Appearance: reddish mid-dark amber; beige head; good lacing. Aroma: caramel-toffee, fruit (date, raisin, hint of apricot), peat, smoke. Taste: toffee and fruit (date, raisin, apricot), peat and hazelnut. Hops can't be tasted in the start, but they're there, keeping the toffee and fruit from cloying. A hint of grass in the swallow. The Duke "darkens" a little (hints of peat and smoke) as it bitters in the finish. Aftertaste: hints of oak. Pleasure-to-alcohol ratio: 12 to 10. A lovely strong ale, this one, a friendly and fetching bottle of delight. A mite less complex than formerly, perhaps, but an ale to cheer up Arthur Wellesley. Or any person who's had a hard day on the battlefield of life.

Iron Duke Porter ★★★★¹/₂

5.7% alc./vol.
O.G.: 1058
Ingredients: two-row pale, crystal,
chocolate and black malts; Magnum
and Mount Hood hops

Here's a wonderful porter: robust, unctuous, fruity and complex. A porter to remind Ontarians of their British heritage. But Ontarians won't find Iron Duke Porter in the Beer Store. It's brewed for the American market! Appearance: cola with dark red highlights; café-au-lait-colored, quiet and stable head; good lacing. Aroma: a teasing combination of toffee, dark fruit, baker's chocolate, and some roasty, almost spicy elements. Hugely roasty flavors mark the initial impression, as does chocolate and fruit (prune, plum, raisin, fig). A flash of fruit sourness in the middle. In the finish, this ale bitters some and dries a touch to a roasty grain bitterness. I find hints of grass, as well as lingering dark fruit in the aftertaste. This is not a quaffing beer. It would work well with game, baked beans and dark treacly desserts. It is splendid on its own. Pleasure-to-alcohol ratio: 13 to 10. Available at the brewery.

Premium Lager ★★★

4.5% alc./vol.
O.G.: 1046
Ingredients: two-row pale and carastan malts; Hallertau-Hersbrucker and Saaz hops; ale yeast

Straw-colored, with a near-white, fairly quiet head, this beer has a dry-grain and hayish nose. Sometimes I get a sense of flowers (Saaz), sometimes not. Premium has a nicely bitter and almost husky graininess in the start, together with a light caramel suggestion. I find a trace of grapefruit skin midpalate, which continues in the finish, where a grassy tart-bitterness shows.

S.P.A. ★★★★

4.5% alc./vol.
O.G.: 1045
Ingredients: two-row pale, crystal and chocolate malts; East Kent Golding, Goldings and Mount Hood hops

Appearance: mid amber; near-white, fairly quiet head; good lacing. Aroma: a fine example of Goldings as a just-so noble hop. Goldings hops are clearly evident beneath the caramel-butterscotch, as are some peaty, plum-apricot, and nutty notes. Malty and hinting at toffee to start, S.P.A. also shows a bit of delicate, plummy sourness. To finish, an earthy-nutshell bitterness with some astringency. Very balanced, excellent carbonation. Pleasure to alcohol ratio: 13 to 10. This classy ale is great with pita rolls, enchiladas, chicken salads, and steak and baked potatoes.

PENNSYLVANIA

A merica starts here," the slogan has it. Beer, too, had an early start in
Pennsylvania. In 1683, William Penn started the Pioneer Brew House at his
estate in Bucks County. A little later, in 1687, an English immigrant, Anthony
Morris, opened a brewery on Front Street in Philadelphia, which operated for
some 200 years. A brewery was built by the Moravian Brethren in Bethlehem
around 1740, and by the 1760s, breweries were operating in Fort Pitt. The state's
growing beer scene reflected the roots of its settlers: English, Scottish, Irish,
Dutch and German.

At one time there were more than 600 breweries in Pennsylvania, with as
many as 100 in Philadelphia alone. Workers in the coal mines and the foundries
were a ready market for local brewers. Pennsylvania's growing wealth and population supported a lively beer scene that grew until Prohibition and the subsequent rise of the megabreweries.

For a time in the '50s, '60s and '70s, Pennsylvania almost lost sight of good
beer — almost, but not quite. Memory of good beer and the continued presence
of the Yuengling brewery helped to ensure that real beer would come back. Just
when it seemed that all hope for flavor and variety in beer was lost, a new wave
of Pennsylvania brewing history began. When Reinheitsgebot-oriented Penn
Brewing and Stoudt started in the mid to late 1980s, they must have felt like
voices in the wilderness, although interestingly, at the same time, Pennsylvania
had more mid-sized "regional" brewers than any other state: Jones, Straub,
Pittsburgh, Yuengling and the Lion. Now, with a dozen or so breweries brewing
an increasing array of beer styles, the Keystone State can boast significant
progress in reclaiming some of its beer history. That's the good news.

The bad news: this good beer renaissance is being thwarted by a state government that is hostile to the interests of consumers and small brewers. Beer
retailing practices in Pennsylvania are foolish and unfriendly. "Beer distributors"
cannot sell single bottles or any quantity less than 24 small or 12 large contain-
ers. Credit cards are not accepted. On the other hand, if you'd like to apply to
sell beer, the Pennsylvania Liquor Control Board will not accept cash or a personal check for carrying out your "request for criminal record check." Indeed, in
this respect and others, the PLCB is a wrathful Jehovah. How would you like to
sign the PLCB's "distributor bond," which reads in part, "And we, and each of
us, do hereby confess judgment against us and each of us for the penal sum as
demanded . . . without stay of execution"?

Being forced to buy in huge minimum quantities discourages the trying of
new beers, and makes it impossible to buy food-suitable brands for a meal. How
can sensible beer attitudes develop or beer culture flourish in such a system?
Restaurants and bars can sell six-packs (maximum, two six-packs) but are not
allowed to sell single bottles. The powers that be in Pennsylvania treat beer as a
generic, high-volume drug, not as a diverse food family.

I asked several people in government, retailing and brewing about
Pennsylvania's retail laws, and the answer invariably was: "That's just the way it
is here."

Considering the fact that the founder of Pennsylvania, William Penn, had a liberal and freedom-inclined state of mind, and considering the fact that the Declaration of Independence was signed in Philadelphia, it would seem that Pennsylvania is long overdue for a revolution in beer retailing.

● ARROWHEAD BREWING COMPANY

1667 Orchard Drive
Chambersburg, Pennsylvania, 17201
717-264-0101
Capacity: 6,000 barrels
Year started: 1991

I didn't get a chance to visit Arrowhead or to interview the brewer.

Red Feather Pale Ale ★★★¹/2

Appearance: orangey mid-amber; pale beige, quiet, stable, slightly moussey head; good lacing. Aroma: caramel, plum-apricot, toasted grain, peat and flowers. Taste: sweetish caramel with some early hop taste and some leathery, resinous tones. In the swallow, Red Feather has some hop astringency, and it finishes with clean, modest hop bitterness, some peaty graininess, and maybe a hint of nutshell. Medium-plus viscosity. Balanced throughout. Very drinkable.

● DOCK STREET BREWING

Suite 110, 225 City Line Avenue
Bala Cynwyd, Pennsylvania, 19004
610-668-1480
Brewpub at Logan Square (18th & Cherry)
Philadelphia, 19103
215-496-0413

Dock Street, a lively Philadelphia brewpub that is well worth a visit, has several beers brewed and packaged under contract by F. X. Matt.

Amber Beer ★★★
5.35% alc./vol.
O.G.: 1050
Ingredients: include two-row pale and
caramel malts; Cascade hops

Appearance: mid amber; pale beige, quiet and stable head; good lacing. Enticing aroma: caramel, grain, flowers, forest and a hint of roastiness. Taste: almost woody, almost husky caramel to start, then slightly out-of-profile hopping shows in early woody tartness. To finish, an earthy-grassy-floral bitterness, some tin. 27 IBUs. Dry hopped. A tad overcarbonated, this ale isn't well-rounded.

Bohemian Pilsner ★★★★

5.33% alc./vol.
O.G.: 1051
Ingredients: include Saaz and
Hallertau hops

Appearance: yellowish light gold; near-white, very quiet, stable head; very good lacing. Aroma: grain, grass, clover, flowers — very attractive, true to style. Here's a lovely lager, similar in some respects to Pilsner Urquell as it was, gloriously, in the 1960s and '70s. To start, a balance of caramel, dry grain and floral-herbal bitterness. There's a tang midpalate, almost like hard fruit or fruit seed — almost woody, almost tannic. Finishes with light floral bitterness, light wood bitterness, lingering grain and tang. 26 IBUs. I like this beer a lot and wish I could buy it in Ontario. It's the tiniest bit too caramelly for the style, and the hopping is a wee bit too grassy, and the "best if purchased before" time period is too long (eight months or more, it seems) — but overall, an excellent North American take on the pilsner style.

Illuminator ★★★★

7.5% alc./vol.
O.G.: 1074
Ingredients: include Tettnang
and Hallertau hops

Illuminators are crocodiles that glow in the dark. The beer is brewed to draw attention to their endangered status. Appearance: mid amber, orangey hint; beige, moussey, quiet and stable head; excellent lacing. Aroma: demerara, toffee, butterscotch and peat; at room temperature, ripe plum and dried apricot are evident. Taste: rich, soft caramel at first blush; toffee and peat follow quickly. A wonderful mélange of plum-prune-apricot mixes with the malts and a hint of smoke. In the finish, Illuminator bitters slowly and modestly (30 IBUs), with a soft ethyl note well married to lingering toffee sweetness. Not huge for the "-ator," double bock style touted on the label, this is still a soft, svelte bock — a beer to illuminate short winter days and cool summer nights. This beer is available in Michigan, Ohio, Pennsylvania and New York.

● INDEPENDENCE BREWING COMPANY

1000 East Comly Street
Philadelphia, Pennsylvania, 19149
215-537-2337
Capacity: 12,000 barrels
Year started: 1995
Tours available Saturdays and by appointment
Glassware and merchandise available

Bill Moore, brewer and hardworking jack-of-all-trades at Independence, had been a "pipe support designer" at a nuclear plant, and he'd seen the nuclear industry decline. He'd been an avid homebrewer ever since it was legalized "back in the Carter administration." And he loved drinking imported beer.

He got to thinking he'd rather work in a job related to his passion — beer — even if it meant less money. And it did mean less money, but Moore has no regrets. He says that his beer-related work over the past decade has been a matter of "being in the right place at the right time." In 1987–88 he worked for an importer-wholesaler, and then he worked for four years at the Stoudt brewery as brewer, cook and delivery man. Now he spends long days brewing independently, after which he faces a long drive home.

Independence Brewing is large, with over 30,000 square feet, sizable fermenting and conditioning capacity, and a state-of-the-art oxygen-free bottling line.

"I'd like to think that we're bringing back craft brew, beer the way it used to be," says Moore. "I'd like to see a return to local and regional breweries. People come back from Germany or wherever and they rave about the beer — but often it's simply because the beer they drank was local." Local beer is best not just because it's usually fresh, he says, but because it's rooted in local culture.

Independence is working to cultivate some of that beer culture itself: it hosts festivals and events throughout the year. In addition to the ale described below, Independence makes a lager and some seasonal specials, and does some contract brewing as well.

Independence Ale ★★★★

4.9% alc./vol.
O.G.: 1050
Ingredients: two-row pale, munich, victory, carapils, caramel and chocolate malts; malted wheat; Cascade, Fuggles and British Columbia Kent hops

Appearance: mid amber; beige, very quiet and stable head; very good lacing. Aroma: beautiful and seductive — dryish, roasty graininess, toffee, roasted nuts (pecans?), brownies, and peat. Taste: an initial soft toffeeish sweetness, plums, and a nice oaky and roasted grain bitterness. Some hop tartness midpalate. The finish is a fading earthy-nutshell bitterness, with some hop taste and lingering toffee. This fine ale illustrates the rewards of complex malt formulations. It also illustrates just how well Fuggles and British Columbia Kent hops, two British-derived classics, work with residual sugars. An interesting comparison is with Wellington County's County Ale. S.P.A. Independence would go well with one of my favorite homemade pizzas: smoked salmon (or trout), smoked mussels, smoked oysters, with feta and old cheddar cheese.

● LANCASTER MALT BREWING COMPANY

Plum & Walnut Streets
Lancaster, Pennsylvania, 17602
717-319-6258
Capacity: 8,000 barrels
Year started: 1995
Tours available daily
Glassware and merchandise available

By 1810, Lancaster county produced 7 percent of all the beer in America. As many as 14 breweries operated in the county in the late 19th century, and then World War I (limited supplies of coal) and Prohibition (limited supplies of something else) slowed things down. Slowed, but didn't stop.

The Riekers Brewery, for example, dealt with Prohibition by going underground. A hose was run through Lancaster's sewers to a warehouse where beer was kegged. You can read this in a thumbnail history of local beer on the menu at the attractive pub-restaurant of the Lancaster Malt Brewing Company.

Christian Heim, Lancaster's affable brewmaster, says his goal is to make beer "of excellent quality, beer of distinction, that still appeals to a wide audience." Lancaster makes an ale, a lager and a porter on a regular basis, as well as many seasonal offerings such as a harvest ale, a rye beer and a maple cranberry beer.

Golden Lager ★★★¹/2

3.8% alc./vol.
Ingredients: two-row pale, carapils and
caramel malts; Cascade, Hallertau and
Saaz hops; Czech lager yeast

Appearance: amber, with a yellow-beige head; good lacing. Aroma: malt, fresh-cut grass, hint of toast. Taste: toffee with a floral, heathery quality, and some bready yeastiness. A balanced finish with modest hop bitterness and taste, hints of malt sweetness and grain.

Porter ★★★★

4.8% alc./vol.
Ingredients: two-row pale, caramel,
chocolate and black malts; roasted barley; Cascade hops; German ale yeast

The fruitiness of this superb porter will surprise some, but I consider this a wonderful contribution to the New World porter style. Cola-colored with glints of
red; mocha-colored, small-bubble head. The aroma is complex and enticing: dark
chocolate, raisin-fig or figgy duff, coffee, roasted grain. Taste: chocolate, raisin-
fig and coffee to start, and then a nice bit of a sour tingle comes in. A short finish
of coffee, and grain and fruit bitterness. This ale is an excellent illustration of the
importance of temperature to beer flavor. At cellar temperature (that is, at a temperature many consider warm), this porter delivers the cornucopia of aroma and
flavor described above. At cold temperature, it would be just another one of those
"dark beers."

Red Rose Amber Ale ★★★★

4.4% alc./vol.
Ingredients: two-row pale, caramel,
vienna and munich malts; Cascade and
Willamette hops; German ale yeast

Red Rose alludes to Lancaster's British roots. It's a good thing the brewery doesn't
make a White Rose (although that would be a great name for a wheat beer). If it
did, they'd have a Wort of the Roses. Mid amber with a pale beige, quiet head,
Red Rose has an intriguing and complex nose: a light caramel or butterscotch, a
green, hoppy, yeasty quality, a heathery, roasted cereal quality, and fruit (melon,
plum) — all can be detected, and all in perfect balance. Taste: slightly sweet and
buttery to start, with a hint of smoke and Fuggles-like hops (Willamette).
Midpalate there's a hint of toffee and fruit sourness. Finishes with a pleasant subdued hop bitterness, with a touch of grain and caramel. Overall: subtle and complex with excellent carbonation — quaffable, but with plenty to think about.
This ale has all the complexity of a bottled pale ale, and yet has some green, draft-
like qualities to it. Pleasure-to-alcohol ratio: 12 to 10. Seek this beer out. It's a
great example of how big the pale ale family is, and of why ales are making a
comeback.

Spring Bock ★★★¹/2

5.5% alc./vol.
O.G.: 1061
Ingredients: two-row pale and
caramel malts; malted wheat;
Hallertau and Saaz hops

Here's an enjoyable, very drinkable, slightly small single bock that would go well with desserts (fruit cobblers, butterscotch desserts, butter pecan pies) as well as with sweet meat dishes (sausage with peaches). This would also be a great cooking beer. Appearance: light to mid amber, with a pale beige, quiet and stable head; good lacing. Wonderful nose: caramel, apricot-dried-apricot, wildflowers and cut hay (note the two hops used). Taste: a soft, buttery caramel start. In the swallow, a hint of soft fruit (peach? nectarine?) and hardwood. The mildly bitter finish has a slight metallic edge as well some peat and the taste of hops. This bock lacks the darker, roasty flavors you find in many bocks; but this is a characteristic, not a defect. Viscosity is appropriate.

● THE LION BREWERY

700 North Pennsylvania Ave.
Wilkes Barre, Pennsylvania, 18703
717-825-8801
Capacity: 340,000 barrels
Tours: not available

Started in 1901 as the Luzerne Brewery, and then sold and renamed the Lion eleven years later, this brewery is the only survivor of four regional brewers in northeastern Pennsylvania. One of these, the Stegmaier Brewery, went out of business in 1974; the Lion bought the rights to Stegmaier labels and hired many Stegmaier employees.

With its 340,000-barrel capacity, the Lion is one of the 12 largest breweries in the United States. It has two bottling lines and a separate kegging line.

Brewer Leo Orlandini is a Siebel Institute graduate. Born near Wilkes Barre, he studied biology at Wilkes University, and started at the Lion as a lab technician in 1988. "I've always loved beer. I grew up with wine and beer in an Italian family," he says.

The Lion has a long line of beers, designed to appeal to various tastes. "We're very quality-driven," says Orlandini. "We'd rather dump beer down the drain than sell poor beer."

Brewery Hill Black & Tan ★★1/2

Ingredients: two- and six-row
pale, crystal, caramel and chocolate malts; Kent Golding,
Cascade, Tettnang (in the porter)
and Mt. Hood, Saaz and
Hallertau-Hersbrucker (in the
lager) hops

This dark red-brown beer has some of the coffee notes and roastiness of a porter, and some of the dry hoppiness of a lager, but isn't quite big enough overall to carry the day. A coffeeish astringency and a thin, slightly sour bitterness mark the middle and the end, denoting a lack of balance. 22 IBUs. I think you can make better black and tans on your own, but given the difficulty of buying single bottles in Pennsylvania, you might have to leave the state to do it.

Brewery Hill Cherry Wheat ★

O.G.: 1052
Ingredients: two-row pale and caramel
malts; malted wheat and cherry juice;
Northern Brewer and Cascade hops

Huge, over-the-top artificial cherry aroma, midway between cherry LifeSavers and bottled maraschino cherries. Very sweet flavor reminiscent of cream soda. May be aimed at people who don't like beer.

Brewery Hill Pale Ale ★★★¹/₂

O.G.: 1052
Ingredients: two-row pale,
caramel and carapils malts;
Mt. Hood, Cascade hops

This straightforward, slightly husky ale shows the benefits of dry hopping. This is the first Lion beer formulated by brewer Leo Orlandini. Appearance: gold-copper; near-white, slightly craggy, fairly stable and quiet head. Aroma: hops (cut grass and flowers), fruit (apricot), and hints of grain huskiness. Taste: butterscotch balanced by the clear taste of hops, followed by a hint of plum and malt sweetness, and increasing bitterness. In the finish, a relatively long hop bitterness, very much like a good best bitter. 28 IBUs. The gradual increase in bitterness in this ale would make it a fine accompaniment to sweet meats like honey ribs, or sweet grain dishes, such as the sticky rice you get at dim sum restaurants.

Brewery Hill Honey Amber ★★

Ingredients: two-row pale and
crystal malts; clover honey;
Mt. Hood, Saaz, and Hallertau-
Hersbrucker hops

This amber, hinting-at-orange beer has a biscuity, honey-caramel and dry-earth nose. It starts sweet (too sweet, I think), with butterscotch and hints of nectarine and honey. The finish is earthy, slightly unbalanced bitterness. Honey is added just prior to final filtration and thus is not fermented.

Brewery Hill Raspberry Red ★

O.G.: 1053

Ingredients: two- and six-row pale
malts; corn syrup, raspberry juice
and flavors; Cascade, Mt. Hood
and Saaz hops

Aroma: artificial raspberry. Fizzy, sweet. Not very beer-like.

Liebotschaner Cream Ale ★★★

O.G.: 1050

Ingredients: six- and two-row pale
malts; corn syrup; Cascade, Mt. Hood
and Saaz hops

Some of Shakespeare's plays have characters who are inoffensive, pleasant, and
necessary for the world to unfold as it should, but they're not terribly, well, characterful. I sometimes think that's what the cream ale style is about, and I don't
say that to be rude. The world needs such people and beers. Appearance: dark
straw below, near-white up top. Head is slightly noisy, dissolves relatively fast.
Aroma: very faint — cut grass, hint of flowers. Taste: true to style, that is, a
slightly sweet, not terribly hoppy lager with some of the viscosity but none of the
maltiness or fruitiness of an ale. Some (not much) huskiness. 15 IBUs.

Stegmaier Gold Medal ★¹/2

O.G.: 1042

Ingredients: six- and two-row pale
malts; corn syrup; Cascade, Saaz, Mt.
Hood and Northern Brewer hops

Before you listen to this straw-gold lager, you can tell just by looking that it's
fizzy. The head collapses in less than 30 seconds. Aroma: corn, paper, some hops.
Taste: sweet and maizy. What little hop bitterness (13 IBUs) there is, is dominated by a distracting adjuncty flavor. This is what Jules Feiffer called a "little
murder": Jimmy Maize killed John Barleycorn, killed 'im dead.

Stegmaier Porter ★★★¹/2

O.G.: 1058

Ingredients: six- and two-row pale,
caramel and chocolate malts; Kent
Golding, Cascade and Tettnang hops

Appearance: very dark brown with burgundy highlights; café-au-lait-colored,
fairly quiet and stable head. Aroma: very fruity (cherry-apricot), with some

licorice and coffee notes. With its high viscosity and soft carbonation, this porter resembles a small stout — not a dry stout, but somewhere between a milk stout and an oatmeal stout. Taste: Soft, almost like almond butter to start, and then a slight bitterness (hops more than grain) and sourness (cherry? plum?) become apparent. Finishes with a mild grain and hop bitterness with some nice licorice notes — very nice, I think, and with a mouth-coating, slightly oily viscosity that helps to produce a good aftertaste. A unique porter, worth trying.

● PENNSYLVANIA BREWING COMPANY

800 Vinial Street
Pittsburgh, Pennsylvania, 15212
412-237-9400
www.pennbrew.com
Capacity: 25,000 barrels
Year started: 1986
Tours available by arrangement
Glassware and merchandise available

A $4-million dollar restoration and renovation has made the old new, and given Pittsburgh-area beer fans a brewery that's listed on the National Register of Historic Sites. Located in the old Eberhardt & Ober Brewing Company (founded in 1848, closed in 1952) in the Deutchtown part of north Pittsburgh, the Penn Brewery is more than a brewery; it's a celebration of American heritage and of Reinheitsgebot lager brewing.

Tom Pastorius, president and founder of Penn, has deep roots in German America. His great-great-great-great-great-great-great grandfather, Franz Daniel Pastorius, founded America's first German settlement, Germantown, which is now part of Philadelphia, and apparently bent elbows on occasion with William Penn. Pastorius himself lived in Heidelberg and Frankfurt, Germany, for 12 years, where he worked in sales and marketing, and where he developed an interest in beer and brewing.

Pennsylvania Brewing had its first beer, Penn Pilsner, brewed under contract. Now it has a 45-barrel, direct-fire brewhouse. It uses German-made copper kettles.

Penn's brewmaster is Alexander Deml, a graduate of the Weihenstephan Institute of Munich. It's a Reinheitsgebot brewery, and I smiled when I read in a note from Mary Beth Pastorius, director of the brewery, that beer should be made out of malted barley, "not adjuncts, fruits, vegetables, syrups or extracts." (I must say that I do like the sentiment: it sometimes seems that the way things are going, every brewery will end up making a Kiwi-Potato Beer.)

"Freshness is important to us; therefore we sell regionally, not nationally," Mary Beth says.

In addition to a Munich-style dunkel (Penn Dark) and Penn Pilsner, Penn Brewing makes a Helles Gold, a weizen and a weizenbock, a märzen, an alt, an oktoberfest, and a strong Christmas bock. The brewery has an outdoor Biergarten, a restaurant, and a Ratskeller.

Penn Dark ★★★¹/₂

5% alc./vol.
O.G.: 1052
Ingredients: two-row pale, munich and
black malts; Hallertau hops

Appearance: dark amber to chestnut; beige or café-au-lait-colored head. Aroma: very roasty, very grainy, plus plum, prune, raisin, and mocha. Taste: mildly sweet, mildly sour chocolate, with raisin and prune elements on a firm malt base. Finishes with a hayish hop bitterness and lingering dark-fruit sourness. This brand tastes different each time I try it. It has a freshness "ensured . . . if enjoyed by" indication on the label. A simple bottled-on date would be more useful.

Penn Pilsner ★★★★

5% alc./vol.
O.G.: 1052
Ingredients: two-row pale and caramel
malts; Hallertau hops

Here's a great, moderately bitter, slightly biscuity lager. It reminds me of some of the better German pilsners I've had. It has a Dortmunderish quality in its dryness and graininess, but it's very much its own beer. Grainy, earthy, and slightly yeasty qualities make me think of bread in a bottle. Appearance: gold to light amber; near-white, fairly quiet and stable head with some big bubbles; excellent lacing. Aroma: dry-biscuity, toasted grain, hay or flowers. Taste: dry grain and caramel to start; adroit hopping produces a perfect balance of peat dryness, hop bitterness and grain bitterness. Sometimes I detect I hint of apricot. A tiny flash of astringency (plums?) midpalate. Finishes with a slightly astringent hop bitterness, beautiful bready graininess, and some peat-oak dryness. This lager would go well with sausages, schnitzel, heavy breads, and bagels with spicy cream cheeses.

● STOUDT BREWING COMPANY

Route 272 (Box 880)
Adamstown, Pennsylvania, 19501
215-484-4386
Capacity: 10,000 barrels
Year started: 1987
Tours available: Saturdays at 3, Sundays at 1
Glassware and merchandise available

The Stoudt Brewing Company strives, according to Carol and Edward Stoudt, "to provide fresh and authentic European-style lagers and ales of the highest quality."

For their honeymoon, Ed and Carol went to Germany, where Edward's ancestors had lived. The variety and the quality of the beer caught their attention. Back in the United States, the couple continued their love affair with each other and with beer — they owned and managed a beer garden and antique shop — but grew frustrated at the absence of fresh, high-quality beer. In 1986, the couple went to Portland, Oregon, for a microbrewery tour (and there they met Phil Gosling of the Wellington County Brewery). Ed and Carol decided to open a brewery, in part to supply their beer garden with fresh beer.

They showed a business plan to an accountant who said that the business wouldn't work. "But I'm a beer lover," Ed Stoudt says, "so we went ahead anyway." In 1987, Carol Stoudt became the first brewster, or female brewer, in modern-day America, and Stoudt Brewing became Pennsylvania's first microbrewery.

Stoudt, which has won many brewing awards, still has a biergarten, and holds summer and Oktoberfest beer festivals. Recently, Stoudt started to produce some cask-conditioned Real Ale.

Amber ★★★

5% alc./vol.
O.G.: 1050
Ingredients: two-row pale, munich and crystal malts; Cascade hops

Appearance: mid amber with an almost white, stable and very quiet head. Aroma: caramel, honeydew, mandarin, with some counterbalancing heather and wood. This ale is very soft and lush: one wonders if some of the British brewers who are ruining traditional beers with nitrogen understand just how soft a beer can be with traditional carbon dioxide. Amber starts with a caramel-toffee tone, and changes to a slightly peaty hop bitterness. Some residual acidity isn't quite integrated into the malt flavor — too aggressively hopped? The suggestion of fruit in the nose isn't evident in the taste.

Bock ★★★

6% alc./vol.
O.G.: 1062
Ingredients: two-row pale, munich and crystal malts; Perle, Cluster, Hallertau and Tettnang hops

Appearance: dark amber-burgundy; yellowish-beige, quiet and stable head. The aroma is fetching: butterscotch, okay diacetyl, plum-berry, toffee, earth, and a wee medicinal undertone. Low to medium bodied and lowish viscosity for a single bock. This beer is, for the style, slightly tart, almost astringent. The flavor remains fairly constant front to back: it's dominated by earthy, peaty, almost smoky flavors balanced by some fruit sourness and subdued caramel tones.

Fest ★★★¹/₂

5% alc./vol.
O.G.: 1050
Ingredients: two-row pale, munich,
crystal and carapils malts; Cluster,
Hallertau, and Tettnang hops

Reddish mid-amber below, beige up top. Very quiet, good lacing. Aroma: roasted grain, some earth, toffee, demerara, apricot. Taste: toffee with hints of peach to start. Peach or apricot sourness shows a little midpalate, as does some märzeny roastiness. To finish, hop bitterness, hop taste, some peat and smoke. Märzens should lean to sweetness; this one's a trifle too sweet for my taste. Still, at only 5 percent alcohol, a rewarding beer (pleasure-to-alcohol ratio: 11 to 10). Bring on the oompah, I'll have another Fest. But I'll go without the feathered green fedora.

Gold ★★★★

5% alc./vol.
O.G.: 1050
Ingredients: two-row pale, munich and
carapils malts; Cluster, Hallertau, Saaz
and Tettnang hops; German lager yeast

Copper-gold in color with a near-white, quiet and stable head; excellent lacing. Aroma: husk, grain (sunlight on barley), hops and wood. "I shall never believe women again," pouted literary critic Cyril Connolly. "I have been perfectly faithful to two women for two years, and now both of them have been unfaithful to me." Mr. Connolly would not have felt so deceived had he been drinking Gold, which is two beers in one. Kind of a gold and a silver, it's the perfect beer for the ambivalent or ambidextrous drinker. The first part is a soft, buttery caramel, but with a hint of peach, and a touch of acidity nicely balancing medium viscosity. Swallow, breathe, and voilà! The second part comes in quickly: a green, draft-like, hops-in-the-beer quality, much as you find in some hoppy lagers. The finish tends to cut grass or hay and earthiness, amounting to a medium bitterness (26 IBUs) nicely carried by the medium body.

Honey Double Bock ★★★★

7.5% alc./vol.
O.G.: 1070
Ingredients: two-row pale, munich,
carapils and crystal malts; honey; Perle,
Hallertau, Cluster and Tettnang hops

What a lovely beer to ogle! Ruby-amber, with a moussey, café-au-lait-colored head that leaves excellent lacing. Aroma: fruit (plum, honey melon, cherry), roasted cereal, nuts, and heather. The beer starts very soft, somewhat vinous and fruity, a tad honeyish. Then, a quick hit of sour fruit. Hop bitterness grows. The long finish is marked by firm hop bitterness, and hints of earth and cola nuts. This lush, mouth-coating bock hides its ethyl well, partly, I think, because of adequate conditioning time. Because the honey isn't overdone, we get a successful "pushing of the envelope" of the bock style.

Honey Double Mai Bock ★★★¹/₂

7% alc./vol.
O.G.: 1070
Ingredients: two-row pale, crystal and
munich malts; honey; Perle, Cluster,
Hallertau and Saaz hops

Appearance: amber hinting at orange below; off-white, fairly quiet head above. The aroma is delicate and subtle: hay, toffee, and mandarin or clementine. Taste: initially, a soft honey-caramel impression; then fruit sweetness and sourness (apricot, mandarin and grapefruit rind). This bock finishes with moderate bitterness and some sourness, which together have a metallic edge. At the very end, there's a taste of Hallertau or Cluster hops and a soupçon of clover honey.

Pils ★★★¹/₂

5% alc./vol.
O.G.: 1050
Ingredients: two-row pale malt; Perle
and Saaz hops

This straw-gold lager has a near-white, fairly stable head and good lacing. Aroma: yeast, grain, Saaz hops, and a hint of grapefruit and herbs. Taste: a malty, buttery start changes quickly to a bitter, metallic taste with some grapefruit acidity. The finish is marked by firm hop bitterness, and then a yeasty-earthy tone with some tin or grapefruit rind. A lovely beer. I see Pils as a very American lager. It doesn't have those rough edges you find in some hophead lagers (although at 35 IBUs, it is adequately hopped), and it doesn't have the soft roundedness of a Czech or Bavarian pilsner. It's very much its own beer. The sudden bitterness and the metallic edges are impressive. This would be a fine accompaniment to sweet and sour dishes.

Scarlet Lady Ale ESB ★★★¹/₂

4.5% alc./vol.
O.G.: 1050
Ingredients: two-row pale and crystal
malts; Perle and Willamette hops

Appearance: reddish amber with a pale beige, quiet and stable, slightly craggy head. Aroma: apricot-tangerine-orange, caramel, and a slight floral suggestion. Taste is a nice balance of three elements: moderate malt sweetness, moderate fruit sourness, moderate hop bitterness. Malty caramel with some soft fruit to start, Scarlet Lady shows some currant sourness and earthy peatiness midpalate. The finish is marked by subdued hop bitterness, a hint of roasted nuts (pecans?) and a metallic edge. This very drinkable, enjoyable ale is a bit quirky in terms of style. It's too thin and not viscous or malty-sweet enough to match a British notion of an ESB (for example, Fuller's). Still, scarlet ladies find their own friends, and I'm sure this one will find many fans who like her on her own terms.

Weizen ★★★★★

4.5% alc./vol.
O.G.: 1050
Ingredients: two-row pale malt (50%);
malted wheat (50%); Hallertau hops;
German weizen yeast

Wow. A very big, unfiltered wheat beer, in which all the elements add up to a magnificent and balanced whole. Appearance: straw, hint of yellow haze; near-white, very stable, very quiet head. The aroma is huge: bananas, citrus zest, fresh bread, yeast, cloves or allspice. In terms of mouthfeel, this wheat beer is soft, firm and velvety, a combination of just-right tartness and bang-on carbonation. Initially, there's a soft lemon and caramel palate, with hints of wood. Then, banana, honey and a touch of metal. Weizen finishes with a very balanced mix of mild bitterness, very mild sourness, and light floral elements. Complex yet clean, big yet subtle, Weizen shows the benefits of yeast sediment and bottle conditioning, and is an example of the judicious use of lightly malted wheat. There's much more to think about here than in most North American wheats. Pleasure-to-alcohol ratio: 14 to 10. If you have the nerve to adulterate this heavenly beer, you could make a great cocktail by adding some raspberry juice, but it would have to be real and fresh.

● WEYERBACHER BREWING COMPANY

20 South 6th Street
Easton, Pennsylvania, 18042
610-559-5561
Year started: 1995
Tours available on Saturdays; phone ahead
Glassware and merchandise available

I did not get a chance to speak to the brewer at Weyerbacher.

Black and Tan ★★

Appearance: dark amber with red highlights; café-au-lait-colored, moussey, quiet and stable head; good lacing. Aroma: some toast or burnt toast, perfumey flowers, hint of caramel. Taste: not a successful marriage, in my opinion. Ms. Black is not suited to Mr. Tan. To start, slightly dry, slightly tart graininess, almost papery, some caramel. To finish, metallic bitterness with woody-earthy elements.

Easton Pale Ale ★★★

Appearance: light amber, with a pale beige, quiet and stable head. Aroma: caramel, lightly roasted grain, grass and flowers. Very nice. Taste: caramel, apricot and a wee bit of diacetyl to start, Easton shows some grassiness and grain midpalate, and finishes with modest hop bitterness and astringency. Slightly sweet and viscous.

ESB Ale ★★¹/₂

Appearance: mid amber; beige, fairly quiet and stable head. Aroma: lightly toasted grain, caramel-butterscotch, tart apricot-plum, and a trace of cut grass — all balanced. Taste: one-third apricot, one-third butterscotch, one-third hoppy-tart, with a slight citric undertone. Slightly fizzy mouthfeel. The finish is a clean, grassy hop bitterness, with some peat and ethyl rawness. Medium in body and viscosity. I've had a three-star version of this when it was fresh; and a two-star, stale version. It's the luck of the draw: there is no production date on the label.

Prime Porter ★★★¹/₂

Appearance: very dark brown with red highlights; mocha-colored head, stable, but a little noisy; some lacing. Aroma: roasted barley, burnt toast, hint of caramel or brown sugar. This medium-bodied porter starts with a caramel-toffee taste, as well as some nicely dry, roasty and burnt flavors, all in balance, and a bit of apricot. Midpalate, I find some inappropriate hop acidity. Finishes with hop and grain bitterness, then some dry graininess and an impression of Turkish coffee.

Summer Wheat ★★

Appearance: light amber to old gold, with a yellowish beige, very noisy head. Aroma: vegetal-cardboard with some lemon skin. Taste: thin and small — hints of caramel, lemon skin, wet paper and cardboard. The cardboard notes indicate that this beer may have too much adjunct or may have been stale. I tried two bottles; each had a similar aroma and taste.

YARDS BREWING COMPANY

5050 Umbria Street
Philadelphia, Pennsylvania, 19127
215-482-9109
Capacity: 15,000 barrels
Started: 1995
Tours available: phone ahead
Glassware and merchandise available

The Real Ale revolution shows no signs of abating. Jon Bovit, one of two partners and a founding brewer at Yards Brewing, is a Tory revolutionary, a conservative who knows that "progress" is often the loss of traditional excellence.

"We brew beers we like. We hope there's a consumer who likes the beers we do. We don't compromise. We're not interested in trends."

When I visited Yards at its original plant on Krams Avenue, beer wasn't yet being packaged. "Only" cask-conditioned versions were available. Bottled beer will be available when the brewery moves to its new digs on Umbria Street. Real Ale is a stay-at-home: Yards' cask-conditioned ales are available only in select, Philadelphia-area pubs.

As Yards gets ready to package beers (mid-1997), Brandon Greenwood has been hired as brewer. Greenwood has a degree in molecular biology from West Chester University and a diploma in brewing and distilling from Heriot-Watt University in Edinburgh, Scotland. Greenwood worked for a short time at Scotland's Caledonian brewery ("I learned cask-conditioned beers") and in Scottish Courage ("I learned forced carbonation"). He came back to the United States to work for Stroh in St. Paul, Minnesota. "At the big breweries, I learned how to run a brewery. What I didn't learn was how to brew quality beer." So Greenwood came home, so to speak (he was born in Unionville, near Philly), to brew for Yards.

Building on Yards' Real Ale history will be a challenge, Greenwood says. Cask-conditioned ale "is a unique product. In the U.S., our warm weather can work against us. Then too, publicans serve the product too cold. You get chill haze and this throws people." Greenwood accepts the challenge. He says that part of his job is to train bar managers how to store and serve Real Ale.

In coming years, Yards will "produce a really high-quality product" and be "flexible and adaptive," Greenwood says.

Entire Porter (Real Ale version)

5.5% alc./vol.
Ingredients: a blend of stout (two-row pale, crystal and chocolate malts; roasted barley) and mild (two-row pale, brown and chocolate malts; roasted barley); chinook, Tettnang, Willamette, Target, East Kent Golding and Bramling Cross hops

Although porter was originally a blend of ales, it isn't every day that one runs into porter made this way. Yards' Entire is a 50-50 blend of a dark mild and a fairly dense stout. The two ales are fermented separately, and then combined, or made "entire."

Extra Special Ale (Real Ale version)

5.75% alc./vol.
Ingredients: two-row pale, crystal,
chocolate and caramel malts; Chinook,
Tettnang, Willamette and East Kent
Golding hops

Dry hopped. Jon Bovit's description: "Very lively. Salient hop flavour, changes radically throughout the barrel. A strong Golding hop and fruity (apple, pear) nose. Earthy. Unique."

Old Bartholomew (Real Ale version)

8% alc./vol.
O.G.: 1076
Ingredients: two-row pale, carapils and
caramel malts; 2–3% malted wheat;
Chinook, Tettnang, East Kent Golding
and Cascade hops

John Bovit: "Varies in sweetness; some Belgian estery qualities." 41 IBUs.

● YUENGLING AND SON

Fifth & Mahantongo Streets
Pottsville, Pennsylvania, 17901
717-622-4141
Capacity: 400,000 barrels
Year started: 1829
Tours available Monday to Friday
Glassware and merchandise available

"America's oldest brewery," built into the side of a hill in the Appalachian town of Pottsville, is a beer historian's dream. Layers of brewing history are evident everywhere in the brewery's buildings, laneways, brewing equipment, and stained-glass ceiling. Tunnels into the hillside are a reminder of the historic importance in brewing of subterranean cooling.

The Yuengling brewery is a family business that has been in continuous operation since it was founded in 1829 as the Eagle Brewery (an eagle still adorns most of the brewery's labels).

In the 19th century, malt was brought by boat on the Schuykill Canal from Philadelphia to Pottsville. During Prohibition, Yuengling made "near beers" (a misnomer: at 0.05 percent alcohol, they were actually "near waters"). When the dry spell officially ended, the brewery celebrated by sending a truckload of "Winner Beer" to President Roosevelt at the White House. I hope he enjoyed it. He wasn't the only winner in the return of legal brewing.

"We'll never be efficient like the big breweries," owner Richard (Dick) Yuengling told the Philadelphia Inquirer. Dick Yuengling is the fifth-generation Yuengling to manage the historic brewery, but he may have to change the name of the company: he has four daughters who are apparently interested in the business.

Yuengling has a beer museum that contains some fascinating breweriana.

Black and Tan ★★

4.7% alc./vol.
Ingredients: six-row pale, caramel and
black malts; corn grits; Cluster and
Cascade hops

A blend of Yuengling's Premium Lager and Porter. Appearance: cola colored with a strong reddish tinge; café-au-lait-colored, quiet and stable head; good lacing. Aroma: roasted grain, coffee, cardboard. Slightly fizzy in mouthfeel, this all-lager B&T is marked by some nice earthy bitterness that loses its fight against a too-sweet (19 IBUs) maizy foundation.

Lord Chesterfield ★★

4.2% alc./vol.
Ingredients: six-row pale
malt; corn grits; Cluster and
Cascade hops

Sheaves of six-row barley are shown on the label; a few ears of corn might also be shown. Yellow-gold in color with a white, moussey, fairly stable head. Aroma: paper, sweet corn, sulfur. Taste: a sweet papery start, some bitterness midpalate, and some astringency in the finish. With 33 IBUs, the best part of Lord Chesterfield is in the hopping; it's dry-hopped with Cascade. Drink this ale on the sofa if you're feeling bitter.

Porter ★★★

4.8% alc./vol.
Ingredients: six-row pale, caramel and
black malt; corn grits; Cluster and
Cascade hops; lager yeast

Wonderful appearance: cola brown with red-ruby highlights; mocha-colored head that is stable and fairly quiet for style; good lacing. Aroma: a mélange of dark malts and roasted barley, hint of hops, very small hint of coffee. Taste: to start, a mix of treacle, caramel and fruit (mango and fig). Coffee notes show midpalate. Hop and some roasted malt bitterness dominate the finish, together with a tiny reminder of fruit sweetness and sourness. I like this porter, and imagine that many others would as well. With higher-than-average viscosity, Yuengling's carries flavors (like the fruit sourness) not often found in porters. This is an ideal beer for those cool, colorless days of November. It would be perfect with baked beans.

Premium ★★
4.5% alc./vol.
Ingredients: six-row pale malt; corn
grits; Cluster hops

Straw-gold in color, and with a white, moussey head and good lacing, Premium promises more than it delivers. The aroma and taste are similar: a sweetish grain and corn flavor predominates; a light metallic edge is evident in the finish. Mouthfeel is a bit fizzy. Some women (and men) wear too much makeup. Premium wears too much adjunct, which smothers and distracts from the hopping. The low level of hopping (12 IBUs) also allows corn to speak too loudly. Were the corn to be reduced by half, some nice six-row huskiness, struggling to assert itself, would show more clearly.

Premium Light ★★★
3% alc./vol.
Ingredients: six-row pale malt; corn
grits; Cascade hops

Here's a light with great technical properties: a quiet, stable, almost white head, with fine bubbles that leave lots of lace. Aroma: delicately hoppy with a hint of grain and corn. Clean and balanced between bitterness and maltiness, Light has more weight and mouthfeel than many "lites," and no over-the-top adjunct taste. I think this is a good example of how six-row barley, with its "huskiness," can be used to good ends. Take me out to the . . . well, this would be a great quaffable beer at a baseball game.

QUEBEC

It would be tempting to call Quebec *le royaume magique de la bière*, if it didn't have such a Disneyesque ring to it. Start by considering the magic of dough — real dough, not lucre. Bouillon was one of the earliest beers to be made and drunk in Quebec. "A ball of raw dough was allowed to rise and to ferment in a solution of spiced water. It was not what might be termed an exquisite drink, but since it was alcoholic, it was thought better than plain water."

For much of the 17th century, brewing in Quebec was heavily influenced by two major institutions, French colonial government and the Catholic church. Beer was brewed on a non-commercial basis by the Jesuits as early as the 1620s. Even earlier, spruce beer "was well known as an excellent cure against scurvy" (both quotations from E. Vaillancourt).

Commercial brewing goes back to 1668 in Quebec City. When New France fell to the English in 1763, British beer influences increased, and curiously, still hold to an extent. Quebeckers drink more ale and less lager than most North Americans.

Two scenes from Montreal show how the image of beer has changed in Quebec.

One: the 19th century. Joe Beef's Canteen, near Montreal's waterfront, was so popular in its day that W. H. Davies, in his *Autobiography of a Super-Tramp*, would remark that "not a tramp throughout the length and breadth of the North American continent . . . had not heard of [the Canteen] and a goodly number had at one time or another patronized" it. Here was a tavern, shunned by respectable Montrealers, that, in addition to beer, served entertainment in the form of parrots, monkeys, wild cats and bears on exhibition. According to Peter DeLottinville, "Joe Beef's first bear, named Jenny . . . never retired sober during the last three years of her life. One of her cubs inherited the family weakness. Tom, who had a daily consumption of twenty pints of beer, was often as 'drunk as a coal heaver' by closing. Indeed, Tom was one of the regulars, usually sitting on his hind quarters and taking his pint between his paws, downing it without spilling a drop."

Two: the present. A stroll down St. Denis, or Crescent Street, or through the Vieux Port area, Montreal's trendy bistro spots. Chic couples sip local beers from a wide variety of styles. On the table or on the wall, there's a beer menu to choose from, and beer is sometimes served in a style-specific glass. Bears are absent.

If Quebec's beer scene is more civilized now than it was a hundred years ago, it's also more feminine. Women are head brewers at two of the larger breweries. I think of that line from "Two Gentlemen of Verona": "She brews good ale — and thereof comes the proverb, Blessing of your heart, you brew good ale."

Several Quebec breweries are unwilling to reveal the ingredients they use. Some brewers told me that other brewers would attempt to duplicate their beers if ingredients were published. This strikes me as unlikely in a province in which each brewery has found a unique niche. And it seems to me that if you don't know the water treatment, ingredient quantities, fermentation temperatures and schedules, and if you don't have identical brewing equipment, you can't duplicate a beer anyway, even with a list of ingredients.

Beer retailing is generally friendly and civilized. Beer is sold in corner stores, called *dépanneurs*. You may have to go to more than one store to find what you're looking for, and sometimes beer is stored under fluorescent light. Most *dépanneurs*, however, do have cold-storage rooms with incandescent lighting, and single bottles may be purchased. Imports are available at the provincial alcohol monopoly, the Société des alcools du Québec, or the SAQ.

● BRASAL BREWERY

8477 Cordner Street
Ville LaSalle (Montreal), Quebec, H8N 2X2
514-365-5050
Capacity: 20,000 hectolitres
Year started: 1989
Tours available: book ahead
Glassware and merchandise available

A respect for German-style lagers, great attention to detail, and a strict Reinheitsgebot orientation characterize the Brasal brewery. Water filtration is emphasized; a Swiss lager yeast in used; and beers undergo relatively long conditioning.

In the mid-1980s, Marcel Jagermann, an Austrian immigrant, started thinking about how beer quality depends on freshness. He found it impossible to get fresh German-style lager in Montreal. His son (and Brasal's managing director) Etan Jagermann explains: "We did a lot of market research. We saw that almost everybody in Quebec bought their beer in corner stores. We also saw that you couldn't find a real German-style beer in these stores." At the SAQ, the provincial alcohol monopoly, imported beer was often stale.

So Brasal decided to fill the void by brewing "all-natural German beers as per the Bavarian tradition and code from 1516," and then selling them fresh in corner stores. In 1989, following construction of a brewery built to specification, Brasal opened its doors. Now Montrealers can drink fresh, local German-style beer — and it's "cheaper than imports, too!" says Etan Jagermann.

Brasal's current brewer, Harald Sowade, graduated from the Doemens Brewing School in Munich, Germany in 1967.

Beyond the *dépanneurs* of the province, Brasal beers are available in many American states. Key goals for the future are to increase penetration of the local market, to sell beer in other provinces, and to export to France and Britain.

Bock ★★★★¹/₂

7.8% alc./vol.
O.G.: 1071
Ingredients: two-row pale, munich and
other specialty malts; Hallertau,
Tettnang and Perle hops

You can't hurry a good bock. High original gravity means that an unhurried approach to fermentation is required. Brasal Bock is at least three months old when bottled, and that, I think, is part of this beer's glory. Appearance: reddish, mid to dark amber; beige, quiet and stable head; good lacing. What a lovely aroma! I smell fresh and dried apricot, dry roasted grain, toffee, sherry-ethyl, floral and grassy hoppiness, and a peaty hint as well. Taste: starts soft, plummy-peachy (almost cherry), and butterscotch, with a mouthfeel that is creamy rather than highly viscous. Midpalate: fruit (apricot, plum, a tiny hint of prune), floral-heather, and a touch of acidity. As for the finish — let me gush — a flirtatious fruit sourness touches the side of the tongue; long, but not overdone, hop and some grain bitterness strokes the back of the tongue. An earthy, slightly nutty effect shows in the aftertaste, as does a slight metallic edge. Pleasure-to-alcohol ratio: 11 to 10. I expect that this suave and gentle beer is widely available in heaven.

Hopps Bräu ★★★★

5% alc./vol.
O.G.: 1047
Ingredients: two-row pale malt;
Hallertau, Tettnang and Perle hops

At first blush this is a clean and simple, well-made lager; closer examination reveals great subtlety. More than most North American micro-lagers, Brasal has let a dry, sunshine-on-barley graininess predominate, as opposed to sweeter malt flavors (which in turn require aggressive hopping). Appearance: yellow-gold; near white, quiet and stable head; good lacing. Aroma: a perfect balance of caramel and dry grain, with some floral hopping. Taste starts fairly clean, a bit green and cerealish. A metallic edge and a touch of fruit show briefly, and then a very well incorporated, long-lasting hop bitterness, as well as some hop taste. Finally, a lingering touch of peat and toffee. All told, soft, but not too soft; floral but not too floral. In other words, a great German premium-style lager.

Légère ★★★

3.1% alc./vol.

Pale amber to copper below; up top, a near-white, fairly quiet head; good lacing. Aroma: cereal, delicate hops. Taste: delicately malty with some grain bitterness, then mildly bitter, with the grassy-hayish taste of hops showing; bit of tin in aftertaste. The world needs more low-alcohol beers. Hop delicacy and small-bubble carbonation make this a reasonably interesting low-alcohol lager. Stales easily; must be drunk very fresh.

Special Amber ★★★★

6.1% alc./vol.
O.G.: 1061
Ingredients: two-row pale, munich and
other specialty malts; Hallertau,
Tettnang and Perle hops

Here's a lovely, viscous märzen-style lager. Appearance: mid amber; light beige, stable, fairly quiet head; good lacing. Aroma: very lush — roasted grain and nuts, toffee and peat, plum or melon. Taste: caramel-toffee with a smoky-roasty undertone. Fruit and fruit acidity show in the middle. In the finish, subdued earthy bitterness, grainy background, almost a hint of Scotch whisky. Great balance and complexity. Pleasure-to-alcohol ratio: 11 to 10.

● BRASSE MONDE

358 Rossy Street
St. André-Avellin, Quebec, J0V 1W0
819-983-3988
Year started: 1996
Tours: on request
Brewery-related merchandise available

I didn't get to visit this brewery, and shame on me: it's not that far from my home. Thiery Vanhavre is the brewer at Brasse Monde, Quebec's newest Belgian-style-oriented brewery. Vanhavre was born in Brussels and did "alimentary and agricultural" studies at the University of Louvain.

The goal of the brewery is simple: "to make good beer."

Plans for the future include making a summer specialty beer and exporting, eventually, to the United States and Europe.

L'infidèle ★★★★

7% alc./vol.
O.G.: 1060
Ingredients: two-row pale malt;
Styrian Golding and Hallertau
hops; Belgian ale yeast

Appearance: old gold to light amber; near-white, very quiet and stable head; good lacing. Aroma: lightly spicy (cloves), yeast-bread, caramel, confectioner's sugar. Taste: caramel, soft ethyl and spice that blend nicely with an early mild bitterness, hint of melon. In the finish, bitterness doesn't increase so much as the other flavors dissipate, leaving a hayish, mild bitterness. Despite the etymology, an "infidel" isn't really someone who lacks faith; it's someone who has his or her own faith. Have your faith restored. Take a leap for this fine ale, a great debut from Brasse Monde.

● BRASSERIE BEAUCE BROUE

295 Industrial Street
St. Odilon de Cranbourne, Quebec, G0S 3A0
418-464-2768
Capacity: 6,000 hectolitres
Year started: 1995
Tours available by arrangement
Brewery-related clothing available

Beauce Broue is a young, family-owned business in the heart of the "Beauce," a charming region of rolling hills, farms and forests south of Quebec City. The area is known for its hardworking, free-thinking people, the sort of folks, one might think, who will welcome and support a local, independent brewery.

I ask brewery manager Pascal Schoune about Beauce Broue's beer philosophy: "*On la fait par amour,*" he says. We make our beer with love. "We're an artisanal brewery," he explains. "We do everything by hand." Schoune's father-in-law, Clément Cliché, is the president of the brewery and one of the principal owners. Cliché says that the goal of the brewery is to offer consumers a refined, but unique, beer.

Beauce Broue's brewer, Belgian-born Benoît Bostaille, uses but doesn't treat the local artesian well water, which is soft. The brewery packages in six- and eight-packs. "You see, if you're drinking with two or three friends," Bostaille says, "six are sometimes not enough. Eight bottles can be just the right amount."

In its early years, Beauce Broue would like to attain a greater share of its local market. As to the future, Beauce Broue is ambitious. In addition to Beauceronne à l'Erable, the first maple beer in modern Quebec, the brewery would like to develop other seasonal beers.

"We want to see the brewery grow," says Schoune. "Eventually, we'd like to export to the U.S., Europe, and maybe Japan."

Beauceronne à l'Erable ★★★

4.5% alc./vol.
O.G.: 1044
Ingredients: two-row pale and munich
malts; rice flakes and (2%) maple syrup;
Willamette, Yakima and Styrian
Golding hops

"When the snows of winter are melting fast, / And the sap begins to rise, / And the biting breath of the frozen blast / Yields to the spring's soft sighs . . ." When, according to Canadian pioneer Susanna Moodie, maple trees yield their "treasure," a young person's fancy turns to beer: maple beer. Keeping in mind that spruce beer was an early Canadian invention — it helped prevent scurvy — it's appropriate that Canada should continue to make "tree beers." But it's a challenge to get maple beer just right. How do you make a beer that lets the maple show, but without overwhelming the malt? Beauce Broue, located in the heart of maple-syrup country, has done just that with this highly enjoyable beer. Golden-amber, with an off-white head, à l'Erable's aroma is a delicate balance of munich malt and maple. The maple comes through midpalate and there's adequate body to allow the maple to linger in the finish. This seasonal ale would be a wonderful ingredient in and with pancakes or crepes, baked beans and sausages. It makes a superb sauce for ham.

Beauceronne ★★¹/₂

6% alc./vol.
O.G.: 1056
Ingredients: two-row pale and carastan
malts; barley flakes; Willamette, Yakima
and Styrian Golding hops

Amber below, with a buttery-beige head, Beauceronne has a butterscotch aroma with a metallic edge. Taste: soft and malty to start, then some acidity and sourness, finishing with a metallic hop bitterness.

La Chaudière ★★¹/₂

4.5% alc./vol.
O.G.: 1044
Ingredients: two-row pale and carastan
malts; rice flakes and malted wheat;
Willamette, Yakima and Styrian
Golding hops

A *chaudière* is a large cauldron, the kind pioneers used in cooking over a fire. It's also a common name in Quebec for the rapids in a river. Light amber in color and with a pale beige head, La Chaudière's medium-size bubbles are a little noisy in dissolving, but leave some lace. Aroma: butterscotch and candied fruit. This ale is soft and buttery to start, then tart, with a metallic bitter finish.

BRASSERIE LE CHEVAL BLANC

5020 St. Patrick
Montreal, Quebec, H4E 1A5
514-362-1551
Capacity: 3,000 hectolitres
Tours available: phone ahead
Glassware and merchandise available at the brewpub (809 Ontario Street East, Montreal)

Since 1937, the Denys family has had a pub on Ontario Street in Montreal. In 1981, Jerome Denys took the pub over from his uncle. As pub manager, his interest in beer grew.

"I got interested in imported beer, partly because I had a sister in England," he says. "We were selling draft imports at the pub, but when I got to know more about beer, I got to the stage where I thought some of the imports were pretty ordinary. Then, when I went on a trip to New York City and discovered the Manhattan brewpub, I got to thinking about building a brewpub here."

He consulted with Pierre Rajotte, a highly knowledgeable beer fan and consultant, and in 1987 the Cheval Blanc (White Horse) brewpub opened.

"Pierre helped me to develop yeast strains. We took a quality-control course together; it focused on dairy products. I've always been impressed by the best bottle-conditioned beers from Belgium, and my first interest was always yeast, not malt or hops."

In 1992, Cheval Blanc bottled its first beer. It was bottle-conditioned, or beer "on lees." In January 1995, Cheval Blanc opened its new plant, close to the Lachine Canal.

"I've learned a lot over the years," Denys says, "mostly by trial and error."

Le Cheval Blanc beers are available in some *dépanneurs* and many SAQ stores.

Bière d'autumne ★★★★
5% alc./vol.

It's easy to fall for this lovely autumn specialty ale. Vivaldi might have forgotten the other three seasons had he had a steady supply. D'autumne is made in French with English yeast in a French-English city. Appearance: orangey mid-amber with some haze; very pale beige, quiet, stable and moussey head; excellent lacing. Aroma: rich and inviting — a perfect marriage of caramel and fruit, plus fresh bread and a hint of peat. Taste: caramel-toffee; lots of fruit, which I find hard to identify (plum? melon? peach?). Dryish, slightly yeasty finish, gentle suggestion of hops, hint of tart fruit.

Bière d'été ★★★¹/₂
5% alc./vol.

Appearance: orange to light amber, hazy; near-white head. Aroma: yeast, lemon-grapefruit skin, bit of caramel. Taste: tart, zesty and a bit too fizzy (this was Cheval Blanc's first batch). It starts light, lemony, with some butterscotch that becomes tart midpalate. A nice tart bitterness (grapefruit zest) marks the finish, as does a small metallic edge. A very refreshing drink, with some wheat beer qualities, good for the verandah on a hot summer day.

La Berlue ★★★★¹/₂
6% alc./vol.

"Reduced vision" is a rough translation of *la berlue*. *Avoir la berlue* means to misjudge. I don't think I misjudge if I say that this is a stunner of a beer. Appearance: orangey mid to dark amber, with a pale beige, very quiet and stable head; excellent lacing. Wonderful aroma: toffee, peat, yeast and wood, with a small suave hint of ethyl. Taste: to put it metaphorically, it's a beautifully crafted tone poem in two parts. First canto: soft, lush, melt-in-your-mouth toffee, crème caramel, and soft fruit (ripe plum and peach). A tiny tang of tartness bridges the two cantos. Second canto: three strands of well-modulated bitterness — a yeasty dry bitterness, with earthy and woody tones; a hoppy grass-hay bitterness; and an ethyl-grainy bitterness. Coda: a flicker of warming and a lovely trace of huskiness. A great dessert beer, La Berlue would also go well with Indian and Indonesian food.

Cap Tourmente ★★★★
4.1% alc./vol.

Appearance: yellow-straw, some haze, with a white moussey head and good lacing. Aroma: delicate and enticing — light grain, yeast and bread, very soft spice. Taste: soft and pretty. (Pretty? Is that beer talk?) Initially, Cap shows adequately firm caramel (especially for the alcohol level) balanced by a slight grapefruit-skin tartness and astringency, with lovely bready and spicy elements. The finish is mild bitterness (yeasty more than hoppy) with mild citric tartness and fading spice. Pleasure-to-alcohol ratio: 12 to 10.

Legendary Red ★★★¹/₂
5% alc./vol.

Some beer zealots (like me) love Belgian and Belgian-inspired ales that emphasize spiciness, fruitiness and sourness, but often find that we can't drink much of them because of alcohol levels that are generally high. Here's an ale that offers lots of Belgian complexity at a relatively modest 5 percent alcohol level. Appearance:

hazy, orangey gold; yellowish cloud-like head; excellent lacing. Aroma: caramel, yeast, flowers, mild hint of nutmeg or cloves, and sun on oranges. Taste: soft and caramel-malty, offset by grain and hop bitterness, yeast dryness, and a hint of cloves. In the swallow, a soupçon of plummy sweetness then tartness. The finish is zesty, slightly yeasty, slightly citric (there's wheat in this beer), and mildly bitter. This charming ale amply demonstrates the rewards of bottle conditioning: very soft mouthfeel, and complexity and delicacy of flavor, especially given the alcohol level. I wouldn't call this a red (at least in the classic Belgian sense), but somewhere between a white and La Chouffe, the Belgian classic. Legendary Red would go well with strong-flavored dishes such as lamb medallions, steak with peppercorn sauce, and baked beans (try baking the beans with this beer).

Loch Ness ★★★¹/2
6% alc./vol.

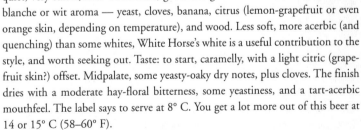

Belgian mother, Scottish father, raised in the streets of Montreal: this might describe the nature and nurture of this superb monster of a beer. With a nose that reminds me of a Belgian spicy ale such as La Chouffe, as well as a hint of the peaty nuttiness found in some of the Scottish ales, Loch Ness hints at a double European heritage. Not so strange, as the Belgians have long had an affection for Scotland's distinctive ales. This reddish amber ale is beautiful to behold, with its very fine beige-butter-colored bubbles in the head (partly the result of bottle conditioning) and its excellent lacing (Belgium is known for its fine lace!). Lees are hard-caked on the bottom of the bottle (a gift for homebrewers), so the beer is clear. There's a coquettish, teasing quality to the taste of Loch Ness: the soft, malty start and lush mouthfeel (from fine-bubble carbonation) is quickly overtaken by some darker flavors: dark fruit and roasted grain. Lovely bitter-sour aftertaste. Pleasure-to-alcohol ratio: 13 to 10. A brewing triumph, this one. Try it on its own, or with strong cheeses.

Original White ★★★¹/2
5% alc./vol.

Appearance: straw-gold (hazy, depending on temperature); quiet, very stable, near-white head; good lacing. Aroma: classic blanche or wit aroma — yeast, cloves, banana, citrus (lemon-grapefruit or even orange skin, depending on temperature), and wood. Less soft, more acerbic (and quenching) than some whites, White Horse's white is a useful contribution to the style, and worth seeking out. Taste: to start, caramelly, with a light citric (grapefruit skin?) offset. Midpalate, some yeasty-oaky dry notes, plus cloves. The finish dries with a moderate hay-floral bitterness, some yeastiness, and a tart-acerbic mouthfeel. The label says to serve at 8° C. You get a lot more out of this beer at 14 or 15° C (58–60° F).

Titanic ★★★★

7% alc./vol.

O.G.: 1060

Ingredients: two-row pale, caramel and chocolate malts; roasted barley; Perle and Tettnang hops; Belgian ale yeast

This may well have been the beer the captain was drinking that cold April evening in 1912, and who could blame him? I'd risk a good deal for this lovely ale. Appearance: dark amber tending to red; café-au-lait-colored head with small bubbles. Aroma: malt, yeast, brown sugar, fruit compote. Taste: big, like the ship. Soft, sweet, firm start, with hints of filbert or walnut; then a tingle of fruit preserve kicks in (marmalade comes to mind), with a touch of sourness. The finish is not a dramatic change, but rather a long bitter, slightly nutty taste on the back center of the tongue, and says encore, encore, which is French for more, and what the genteel folks on the Titanic were shouting to the band as the ship made its way through "iceberg alley" off Newfoundland. Bottle conditioning results in a lovely small-bubble carbonation and mouthfeel. I see this beer as a great winter warmer that suggests the stronger ales of Scotland as well as some Belgian bottle-conditioned beers. The label says "Best Before 2000." I haven't had an older bottle, but this one is likely to be even better 12 to 18 months old.

Tord-Vis ★★★

6% alc./vol.

Tord-vis is an expression loosely translated as "damn!" The label shows a man using an auger to tap a maple tree for its sap. Go figure. "Do not pour this beer on snow!!!" exhorts the label. But of course, that makes me wonder if doing so mightn't be a good idea: glace à l'érable for dessert? Appearance: orangey gold; very pale beige head, quiet and stable. Aroma: yeast, smoke, faint cloves and lemon skin; surprisingly, for a maple beer, no maple. Perhaps the maple syrup has been attenuated. Taste: soft and sweetish to start, plummy, trace of maple syrup flavor. In the middle, some wood-smoke bitterness. The finish is warming, with attractive earthy and cereal notes, and a hint of maple in the ethyl.

Traditional Amber ★★★★

5% alc./vol.

Appearance: mid amber with an orangey hue; very pale beige-orange head. Lovely aroma: butterscotch, yeast-bread, dry wood, spice (allspice?), hay. Taste: a not-sweet caramel taste, almost peachy, with undertones of yeast and grain. Amber finishes with gentle yeast bitterness, hop bitterness and earthy tones. Sometimes I think there's a lingering impression of peaches. Here's a beer I could drink for a whole evening (low to medium viscosity, low to medium body) — or have but one glass, and derive great pleasure just by paying close attention to each sip.

● BRASSERIE SEIGNEURIALE

135-D du Tremblay Road
Boucherville, Quebec, J4B 7K4
514-641-6433
Capacity: 1,000 hectolitres
Tours not available

Three hundred and twenty-five years ago, the Montreal suburb of Boucherville was a "seigniory," a piece of land granted to a *seigneur*, with a view to "colonizing" New France. Brasserie Seigneuriale is a colony, if you will, a beer colony, presided over by Marcel Laflamme (president) and his son Guy (brewer).

While the name may derive from New France, the styles produced by this brewery have their roots in old Belgium. Guy Laflamme was a homebrewer who became increasingly interested in the technical side of brewing. In the fall of 1994, Guy and his father toured some of the small breweries of Belgium and France, noting the methods and the equipment used.

"We take the time required to brew a quality bottle-refermented ale. We believe in craftsmanship," says Guy Laflamme. The brewer emphasizes two advantages of bottle conditioned or "refermented" beer, the second of which is perhaps not as well known as it should be. First, "it gives you a soft, subtle carbonation"; second, "it contributes to aroma — depending on the yeast: more fruitiness, more esters, more spiciness."

La Seigneuriale employs an open fermentation system, so that, according to Guy Laflamme, "yeast can be at its ease." Father Marcel adds: "We try to buy the best ingredients we can. We don't scrimp."

Plans for the future include expanding the brewery and exporting to the United States.

Seigneuriale ★★★★
7.5% alc./vol.
Ingredients include two-row malt
and hops

Appearance: orangey mid-amber, slightly hazy; beige, quiet, stable and moussey head; good lacing. Aroma: gentle spice bouquet (hints of cloves or nutmeg, coriander seed and, perhaps, toasted cumin seed), yeast, hay, bread. This dry-hopped ale has a complex start: caramel-toffee, spice (nutmeg-allspice, coriander-cardamom), yeast, fruit (apricot, mango, peach), and a well-integrated ethyl note. To finish, a very gentle bitterness, some yeasty dryness, lingering spice and a touch of earthiness. Pleasure-to-alcohol ratio: 10 to 10.

Seigneuriale Blonde ★★★¹/₂

7% alc./vol.
Ingredients include two-row malt;
wheat malt and honey; hops

Appearance: yellow-straw; near-white, fairly quiet, very stable head with smallish bubbles; good lacing. Aroma: yeasty-grainy, cloves-nutmeg, lemon zest. Taste: honey-caramel to start, offset by a light citrus astringency and taste, and some spice (ginger, cloves). Long, dry-yeasty finish, with toffee and earthy notes as well as ethyl warming. Pleasure-to-alcohol ratio: 9 to 10. Style? This mildly spicy beer strikes me as a cross between something like Leffe Blonde (for its softness and lightness) and a saison (for its citrus-spicy quality).

Seigneurial Reserve ★★★★¹/₂

7.5% alc./vol.
Ingredients: include two-row malts
and hops

This splendid Belgian-inspired ale shows the benefits of long conditioning and dry hopping. It has some of the toffee complexity of La Divine from the Silly brewery of Belgium, but with less alcohol. Mid amber in color, with a very quiet, pale beige head and good lacing. Aroma: yeasty-spicy (coriander, cloves or nutmeg), demerara-toffee, hay-flowers. Taste: soft, slightly sweet toffee and treacle, a clove spiciness that the ethyl reinforces rather than fights, plus hints of peach and peat or tobacco. Finishes with a lovely long fade, with both stale hop and yeasty dryness, a mild hay bitterness, and a toffee-ethyl kiss that you can feel above your two front teeth. Medium viscosity. Pleasure-to-alcohol ratio: 12 to 10. An unreservedly great ale that can serve as a dessert beer, but I like it best as an aperitif.

● BRASSEURS DE L'ANSE

182 Route 170
L'Anse St. Jean, Quebec, G0V 1J0
418-272-3045
Year started: 1995

I didn't get a chance to visit this brewery, located in the beautiful Saguenay Valley northeast of Quebec City. The brewery aims to build on the region's tourism. Peter Austin and Partners had a hand in formulating the recipes.

Illégal ★¹/₂

5.08% alc./vol.

Appearance: gold or pale amber; near-white craggy head; bit noisy. Aroma: light caramel, some dry grain, dry leaves. Taste: starts with caramel, corn sweetness and grain huskiness. Astringency and vegetal bitterness in finish.

Illégal Dry ★★

5.5% alc./vol.

Appearance: gold or pale amber; near-white craggy head; bit noisy. Aroma: maize-cereal, faint hop trace. Taste: very noticeable adjunct (cardboard, vegetal). Starts sweet and papery and finishes astringent with cardboard flavors.

Folie Douce ★

5% alc./vol.

Ingredients: include wild blueberries

I like the idea of a blueberry ale. To make it work, I think you'd need a good amount of sourness, and you'd need a firm pale malt base and judicious hopping. Appearance: very reddish amber; apple-blossom-pink head. Aroma: a trace of blueberry and wildflowers. Taste: cream soda, though slightly drier. No discernible blueberry taste. Very fizzy. More like a cooler than a beer.

● BRASSEURS DU NORD

875 Michèle-Bohec
Blainville, Quebec, J7C 5J6
514-979-8400
Capacity: 40,000 hectolitres
Year started: 1988
Tours not available

Founded in 1988 as a draft-only microbrewery, Les Brasseurs du Nord has grown to be a significant presence in the Quebec brewing scene.

Laura Urtnowski, president and head brewer, is not interested in "trying to reproduce Old World beers." Rather, "as North Americans, we get to take the best from the Old World and make something new, something special."

As a female in a male-dominated industry, Urtnowski is something of a pioneer. A native Montrealer, she studied history at the University of Quebec at Montreal, and got started in homebrewing with a fellow named Bernard Morin, now her husband. She managed a homebrew supplies store, and did a two-week apprenticeship at the Wellington County Brewery in Guelph, Ontario. Together with Morin and Morin's brother Jean, Urtnowski put together a business plan, and, with a loan from the government, Les Brasseurs du Nord was founded. The first kegs of beer rolled out in June 1988.

Two years later a bottling line was added. Recently, the brewery moved to larger quarters. Almost 50 percent of current production is sold in draft format.

"We don't go down the beaten path," says Urtnowski. "We try to be innovators. We want our beers to taste new and different, not an imitation of something." The trick for the brewer, she explains, is to give the drinker "the kind of pleasure you want to come back to. At first there's the element of discovery, but the taste must be there that makes you want to come back."

In coming years, the brewery would like to further improve the brewhouse to allow, for example, more elaborate protein rests, to obtain better bottling equipment, and to continue to improve its service.

It's easier for women to make their way in microbreweries than it is in large commercial breweries, Urtnowski says. "In olden times the beer maker had a prestigious position. For me, brewing is a continuation of times when brewing was associated with magic."

Boréale Blonde ★★★¹/₂

4.5% alc./vol.
O.G.: 1044

Appearance: pale amber; near-white, quiet and stable head; good lacing. Lovely aroma: dry grain, white bread, caramel, grass-hay, hint of grapefruit skin and flowers. Taste: initially, caramel with some mandarin or apricot, balanced by dry hoppy and oak-peat bitterness. Midpalate: grain and hop bitterness with hints of plum and bready yeastiness. In the finish, a grassy-woody hop bitterness with a wee bit of zest astringency. I like this deftly hopped, adequately firm pale ale. Quebeckers pun with the word "blonde," which denotes "girlfriend" as well as the color. To say *j'aime ma blonde* may indicate a greater fondness for this kind of beer than for one's sweetheart. Pleasure-to-alcohol ratio: 11 to 10.

Boréale Forte ★★★

8% alc./vol.
O.G.: 1072

Appearance: pale amber with a hint of orange; very pale beige, fairly quiet, moussey head; good lacing. Fetching aroma: sweet, caramel-butterscotch, toast or grain, light suggestion of fruit (dried apricot), plus hints of peat and flowers. Is there corn as well? The taste vacillates along a line. On the one side, the soft side, there's caramel, peach, apricot, a hint of plums and maybe vanilla. On the other side, the hard side, there's husky-grainy, nutshell bitterness, and a not-quite-suave ethyl edge. The soft side dominates the initial impression; the hard side, the finish. Some metal in the aftertaste. Pleasure-to-alcohol ratio: 8 to 10. Overall, well behaved for a muscular beer, but lacking in complexity for the alcohol level. It would be interesting to try this in a cask-conditioned format.

Boréale Noire ★★★¹/₂
5.5% alc./vol.
O.G.: 1060

This isn't really a black beer (as in preta or schwartz); it's a stout of which I've drunk more than a few glasses. Its licorice profile makes it complement desserts with a vanilla touch, such as crème caramel. Appearance: dark cola-brown with red highlights; mocha-colored head, quiet and stable. Aroma: licorice, espresso, prune-date, burnt toast, peat and flowers. Taste: overall, this medium-bodied stout tastes about two-thirds licorice and one-third espresso, on a honey-toffee base. There's the smallest suggestion of fruit in the start (raisin or fig), a hint of (nice) sourness just as you swallow, and a dry, medium-bitter earthy-graininess in the finish, along with lingering licorice and fresh hop taste.

Boréale Rousse ★★★★
5% alc./vol.
O.G.: 1047

This lovely ale must have voted communist in its youth; I can't see any other reason to call it Rousse, which translates as rusty-reddish. My eyes see mid amber, as well as a very stable head of fine bubbles; excellent lacing. Aroma: roasted malt, a hint of fruit (plum-orange) and oaky-hoppy undertones. Taste: a soft, buttery start changes quickly to fruit (plum, melon, berries), heather or peat, and caramel. Rousse finishes with the hop and grain bitterness dominating, and just a soupçon of licorice, fig, and fruit sourness. A thought-provoking and highly drinkable pale ale.

● LES BRASSEURS GMT

5585 de la Roche
Montreal, Quebec, H2J 3K3
514-274-4941
Capacity: 35,000 hectolitres
Year started: 1988
Tours available on Saturdays and by appointment for groups
Brewery-related clothing available

The year 1988 was a memorable one for Quebec beer drinkers. Three breweries, Massawippi (now defunct), les Brasseurs du Nord, and les Brasseurs GMT were born.

GMT founder André Martineau had been given a bottle of good microbrewery lager from the Granville Island brewery in Vancouver, and he was impressed. To his two partners, the G and the T of GMT, Gilbert Gravel and Yves Thibeault, Martineau presented the challenge: Why don't we try to make great-tasting, characterful beer?

Originally, Martineau and his partners wanted to open a brewpub, but then decided on a small brewery. Georges Van Gheluwe, a retired brewer with Flemish roots, who had brewed in Belgium, acted as a consultant to the fledgling brewery.

André LaFrenière started brewing for GMT in 1990. Born in eastern Ontario and raised in Montreal, he'd been homebrewing since 1983. In 1988 he took a brewing course in London, England. "Beer is one of life's simple pleasures," he says, "something that makes life more enjoyable. I like beer to have a definite personality or character. I don't like to appeal to the lowest common denominator, and yet your beer has to appeal enough to sell, to find its market."

GMT was a lager-only brewery until 1996, when Blanche de L'Isle, a wheat beer, was launched. In the same year, a vacuum bottling line was added. Plans for the future include making a pilsner-style beer, more seasonal beers, and exporting to the United States.

Belle Gueule ★★

5.2% alc./vol.
O.G.: 1051
Ingredients: two-row pale and caramel
malts; hops not disclosed; Belgian
lager yeast

Think of "gullet." *Belle gueule* means "nice mouth" in French. Appearance: copper to old gold; very pale beige, quiet and stable head; some lacing. Aroma: caramel, paper, dry grain, faint butterscotch. Taste: a mélange of caramel, paper, earth and grain, all fairly bitter. To finish, a paper-wood, earthy bitterness.

Bière de Noël ★★¹/2

6% alc./vol.

Appearance: russet, mid to dark amber; pale beige, fairly quiet and stable head. Aroma: light toffee, very faint spice, paper. Taste: caramel-toffee, with a sweet papery edge that hides the spice in the aroma. To finish, a woody bitterness; earthy aftertaste.

Blanche de l'Ile ★★★¹/2

4.8% alc./vol.

Appearance: gold, with a white, slightly noisy head that leaves little lacing. Aroma: dry grain, fresh bread, banana skin and lemon skin. Here's a great banana-ish addition to North America's wheats. To start, caramel with banana esters and a touch of citrus skin. Finishes with a very mild bitterness and yeasty dryness. The island in the name is the island of Montreal.

Canon ★★★
7.6% alc./vol.
O.G.: 1071

Appearance: reddish amber, with a beige, fairly quiet and stable head. I like the aroma: brandy-ethyl, malt-toffee, and traces of flowers, roasted nuts and (maybe) licorice. Taste: a quick warm sensation at the front of the tongue, together with a bit of fruit sweetness and brown sugar changes midpalate to fruit sourness (unripe plum) and sweetness (ripe plum, raisin). There's a brandy-like warmth in the finish, as well as some bitterness, some sugar, and some roasted grain. Pleasure-to-alcohol ratio: 8 to 10. The neck label calls Canon a "bière de garde," but unlike some examples of the style (for example, Trois Monts), the ethyl here weighs heavier than malt-fruit complexity.

● MCAUSLAN BREWERY

4850 St. Ambroise, suite 100
Montreal, Quebec, H4C 3N8
www.mcauslan.com
514-939-3060
Capacity: 30,000 hectolitres
Year started: 1989
Tours available by arrangement
Glassware and merchandise available

Education, like fermentation, is the art of change. Peter McAuslan, president of the McAuslan Brewery, has a background in this art. As a teenager, he made wine from wild grapes, dandelions, even raisins. As a student at university, he home-brewed. He joined Dawson College in Montreal as an admissions officer in 1972, and continued in various administrative posts until 1987.

As funding for colleges began to be squeezed, McAuslan began to think that opening a brewery, an idea he'd nurtured for a while, might be less risky than the "safe" college job.

McAuslan's head brewer is his wife. Ellen Bounsall also worked at Dawson College, and brings an academic background in biology to brewing. "Our goal is to maintain British brewing traditions using New World ingredients," she says. He says: "We think of our beer as world class. And we like to have fun." The press kit describes the brewery as an "artisanal brewery with a human face," which is true, I think, but only hints at McAuslan's and Bounsall's interest in community life and beer culture. The brewery has supported many Montreal-area cultural activities, including the International Film Festival, the Montreal Chamber Orchestra and the International Festival of Contemporary Music.

McAuslan and Bounsall's sense of tradition and history is evident in the names of many of the brewery's beers. Bounsall notes, for example, that McAuslan's first beer, St. Ambroise, is "named after Frère Ambroise, a member of the Sulpician religious order granted the territory of Montreal by Louis XIII of

France. Brother Ambroise was reputed to be the first brewer in New France."

The brewery uses Ringwood yeast and ferments in open vessels. Alan Pugsley helped to design the brewery. Of all the new-generation Ringwood breweries I know, McAuslan produces the beers that leave the smallest "thumbprint" of this distinctive, hard-working yeast.

Beyond Quebec, McAuslan ales are often available in the northeastern United States, Ontario and Europe.

Frontenac Extra Special Pale Ale ★★★¹/₂

5% alc./vol.
O.G.: 1049
Ingredients: two-row pale
and specialty malts; four
types of hops

There are three chicken feet on the label. I believe this refers to a prediction made by Count Louis de Buade Frontenac, who, when he was Governor of New France, said that in 300 years, three brewers would dominate brewing in Quebec, and that their beer would smell like chicken feet. The prediction came true, but fortunately those dark days are over. Appearance: gold to pale amber; near-white, very quiet head; good lacing. Aroma: delicately floral, not at all like chicken feet. Taste: a simple, moderately hoppy start, with just enough caramel-flavored malt to carry the hops. Some soft fruit (peach-melon) in the middle. Finish is mildly fruity with some balancing grain and hop bitterness. 25 IBUs.

Griffon Brown Ale ★★★★

5% alc./vol.
O.G.: 1049
Ingredients: two-row pale and specialty
malts; four types of hops

Griffon Brown ale isn't my idea of a brown ale, but it is a great beer. I think of English brown ales as soft, sweetish, with relatively low alcohol (by North American standards), modestly bitter, and often with some nuttiness. Griffon Brown (called Rousse in French) is grainy and moderately bitter. I'd call it a best bitter or pale ale. Appearance: mid to dark amber; beige, quiet, stable head; excellent lacing. Aroma: balance of bittering and noble hops over a lightly toasted grain base. Taste: grainy, almost husky malt base, hints of melon and oak (effect of Ringwood yeast, I think). Finishes with moderate hop bitterness nicely complemented by some grain bitterness.

Griffon Extra Pale Ale ★★★★

5% alc./vol.
O.G.: 1049
Ingredients: two-row pale and carastan
malt; four types of hops

The appearance — straw-to-gold; near-white, craggy, moussey, stable and very quiet head — lets you know that you're in refined company with this ale. EPA's delicacy of flavor isn't often found in an ale of such substance and firmness. The aroma is complex: hard fruit, caramel, cereal, hops. Flavor starts soft and butter-scotchy (but not sweet); then I find some delicate peach and melon tones as well as hop and grain bitterness. The finish is soft with lingering hop bitterness and a trace of roasted nuts. Some lions do have wings.

St. Ambroise Oatmeal Stout ★★★★¹/2

5.5% alc./vol.
O.G.: 1060
Ingredients: two-row pale and specialty
malts; rolled oats; four types of hops

Dark cola brown; mocha-colored, quiet, stable head. Excellent lacing. Aroma: baker's chocolate, toffee, coffee, biscuit, molasses, tar, prune and fig. The taste starts soft, with smooth toffee and malt, roastiness and mocha, and fruit (fig, prune, almost cherry). Some biscuit and further chocolate hints midpalate. Firm hop (grassy-minty) and grain bitterness in the finish (39 IBUs), with hints of cof-fee, roasted nuts and burnt biscuit. An excellent medium- to full-bodied stout. The profile changes gracefully from a slightly sweet toffee-fruit start through the biscuity middle to the dryish, expertly hopped finish. The oats are perfect and work with low carbonation to produce a silky mouthfeel and the suggestion of biscuit. Pleasure-to-alcohol ratio: 12 to 10. A great stout to go with barbecued meats, or, surprise your friends: serve it as a before-dinner drink.

St. Ambroise Pale Ale ★★★★¹/2

5.5% alc./vol.
O.G.: 1049
Ingredients: two-row pale, chocolate
and one other specialty malt; wheat;
Cascade, Willamette, Kent Golding and
Hallertau hops

Appearance: copper to mid amber; pale beige, quiet and stable head; excellent lacing. Aroma: three elements all in balance: caramel, lightly roasted grain, and hay, plus a mild Ringwood (oaky-earthy) thumbprint. Taste: great. Is that precise enough? This is a rounded, flavorful pale ale with lots of fruit and just the right amount of graininess and bitterness. To start, caramel, dry grain (hint of huskiness) and fruit (plum, unripe apricot). Fruit tartness builds. Finishes with moderate-plus bitterness exaggerated a little by a slightly acerbic mouthfeel, clear hop taste, earth, and hints of oak and citric zest. 35 IBUs. A real contribution to the world of pale ale.

St. Ambrose Raspberry Ale ★★★★

O.G.: 1049
Ingredients: two-row pale and specialty
malts; raspberry concentrate with
essence; four kinds of hops

Appearance: russet-amber; pale pinkish-beige head, quiet and stable. Excellent lacing. Aroma: delicate but pure raspberry, traces of hay and flowers. Taste: soft toffee and raspberry to start; then hops show quickly and firmly, leaving a raspberry seed bitterness. Lingering bitterness in the aftertaste. A firm toffee base and adroit hopping make this honest, unusual fruit beer one of North America's best. Fruit bitterness makes this ale go well with mixed green salads (use the beer in the vinaigrette) and with fruit custards.

● UNIBROUE INCORPORATED

80 Des Carrières
Chambly, Quebec, J3L 2H6
514-658-7658
Year started: 1992
Capacity: 180,000 hectolitres
Tours available: phone in advance
Glassware and merchandise available

Take a big pot, throw in some business savvy, a great deal of respect for the Belgian refermented beer tradition, and one very knowledgeable and charming Belgian-born brewer — the result is Unibroue, one of the crown jewels of the Quebec brewing scene.

Located just west of the Richelieu River and the historic Chambly canal, a canal that makes small-boat navigation possible between the St. Lawrence and the Hudson Rivers, Unibroue was born of . . . well, let president André Dion explain: "I was in the hardware business. Customers are always unhappy when they come in to a hardware store: they're there because something's gone wrong! But I noticed that the person buying beer was usually happy. The beer business is the happiness business." Together with Serge Racine, a partner with a background in the furniture business, and Gino Vantieghem, Unibroue's head brewer, Dion has built Unibroue into a kind of Belgium-on-the-Richelieu.

To the Unibroue cauldron, add some fun, or spice: Robert Charlebois, a Quebec-based pop singer and songwriter, is also a partner, and helps with marketing. A musician as a brewery worker? Well, why not? Charlebois's international career took off in Belgium, and it was there that he started to develop a taste for Belgian beer, especially whites, the Belgian version of wheat beer. Charlebois would fly home from concert dates in Europe, carefully tending his guitar and several bottles of white beer. What, he says, could be more natural than linking two of the world's greatest pleasures — music and beer?

The brewery is spotless. Brewer Gino Vantieghem is extremely knowledgeable. I feel that I know little about beer in his company. Not that he tries to make me feel this way; he is modest and courteous. Born in Flanders, he studied at the university in Louvain, and worked for the Riva brewery before coming to work for Unibroue.

Unibroue beers are available in Michigan, Pennsylvania, Ohio, New York, Vermont and Ontario. Many of the brewery's beers are available both in standard bottles and in 750-ml corked versions. I think the corked versions taste better, and often have better carbonation.

Blanche de Chambly ★★★★★

5% alc./vol.
O.G.: 1048
Ingredients: two-row pale malt, malted
wheat and raw wheat; Curaçao orange
peel and coriander; Hallertau hops

Take one: The blanche, or white beer, style is a major Belgian subset of the family of wheat beers. During the 18th century, many brewers of white beer, or "witbier" as it's called in Flemish, were concentrated around the town of Hoegaarden. The style almost died out in the 1950s when the last white-beer maker closed, and then in the mid-1960s, the style was revived, in part because of a certain Pierre Celis of the Hoegaarden Brewery. Celis went on to build a brewery in Texas, but before he did, he advised Unibroue on this beer, the first white to be brewed in North America. Even within the relatively small world of white beers, there's a lot of variety. White beers can range widely in sweetness, tartness and sourness, as well as in how they hint at spices and fruits. Unlike some of the Belgian white beers that have about 5 percent unmalted (raw) oats in addition to the roughly 45 to 50 percent wheat, Blanche de Chambly is all wheat (malted and raw) and barley. Unibroue spices this Blanche with Curaçao orange peel and coriander seed, and ferments at a high temperature (25–26° C). Blanche de Chambly benefits from being bottle-conditioned. It's loosely filtered, leaving some yeast in suspension, to provide flavor and to allow a slow secondary or tertiary fermentation to occur in the bottle. Suspended yeast also accounts for Blanche's soft, opaque pale yellow color. Because the yeast is such a vital element in the appearance and the flavor of the beer, many drinkers like to turn the bottle upside down (gently) before pouring. This will make the beer cloudy and add a small yeast bite. I find Blanche de Chambly's tartness and sourness more pronounced in its draft version.

Take two: Don't be too analytical with this beauty of a beer; instead, capture the right mood. Think of a summer day when dreams stretch to heaven.

Think of a waterside café on a warm windless afternoon. Picture in front of you a tall, thin wheat-beer glass filled with hazy, straw-gold colored Blanche de Chambly. Citric-sour in flavor, lightly lemony, and yet balanced with detectable sweetness, Blanche is a perfectly appropriate beer for al fresco dining, for afternoon sipping, for dreaming. It is also, I believe, a real contribution to the white beer style. On a hot day, try this refreshing beer cool, a little warmer than fridge temperature. I like mine without lemon but I never argue on a hot day. Surprisingly, Blanche is also a good winter beer; it goes well with strada and other bread-based dishes.

Eau Bénite ★★★★
7.7% alc./vol.

Appearance: old gold with a near-white, moussey, fairly quiet, very stable head; good lacing. Aroma: yeasty, lightly spicy (a delicate combination of cloves, nutmeg and pepper), caramel hinting at butterscotch, and hay. Taste: holy water indeed. To start, caramel, butterscotch, brandyish ethyl, fruit (peach, mango), and nutmeg-ginger. A bit of oak in the swallow, and to finish, a mildly bitter, slightly warming balance of earth and grain. Pleasure-to-alcohol ratio: 11 to 10. The name suggests water, but I'm reminded of fire. A great beer to sip in front of a fireplace in winter, or in summer, beneath the stars.

La Fin du Monde ★★★★¹/₂
9% alc./vol.
Ingredients: two-row pale malt; corn
flakes; coriander and Curaçao orange
peel; Cascade, Mt. Hood, Perle and
Saaz hops; Belgian ale yeast

The End of the World is at hand, and I, for one, am cheering. La Fin du Monde is a strong, soft, silk-smooth ale — the first true tripel-style beer to be brewed in North America. Tripel, a beer style originating in Belgium, is complex and slowly fermented — that is, often in three stages. At 9 percent alcohol, La Fin is definitely a sipping beer. Like Duvel, the Belgian classic that might be used as a reference point for this beer, La Fin is soft and refined, but I think even more complex and rewarding than its Belgian counterpart. Appearance: pale straw-yellow (I like to pour it so that it's a little cloudy); whipped-cream head with very tiny bubbles, craggy and stable; excellent lacing. Aroma: a bouquet of lemon, fresh bread, yeast, orange peel, toffee, hay, and a soupçon of cloves or nutmeg. Taste: a wonder. A soft, cloudlike initial mouthfeel; very light toffee overlaid by five elements: soft, warming ethyl, delicate spiciness (allspice?), a mild citric tang (almost grapefruit), hayish bitterness, and a hint of brandied fruit. A long malty finish with waves of yeasty dryness, herbal-bitterness and hints of orange and oak. After the finish, breathe in: you'll get a touch of orange zest. Strong beers should provide depth, complexity, and integration of flavors. Thanks to its slow, triple fermentation and use of first runnings only (to avoid the polyphenols that come from long sparging), La Fin du Monde delivers all this in spades. Given the alcohol level, you might want to split a bottle with a friend. Serve La Fin at cellar temperature in large balloon glasses. Pleasure-to-alcohol ratio: 11 to 10. Compared with Duvel, La Fin is a little darker, yeastier and spicier (but subtle and soft), with hints of orange as opposed to pear. Brewer Gino Vantieghem recommends that you put a few bottles away in the cellar to see how they age. Were I to believe that the end of the world were tomorrow, I'd get mine out of the cellar now; this is the drink I'd choose to witness "God's temple in heaven . . . flashes of lightning, voices, peals of thunder, an earthquake and heavy hail." But don't wait. This is an excellent beer to help you meditate — anytime — on the ends of things.

La Gaillarde ★★★★★

5% alc./vol.
Ingredients: two-row malts; malted and raw wheat, raw corn; herbs, spices and wood; Kent Golding and Tettnang hops

What's the reference point for this delightful ale? I think of lightly spicy Belgian ales, but I haven't had one quite like this. There are also some wheat-beer qualities here, but this is no ordinary wheat beer. Appearance: straw-colored with a near-white, very moussey, fairly quiet and stable head. Aroma: lightly spicy, delicate and complex (lemon, cloves, banana, coriander leaves, orange zest). Taste: much like the nose, but with very refined pale malt qualities that show brilliantly. The spice and fruit move toward a slightly tart, slightly metallic finish. Flavors are very well integrated. Very little dry yeasty flavor. Pleasure-to-alcohol ratio: 12 to 10. If Unibroue keeps making beers like this one, we're going to see plane loads of Belgian beer tourists in Canada. This would be a great beer with which to make a lightly spiced bread, or to serve with a loaf right out of the oven. Firm, but delicate and subtle, this ale is a significant and unique contribution to the world of beer style. Drink this one as fresh as possible.

Maudite ★★★1/2

8% alc./vol.
O.G.: 1068
Ingredients: two-row pilsner and caramel malts; caramelized sugar and corn (about 10%); coriander seed and other spices; Saaz and three other hops; Belgian ale yeast

For this beer, I think it helps to know the legend depicted on the label. The *chasse galerie* is the story of lumbermen who make a pact with the devil. The context: it is New Year's Eve, and the lumbermen want a quick trip home to visit their lovers. The deal: the devil gives the men a flying canoe; the men must refrain from saying any Christian or holy word or the canoe will fall from the sky and the Devil will take their souls. The outcome? Well, let's look at this beer. *Maudite* means damned, or cursed, in French. This is a damned good beer. Orangey mid-amber in color, with a beige, quiet, stable head and excellent lacing, Maudite has a surprisingly delicate nose: yeast, toffee, soft spice (nutmeg), oak and hay. Taste: caramel or light toffee and cinnamon-nutmeg which, with ethyl, produces a spicy warming. Some brandied fruit midpalate. Finish is not so much bitter as earthy-yeasty; spicy ethyl lingers. Usually I'm indifferent to how I pour a beer on lees. For this one, I like two-beers-in-one: a clear first glass and a hazy final glass. Pleasure-to-alcohol ratio: 9 to 10. Style? No damned idea. This beer is unique.

Raftman ★★★

5.5% alc./vol.
Ingredients: two-row pale,
caramel and whisky malts;
caramelized sugar; Kent Golding
plus one other hop

The raftmen of Quebec and Ontario were the fellows, celebrated in song, who, at the end of a log drive on a smaller river, turned the pine logs into huge rafts. The rafts were steered down the large rivers, like the Ottawa, to mills or to ships that would carry the wood to Europe. Joseph Montferrand, once a lumberjack and raftman in the Ottawa Valley, is said to have been so quick, such an energetic dancer, that he'd leave his footprints on the ceilings of the shanties in which he danced. The raftman tradition has disappeared, but only recently. The last of the log drives occurred in the 1980s. Raftman is not unique in using "whisky malt," a lightly smoked malt, but the malt is not commonly used. Appearance: amber-orange, off-white moussey head. Aroma: spicy-yeasty, with an orangey apricot tone. Taste: very soft and lush to start; smoky and mild-bitter notes midpalate (16 IBUs), with a peaty-smoky, slightly sour finish. If you've tried a rauchbier and found the smoke a bit over-the-top (my wife described her first rauch as like licking an ashtray), try this intriguing ale. The smoke is just right, a bit like catching a whiff of a bonfire from the shore as you drift past on a raft.

VERMONT

Given its small size, its topography, and its concentration of breweries, perhaps Vermont should be called the Beer Mountain State. After Maine, it would seem that Vermont has the most breweries per capita in the United States. Despite Vermont's love affair with brewing, I couldn't find any histories of brewing for the state. Vermont doesn't appear in the index of Gregg Smith's *A History of Suds*; in Stanley Baron's *Brewed in America: The History of Beer and Ale in the United States*, the only index listing is "Vermont, prohibition legislation in." Poor Vermont!

The motto of this lovely state, which was founded in 1777 by Bob Newhart and the Green Mountain Boys, is Drink Ale or Die. Ale is often easier to produce for the small brewer than lager. To the best of my knowledge, there are no lager breweries in the Vermont — is this an export opportunity for Brasal, in nearby Montreal?

For the lover of ale who enjoys beer tourism, Vermont is ideal. Given its size, all the beer shrines can be visited in a one-week visit. And beer tourism can be combined with hiking, cycling, skiing, antique shopping and so on.

Vermont has some bizarre beer legislation. Saying on a label that a beer has four percent alcohol by volume is not a crime, but to say so in an advertisement is a crime. The Department of Liquor Control person I spoke to said that a desire to prevent alcohol abuse motivated Vermont's beer legislation. Why then is three percent beer taxed as heavily as six percent beer? Why is six percent beer taxed at less than half the rate of seven percent beer?

Beer is sold in private, competitive stores, unless the folks in Montpelier say that a beer is not beer. A beer *is* beer if it has less than six percent alcohol, or if it has "more than six percent and not more than eight percent and has a terminal specific gravity of [more] than 1.009." Six to eight percent beers with a final gravity of less than 1.009 and beers with more than eight percent alcohol are "deemed to be a spirit and not a malt beverage." These "spirits" are spirited out of public view and, if the Liquor Control folks allow it, sold in out-of-the-way, state-run liquor stores.

I would like to have heard the discussion when these laws were passed. Sweetish seven percent beers can be bought with a loaf of bread; dryish seven percent beers cannot be. Vermont was the first state to prohibit slavery, but it does not prohibit wacky laws.

Fortunately, advertising of beer "on vehicles drawn by horses" is permitted in Vermont.

● CATAMOUNT BREWING COMPANY

58 South Main Street
White River Junction, Vermont, 05001
802-296-2248
Capacity: 70,000 barrels
Year started: 1986
Tours available
Glassware and merchandise available

Tony Lubold, Catamount's cheerful brewer, used to be a pattern maker in a Vermont foundry. When I ask him about patterns in Catamount brewing, he talks about consistency and tradition. "Consistency is important. Even a seasonal beer should be the same one year to the next." When Lubold says that Catamount sticks to traditional styles, he emphasizes that this means, by and large, New England styles, which are, he says, "a little drier and a little hoppier" than their British equivalents.

Lubold is one of the few brewers I've met who continues to brew at home: "thirty-five batches a year, maybe," he says. "We don't have a pilot plant here, so if we want to develop a new beer, I try to do it at home."

On my last visit to the brewery, Lubold was adding hop flowers to the wort when I walked in. Catamount uses only fresh hop flowers, never pellets or oils, and uses no rice or corn adjunct. For two of its ales, the brewery uses six-row barley malts, an ingredient that isn't commonly used in microbreweries. Six-row barley has a reputation (both good and bad) for "huskiness," which Lubold thinks it doesn't necessarily deserve. Catamount uses an ale yeast obtained from a Pennsylvania brewery.

Catamount has been happily ensconced on Main Street in White River Junction since it was founded in 1986, but success has left the brewery constrained by the size of the premises (an old meat-packing plant), even after two expansions. Catamount has therefore built a new 25,000-square-foot brewery in Windsor, just south of White River Junction. The new facility adds 50,000 barrels capacity to the White River Junction plant's capacity of 20,000 barrels.

"Beer is life," Lubold tells me. "It makes life happy. Hops make me happy," he says pointing to a photograph of ripe hop cones. "Beer goes well with food, with friends, even with moments when you're alone. Add that up, and that's life."

In addition to four ales in the permanent line-up and five seasonals, Catamount brews three draft-only beers: ESB, a double bock and a red ale.

Amber ★★★¹/₂

4.8% alc./vol.
O.G.: 1049
Ingredients: two-row pale,
caramel and carapils malts; Perle
and Willamette hops

Appearance: mid amber, with a yellowy beige, quiet and stable head; good lacing. The aroma is light and delicate — lightly toasted grain, caramel, peach, fresh white bread and hay. Taste: a slight tartness mingles with caramel and peach, all balanced by some graininess. Finishes with delicate hoppy bitterness (36 IBUs), with some floral taste and a touch of earthy astringency. Simple, well-balanced and refreshing.

American Wheat ★★★¹/₂

4.48% alc./vol.
O.G.: 1043
Ingredients: two-row pale malt; malted
wheat (50%); Kent Golding and
Hallertau hops

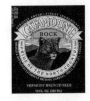

Appearance: pale gold (yellow-straw tinged with green); white, very quiet and stable head; excellent lacing. Aroma: sun-on-grain, fresh bread, traces of banana skin and lemon skin, delicate Hallertau leafiness. Taste: baguette in a bottle. Caramel and grainy-bready to start, with some yeast and green, draft-like flavors. To finish, very mild citric tartness, allowing the rounded taste of Kent Golding to show. This enjoyable beer is an example of the developing American wheat style.

Bock ★★★

7% alc./vol.
O.G.: 1064
Ingredients: two-row pale, caramel and
munich malts; Northern Brewer and
Hallertau hops

Mid to dark amber, with a beige, slightly noisy (but stable) head, this seasonal offering has an aroma of grain and caramel with tart and bitter edges. To start, caramel-toffee with early earth and hop bitterness; some astringency. Ethyl warming midpalate, with a wee hint of fruit (cherry?). A hoppy-peaty bitterness in the finish with ethyl lingering. More woody and earthy than most bocks. Pleasure-to-alcohol ratio: 9 to 10.

Gold ★★★¹/₂

4.2% alc./vol.

O.G. 1045

Ingredients: six-row pale, carapils and
caramel malts; Willamette hops

Appearance: yellow gold; near-white, fairly quiet and stable, craggy head. Aroma: dry grain, fresh bread, hay, trace of wildflowers. How can an aroma so light be so attractive? Balance, I think. Taste: dryish caramel, hints of apricot or peach, and oak. Midpalate, there's a wee touch of citrus rind. Finish is dry, hayish and lightly grainy. There's a delicately earthy, almost husky aftertaste. I like the progression of flavors here, with most elements detectable at each stage, but with more or less prominence.

Oatmeal Stout ★★★★

4.8% alc./vol.

O.G.: 1052

Ingredients: two-row pale and crystal
malts; rolled oats and roasted barley;
Northern Brewer and Fuggles hops

Here's a lovely contribution to the style. Enough oats for a silky mouthfeel, but not overly viscous. Appearance: cola brown with burgundy highlights; café-au-lait-colored head, quiet and stable; excellent lacing. Aroma: roasted grain, molasses or demerara, prunes, Turkish coffee, licorice root. Taste: a balance of fruit (prunes, apricot) and toffee with lots of not-quite-burnt toastiness. Maybe a hint of oaty cerealness. To finish, firmly hoppy (a bit too), almost minty, some espresso and dry grain. Pleasure-to-alcohol ratio: 11 to 10. Seasonal (spring).

Octoberfest ★★★

5.3% alc./vol.

O.G.: 1056

Ingredients: two-row pale, caramel and
munich malts; Northern Brewer,
Tettnang and Ultra hops

Light to mid amber in color, with a yellowy, light beige, very quiet and stable head, this fall seasonal has a nose that includes caramel and toffee, plum, roasted grain, and some floral accents. Taste: caramel offset by a light hoppiness and some nice plummy notes. The finish has some hop and fruit astringency as well as a tiny hint of ethyl. This beer is "green" from start to finish, meaning tart, fresh and draft-like, as well as grassy-hoppy, making it ideal for sausages, ribs, wings, or other oily meats. I'm not sure I'd call this an oktoberfest, even if it is spelled with a "c" — it's not as firm, dark or malty as most beers in that style. Perhaps it's something along the lines of a "harvest ale."

Pale Ale ★★★★¹/₂

5% alc./vol.
O.G.: 1049
Ingredients: two-row pale, caramel,
carapils and black malts; Cascade, Kent
Golding and Fuggles hops

Appearance: orangey mid-amber; pale beige, very quiet and stable head; excellent lacing. Aroma: a balance of malt, grain or toast, plum and hay, plus a hint of smoky peat. Taste: to start, toffee, grain, oak and some early hop tartness. To finish, a clean hop bitterness (40 IBUs), with lingering grain flavors and a slight suggestion of smoke. Medium in body and viscosity, this is a delightful and satisfying American pale ale. More hoppy than many British pale ales, but less than many on the West Coast, this ale shows balance and subtlety. I like roasted vegetables, and I think this hoppy, slightly tart ale would go well with roasted veggie pita rolls or roasted veggie pizza.

Porter ★★★★★

5.3% alc./vol.
O.G.: 1053
Ingredients: six-row pale, caramel, carapils and black malts; roasted barley and
black barley; Galena and Cascade hops

Always a favorite of mine, and an outstanding example of the style. Perhaps more than three other porters that I also love (Anchor's, Sierra Nevada's, Wellington County's), Catamount's porter shows two aspects of porter brewing I consider important: appropriate density and the judicious use of roasted barley. Appearance: dark amber hinting at red; café-au-lait-colored, fairly stable, fairly creamy head; good lacing. Aroma: dryish, roasted barley intermingled with floral hops, almost-burnt toast, notes of toffee, and wild flowers. Sometimes I detect fruit as well: a mélange, perhaps, of plum, prune and cherry. Taste: a soft and caramelly start changes quickly to a dry, toasty, grainy midpalate with pruny hints. Hop flavors (grassy, not metallic) and a gentle burnt-grain-and-baker's-chocolate bitterness show in the finish, as does a touch of plum-cherry sourness. Is there a touch of bitter licorice in the aftertaste? Medium body, medium viscosity. There's a big movement in the taste from the initial soft and slightly sweet to the later sour and bitter, and the flavors are very well married throughout. Please give me more, lots more. I'd like a big amount, please, not just a cat amount.

LONG TRAIL BREWING COMPANY

Junction, Route 4 & 100A
Box 168, Bridgewater Corners, Vermont, 05035
802-672-5011
Capacity: 20,000 barrels
Year started: 1989
Tours available

It was in 1990, I think, when I was looking for a new brewery in Bridgewater, Vermont. Bridgewater is small, but still, the brewery wasn't easy to find. It was located in the village's historic woolen mill, and I remember, after finding it, thinking that the minuscule brewing company might be easy to overlook among the gift shops also located in the mill.

Long Trail, formerly called Mountain Brewers, has come a long way down the trail since that time. In 1995, the brewery moved to a custom-built plant west of Bridgewater. There's a well on site, and the plant is large enough to accommodate expansion in capacity.

"Imported beer brewed in Vermont" was the original idea at Long Trail, an expression that encapsulates so much of the early days of the beer renaissance. Andy Pherson, chief of the brewery and an electrical engineer, was inspired to get involved in microbrewing by the success of imported beer in the United States. Watching skiers at Killington drink British ale made him think that there might be a market for locally produced quality beer.

Matt Quinlan, brewer at Long Trail, says that the brewery tries to brew "the best beer we can" while brewing to style. "We use classic recipes and a single stage infusion process." In its early years, Long Trail was happy to discuss its ingredients. It no longer does, making Long Trail the only brewery in Vermont that considers ingredients a secret.

Quinlan said that it's possible that the brewery will grow its own hops and perhaps even its own barley. The brewery has plans to sell cask-conditioned ale.

Blackbeary Wheat ★★
O.G.: 1036

Appearance: straw to pale gold; near-white, quiet and stable head; largish bubbles. Aroma: sugars, fructose, cream soda. Taste: more like a cooler than beer. Fizzy mouthfeel, a papery taste, and hops all work at cross-purposes with the malt. The fruit is not clear or distinctive. No sourness.

Brown Ale ★★★¹/₂
O.G.: 1040

As bitter (25 IBUs) but more acerbic than many British brown ales, this is a lovely, thought-provoking beer. Appearance: dark reddish brown; café-au-lait-colored, quiet and stable head; good lacing. Aroma: unique and engaging — mocha and soft fruit on a roasted barley base. Taste: to start, soft, mildly bitter, slightly grainy and nutty, and with a slightly thin mouthfeel due to aggressive hopping. In the finish, the beer actually sweetens to a malty-mocha effect with roasted barley lingering. Aftertaste: subtle hop bitterness balanced by grain dryness. I think this ale would be ideal with tacos, meat fondues, couscous, or any sweet and spicy dish.

Brown Bag / Double Bag Ale ★★¹/₂

Appearance: reddish mid-amber, with a beige, quiet and stable head; good lacing. Aroma: toffee-ethyl, fresh-cut grass, diacetyl, all equally prominent. The start is sweet, viscous, toffeeish and brandyish. Not much fruit. The finish is peaty-bitter, ethyl-warming bitter, and ethyl metallic. Long Trail has not indicated the alcohol level on the label of this ethyl-tasting beer. If the alcohol is 6.5 percent by volume, I would rate the pleasure-to-alcohol at 8 to 10; at 7 percent, 7 to 10. Better and maltier than some of the inexpensive high-octane suds, Double Bag lacks the fruitiness and complexity of most winter warmers, to which, in the absence of any useful style information on the label, I would compare this rather raw, ethyly ale.

India Pale Ale ★★¹/₂
O.G.: 1060

Appearance: mid amber; yellowy pale beige, quiet and stable head; good lacing. Aroma: butterscotch, fresh cut hay, some okay diacetyl and flowers. Taste: to start, butterscotch-diacetyl with strong hop taste, the combination of which produces tart-acidic plumminess. To finish, a long grassy bitterness. This ale has all the hoppiness you'd expect in an IPA but little of the firm, dry, cereal maltiness or "roundedness" that marks the style. An interesting blind tasting would be this with two other American IPAs: Grant's (Yakima Brewing, Washington state) and Brooklyn's (New York state).

Kolsch ★★¹/₂

5.1%
O.G.: 1040
Ingredients: include Saaz hops

I don't understand the low, 1040 starting gravity (according to the brewery's literature) and the relatively high 5.1 percent alcohol (what I was told). Appearance: gold to old gold; near-white head; excellent lacing. Aroma: dry grain, grass-hay, hint of caramel. Taste: a green, worty pale ale. Very fizzy caramel with grassy hop astringency to start. Unripe plum middle. Clean, acerbic hop bitterness in finish. Very big bubbles. Too fizzy, not soft enough for style. As a pale ale, three stars; as a Kolsch, two.

Long Trail Ale ★★¹/₂

O.G.: 1050

The label says "Premium altbier," but Long Trail's flagship brand doesn't taste like any German alt I've had. Rather, it strikes me as a hoppy, moderately bitter pale ale — not a hophead beer, but a beer for someone who likes the taste of fresh hops. Appearance: mid amber; yellowy beige, quiet and stable head; good lacing. Aroma: grass, yeasty bitterness (like Ringwood bitterness); dry grain, butterscotch and plum. Taste: initially, caramel, hop grassiness and acidity, and tart apricot-plum. A flash of earthiness midpalate, and then a long, firm, clean hop finish. Aftertaste: a touch of citrus zest. As a pale ale, three stars, as an altbier, only two.

Long Trail Stout ★★¹/₂

O.G.: 1042

Appearance: cola brown with red highlights; mocha-colored, quiet and stable head; good lacing. Aroma: chocolate, molasses, biscuit, fig and prune, grass, coffee. Taste: biscuity chocolate (dry and bitter due to early hoppiness) with hints of dark fruit, all in a tart, acerbic hop bath. The finish is coffee, some burnt toast, raw hop flavor, acid. Too much of the dryness in this "dry Irish style" stout is merely hop bitterness. Pretty skinny for the style, and too thin to support the hopping. 40 IBUs.

● MAGIC HAT BREWING COMPANY

180 Flynn Avenue
Burlington, Vermont, 05401
802-658-2739
Capacity: 6,200 barrels
Year started: 1994
Tours available: phone ahead
Glassware and merchandise available

To get the financing to start a brewery, one would pretty well have to pull it out
of a hat. A magic hat. So says brewer Bob Johnson in explaining the brewery
name.

Johnson thinks it's important to study historic beer styles, to know their
parameters and their historic evolution, and then to "break the rules. Kind of like
Picasso: he knew the major art styles, but he broke loose of them."

Magic Hat uses Ringwood yeast, and after almost 300 generations of cultiva-
tion, the yeast is starting to take on a house profile. When I visited, Magic Hat was
brewing a seasonal wheat beer in a rectangular open fermenter, an old cheese-vat.

Johnson sees the beer market as increasingly educated, and thinks that to survive, brewers need to make beer that is not only of high quality, but distinctive.

Magic Hat's Blind Faith, an IPA, is sold in cask-conditioned format in
Burlington and Stowe. Magic Hat brews other ales in addition to the ones
described below, including an oatmeal stout, a raspberry stout, and an unfiltered
wheat beer.

Magic Hat hopes to lease new premises sometime in the future, but will stay
in the Burlington area.

Blind Faith ★★★★

6.2% alc./vol.
O.G.: 1056
Ingredients: two-row pale, crystal and
chocolate malts; malted wheat; Cascade
and Progress hops

Here's a new style of beer: I'd call it a Yorkshire-Vermont IPA. Appearance: mid
amber; pale beige, quiet, stable, craggy head; good lacing. For me, the aroma was
a sense of *déja senti*: it is eerily similar to the nose of Hart Amber (Hart Breweries,
Ontario) when it was first brewed — very tart. It's that smell associated with the
distinctive Ringwood yeast (which comes from Yorkshire, England) and open,
relatively fast, fermentation. Blind Faith has a citric-tannic tart aroma over a
toffee base. Taste: shockingly, pleasingly tart, green and worty, plus caramel and
nectarine-peach over a woody bitterness. Finishes with tart hop bitterness (45
IBUs), firm grassy hop taste, some lingering toffee with a nutshell-bitter edge.
Blind Faith is dry hopped with Cascade.

Hocus Pocus ★★★¹/2

5% alc./vol.
O.G.: 1050
Ingredients: two-row pale malt;
malted wheat; Tettnang and
Cascade hops

The word hoax may be a contraction of hocus; hocus pocus is likely a parody of *Hocus est Corpus*, the words said to consecrate the bread in the Latin mass. Magic Hat's Bob Johnson said that he didn't know this when I mentioned it on a visit to the brewery. It must be serendipity then that this ale, a hoppy version of a plain or best bitter, ended up with a bread- and spirit-related name. Appearance: gold to light amber; near white, fairly quiet and stable head. Aroma: grassy hops, some floral hops, sun on grain. Taste: caramel and dry grain with some hop bitterness (26 IBUs) and Ringwood tartness to start; moderate hop bitterness and astringency to finish. Lightly fruited versions of this ale (raspberry, blueberry) are also brewed.

● MCNEILL'S BREWERY

90 Elliot Street
Brattleboro, Vermont, 05302
802-254-2553
Tours available by arrangement
Brewery-related merchandise available

Ray McNeill, cellist, brewmaster and vice president of McNeill's Brewery, apprenticed at the Catamount brewery. He says that his brewery has a unique niche in Vermont brewing: "What we're doing is very different. We don't filter any of our beers."

For McNeill, this is central to his beer philosophy. Filtration, he says, strips out "proteins, flavor and mouthfeel. Clear, unfiltered beer tastes best." Long conditioning helps McNeill to achieve clarity in his beers: most beers require 25 to 28 days from initial fermentation to bottling, a long period for ales. McNeill points out that having some residual yeast can also contribute to shelf life: "Yeast is an anti-oxidant."

"Filtration is a crutch," he says. "It covers problems in the beer. Not using a filter forces you to do things right in the brewhouse, particularly during the boil and the sparge."

Most McNeill ales are dry hopped. McNeill points out that aromatic hop constituents are lost in the boil and during fermentation. Dry hopping allows him to achieve the aromatics he seeks.

McNeill's bottles a long line of beers for a small brewery. It also operates as a pub-restaurant.

Acme ★★★¹/₂

5% alc./vol.

O.G.: 1048

Ingredients: two-row pale, moravian
and crystal malts; Perle, Fuggles and
Tettnang hops

I call myself promiscuous, but were I to become monogamous (or is it moniverous?), I could do worse than to stick with this complex and beautiful ale. Mid amber with a slight orangey haze, Acme has a very pale beige head that leaves some lacing. The aroma is complex: something akin to lactose or warm milk, roasted grain, toffee, forest, walnut and flowers. At warmer temperatures, some leather and okay diacetyl. Acme starts soft, with not-sweet toffee and hints of apricot or even mango. A quick blush of sourness midpalate. A lovely soft-bitter finish, with hops perfectly married to the roasty-grainy, peaty, nutshell malt base. Acme is much like a well-scored violin duet: it celebrates malt in the melody, and hops in the counterpoint. Malt dominates, but is never cloying. Hops are always there, but never harsh (25 IBUs). Medium viscosity and perfect carbonation make it hard to stop sipping. Style? In flavor, if not in alcohol, it's ESBish, with some old-style buttery qualities.

Alle Tage Altbier ★★★¹/₂

5.2% alc./vol.

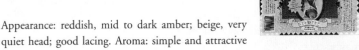

Appearance: reddish, mid to dark amber; beige, very
quiet head; good lacing. Aroma: simple and attractive
— light caramel-toffee, hay or forest, hint of peat. Taste: a lightly metallic, firmly malty start with toffee and caramel and some peat. There's a touch of fruit (apricot, plum) midpalate. The finish is grassy, bitter hoppiness, some yeasty dryness. Alt flavors show in the very nice metallic (copper or tin) aftertaste. I like a bit more of a grainy and cereal-dry character in my alts, but this is a very drinkable ale.

Big Nose Blond ★★★¹/₂

5.2% alc./vol.

O.G.: 1048

Ingredients: two-row pale and crystal
malts; malted wheat; Hallertau-
Tradition, Chinook, Cascade, and
Hallertau hops

Here's an ale for hop lovers, not because of the quantity of hops used, but because of how they come across: clear, fresh and floral. Appearance: yellow gold; near-white, creamy, quiet and stable head. Aroma: perfumey hops very much like lemon grass (or fresh cut hay, flowers and lemon zest) on a light caramel base.

Taste: a soft, floral and bitter hoppiness comes across almost like citrus zest (that's the wheat) mixed with lightly toasted grain. Bitterness actually decreases in the finish; in addition to the taste of fresh hops, caramel and a hint of plums come through.

Duck's Breath Ale ★★★¹/₂

5% alc./vol.
O.G.: 1048
Ingredients: two-row pale, crystal and
mild malts; Fuggles and Goldings hops

Appearance: orangey, slightly hazy amber; yellowy beige, fairly quiet and stable head. I like the aroma of this fruity, slightly hoppy ale. Not at all like a mallard's exhalation: rather, a delicate suggestion of hop flowers, plus some caramel and apricot. Taste: to start, caramel with apricot and plum, offset by a mild hop astringency. Some fruit tartness midpalate. To finish, moderate hop bitterness, grass, metal, and a nice touch of residual fruit sourness. The fruity tartness and delicate metallic edge of this ale would make it a quacking good accompaniment to canard aux bluets.

Extra Special Bitter ★★★¹/₂

5.75% alc./vol.
O.G.: 1054
Ingredients: two-row pale and crystal
malts; Bullion, Northern Brewer and
Cascade hops

Appearance: orangey mid-amber below; yellowy beige up top; quiet and stable head. Aroma: fresh aromatic hops over a light grainy base. Taste: Is cohabitation better than marriage? This medium-bodied ESB has two clear flavors — fresh hops and caramel-apricot — living together yet leading separate lives. Initially, the impression is one of caramel-apricot and, thanks to aggressive hopping, bitterness that resembles tartness. The finish is grassy (but not harsh) hop bitterness, with traces of lingering caramel and some nice earthiness. I bet this one would be even better cask-conditioned at the brewpub.

Firehouse Amber Ale ★★★★

5% alc./vol.
O.G.: 1048
Ingredients: two-row pale, crystal and
munich malts; Northern Brewer,
Chinook and Cascade hops

Appearance: mid amber; beige, fairly quiet head. The aroma is unique and attractive — fresh grassy and floral hops over a caramel and plum-melon background, with an overall impression of forest and freshness. Taste: butterscotch and peach, thinned and made slightly tart by hops (but oh-so-fresh hops). A grassy hop bitterness (firm, but not raw) marks the finish, as does a faint memory of the butterscotch and peach. Slight metallic edge in the aftertaste. Medium body, more than medium viscosity. I like to bake or fry meats with fruit (for example, sausage with peaches, chops with apples and pears). This would be a fine ale to use as an ingredient in such dishes, as well as to serve with them.

● OTTER CREEK BREWING

85 Exchange Street
Middlebury, Vermont, 05753-1106
802-388-0727
Capacity: 40,000 barrels
Year started: 1991
Scheduled tours available
Glassware and merchandise available

"I picked Vermont simply because it's a nice place to live," says Lawrence Miller with a smile, explaining why a lad who'd grown up in New Jersey and Massachusetts, gone to college in Oregon, and traveled in Germany and Belgium had built a brewery in western Vermont.

Miller, the president and brewmaster of Otter Creek, started brewing at home. He says that Otter Creek makes "novel interpretations of traditional styles." Miller thinks a brewer should understand the parameters of given styles, and then use his or her creativity to make something new.

Otter Creek uses one yeast for all its beers — beers brewed in what Miller calls an "Ameri-German context" — an alt yeast. Fermenting and conditioning is done at cooler-than-ale-average temperatures.

Otter Creek's goal is to "brew beers of national distinction for local and regional distribution." Adds Miller, "We sell to a cross-section of Vermonters," from people at beer specialty bars to folks at the American Legion.

Miller sees the Vermont market as more mature than those of some other states. He thinks that the variety of beers available is not only a response to increasingly educated consumers, but also tends to feed further interest in beer. Likewise, he not only tries to develop the market for his beer, but he listens and responds to comments on his beer, which, Miller says results in better beer.

While Otter Creek continues to try to expand its market, "we don't want to sell further than we can send a truck and get it back the same day."

Copper Ale ★★★★

5.4% alc./vol.
O.G.: 1050
Ingredients: two-row pale,
munich, caramel and carapils
malts; roasted barley; Chinook,
Hallertau and Tettnang hops

Light to mid amber, with a pale beige, quiet and stable head, Copper has a faint but appealing aroma: light caramel, hay, apricot, traces of grain, and an alty-metallic edge. Taste: the initial impression is of a balance between, on the one hand, soft caramel and fruit (plum, apricot), and on the other, crisp, almost dry, cereal flavors. Copper finishes hoppy (grass and hay) with some dry grain and a hint of peat. 21 IBUs. Medium body, medium viscosity. Highly drinkable; an American take, perhaps, on the altbier style.

Hefeweizen ★★★

4.8% alc./vol.
O.G.: 1044
Ingredients: two-row pale malt; malted
wheat; Willamette and Cascade hops

Appearance: hazy yellow-straw with a hint of green; white, quiet and stable head. Aroma: yeasty-bready, dry grain, hint of citrus skin. Very lemony with some tartness to start, this seasonal offering bitters a little in the finish, showing a nice touch of grapefruit skin and just the right amount of acidity. This easy-drinkin' wheat would go well with Key lime pie, lemon pudding, or crackers with jalapeno cheese.

Helles Alt ★★★¹/2

4.9% alc./vol.
O.G.: 1046
Ingredients: two-row pale, munich and
carapils malts; Chinook, Hallertau and
Tettnang hops

Appearance: yellow gold; near-white, quiet head. Aroma: dry, husky, lightly roasted grain, and hay — very pleasant. Whereas I think of Otter Creek's Copper as a good American take on altbier, the huskiness and dry, hay-like bitterness of Helles Alt makes me think that this ale is somewhere between an alt and the old Canadian ale style. To start, a dryish, grainy, caramel flavor with some fruit (apricot with a citric tinge). Hops show in a dry, slightly metallic ("alty"), slightly woody or earthy finish. I could drink lots of this quenching but characterful beer.

Oktoberfest ★★★

4.8% alc./vol.
O.G.: 1049
Ingredients: two-row pale, munich,
carapils and caramel malts; Chinook,
Hallertau and Tettnang hops

Appearance: mid amber; yellowy beige, quiet and stable head. Aroma: toffee, peat, roasted grain, grass — fresh, and a little tart for the oktoberfest style. Taste: smoky-toffee, touch of apricot, some astringency to start, and then hop bitterness, grain bitterness (but only 19 IBUs) and a lingering touch of smoke. Less malty and more astringent than many oktoberfests, this autumnal beer would, with its smokiness, appeal to many scotch drinkers.

Stovepipe Porter ★★★

5.5% alc./vol.
O.G.: 1054
Ingredients: two-row pale, munich,
caramel, chocolate and carapils malts;
roasted barley; Chinook, Cascade and
Willamette hops

Cola colored, with a café-au-lait-colored head that is quiet and stable, Stovepipe has a simple, attractive aroma: roasted grain, coffee, grass-forest, and a hint of licorice. Taste: a bit thin, dry and toasty, not quite burnt, with a licorice undertone. Finish: grassy-hoppy, bitter, astringent and dry. 30 IBUs.

Summer Wheat Ale ★★★

4.8% alc./vol.
O.G.: 1044
Ingredients: two-row pale
malt; malted wheat;
Willamette and Cluster hops

Appearance: straw colored, with a near-white, quiet and stable head. The aroma is small and delicate: butterscotch, fresh bread, hint of lemon. This light and refreshing American wheat starts mildly tart and acerbic: caramel with a grapefruit-rind edge. Finish is of moderate grassy hop bitterness (17 IBUs may seem low, but is actually higher than some wheat beers), with some grapefruit zest and earthiness.

8

SOME MASS MARKET BEERS

The beers reviewed in chapter 7 represent about five percent of the beer sold in the Great Lakes region. Imported beer represents another few percent. The big breweries have the rest of the market.

Big brewers dominate the market to a greater extent in Canada than in the United States In the U.S., Anheuser-Busch, Miller and Coors, have "only" 77 percent of the national market. Stroh and Pabst have about 12 percent; imports account for about 5 or 6 percent; micros have the rest. In Canada, two foreign-owned breweries, Molson and Labatt, have about 90 percent of the national market.

Anheuser-Busch is the largest brewer in the world, selling over a hundred million hectolitres of product per year, or just over 44 percent of the American market. Miller is the third largest after Heineken of Holland; it manufactures 54 million hectolitres, giving it just over 22 percent of the American market. In sixth place (after SAB of South Africa and Brahma of Brail) is Interbrew, owner of Labatt, which makes 35 million hectolitres. Then, following Kirin (Japan), Carlsberg (Denmark) and Foster (Australia), is Coors, which turns out about 26 million hectolitres of product (10 percent of the American market).

This fact alone — market dominance — makes it worthwhile to pay at least some attention to the big breweries' product. Some beer writers take great pains to say that megabrewery beer isn't bad beer. Huge brewers have excellent quality control, it is said, and after all, they're just giving people what they want. The numbers prove it.

I don't agree. I don't think that all microbrewery beer is good, and I don't think that every brand produced by every large brewery is bad, but I do think that the leading North American brands taste bad. Horrible even. Not "bland" or "insipid" or "middle-of-the-road" or "uninspiring." Bad. The brands reviewed below are nowhere near as good as (say) water. If they were bland or lacking in flavor, they would be better.

How is it possible, one might reasonably ask, that most of the beer sold tastes bad? Might I be wrong? Am I a snob? Perhaps, but consider the following. Most big brewery beer is drunk very cold, at temperatures at which most flavor is hidden. Few people who drink the major brands have drunk a variety of all-malt beers with which they could compare their favorite brand. Finally, it may be that some people who are "brand-loyal" to a mass-market beer lead cloistered lives.

If you've never formally evaluated a major brand, it's an enlightening experience.

Serve four lagers, two of them all-malt lagers (for example, Penn Pilsner, Brick Premium, Great Lakes Dortmunder, Brasal Hopps Bräu) and any two major brand lagers. Serve them at cellar temperature or warmer. Make notes on appearance, aroma and taste. Enjoy.

Budweiser ★ (Anheuser-Busch)

This beer is nothing if not good, and it is not good. It isn't even mediocre. Poor technical properties: big bubbles, noisy and quickly collapsing head. Aroma: combination of fine paper and wet newsprint. Taste: one-tenth sake, nine-tenths soda water. Wet brown-paper-bag aftertaste. Beer is supposed to be made from barley, not rice, and this beer is, I would guess, at least one-third rice. Drink this concoction and, as they say, you'll be sadder, budweiser.

Original Coors ★ (Coors)

Life is a comedy to those who think, and a tragedy to those who feel, according to Horace Walpole. To the thoughtful, sensitive beer drinker, Coors is comedy and tragedy. It insults the brain and tortures the heart. Predominant flavors are wet newspaper, cooked rice and white sugar. Very, very fizzy.

Blue ★ (Labatt)
5% alc./vol.

Aroma: cardboard, wet newsprint; no hops discernible. Taste: sugar, paper mâché, canned cream of corn, with a vegetal, wet cardboard finish. Michael Jackson calls Blue "bland." I think bland would be better. For reasons lost in history, Labatt puts "Pilsener Beer" on the label.

Miller Beer 1/2★ (Miller)
5% alc./vol.

While I'm grateful for Miller putting the alcohol level on the label, this is, undoubtedly, one of the worst beverages I've ever drunk. The eagle on the label, the one with the barley and hops in his talons, has obviously made off with the ingredients that should have been used. Aroma: pulp and paper, not unlike the air in a kraft pulp mill. Taste: a sweet corrupt flavor rather like corn silage mixed with sugar and rancid vegetables. Very fizzy.

Export ★1/2 (Molson)
5% alc./vol.

The only ale in our line-up has an aroma of paper, faint caramel, and a touch of hay. Taste: sweet, papery caramel, then bittersweet wood-pulp, with a maizy sweet finish. This was actually a reasonable ale in the 1960s when it was more bitter. The most interesting thing about this beer is the fact that if you turn the two-masted sailing ship on the label sideways, it looks like an armadillo.

9
AN EXULTATION OF BREWERS

Other than the five products described above, almost all the beers listed in this book are a pleasure to drink. I hope you seek them out.

All breweries listed in this guide (even, on occasion, the Big Five) are making some fine beer. Most of the region's breweries are helping to create a healthier beer culture. I thought it a good idea to finish this book with a salute to the breweries (as opposed to the brands) of the region.

To this end, I decided to cite some breweries for their overall excellence. A dozen seemed about right — small enough to make choosing hard, large enough to recognize the widespread brewing prowess of brewers in the region. Brewpubs weren't considered. No objective criteria were used, just my recollection of the pleasure that various beers have given me.

An exultation? I've always been fascinated by those collective names for animals: a charm of goldfinches, a team of ducks, a barren of mules, and of course, the euphonious exaltation of larks. To exalt means to raise high, to elevate in rank, to elate with joy — so exaltation wouldn't have been a bad word to use as a collective for superb breweries, but I'm in less of a position to exalt a brewer than I am to exult in the fruit of their work — that is, to "rejoice exceedingly," to "leap for joy," and to feel "rapturous delight."

The thirteen I've chosen are what is called, I believe, a brewer's dozen.

THE EXULTATION

Brasal

Brooklyn

Catamount

Cheval Blanc

Creemore Springs

F. X. Matt

Great Lakes

McAuslan

Motor City Brewing Works

Niagara Falls

Stoudt

Unibroue

Wellington County

BEER WORDS: A TASTER'S LEXICON

The difference between the right word and the almost right word, Mark Twain noted, is the difference between lightning and the lightning bug. Or between genuine draft and Genuine Draft, he might have added, had he lived longer.

Beer fans face two contradictory needs: the need to have a meaningful, reasonably precise vocabulary with which to think about beer, and the need for simplicity and clarity in language. Beer fans (and Monty Python fans) may laugh at the oenophiles' vocabulary: "Ah! A phenolic, hickory-tinted start and a buttercup-lilac middle leading to a rounded passionfruit finish." We can laugh, but we need a vocabulary that goes beyond "sweet," "smooth," "refreshing." Words are the best tool we have for understanding and discussing beer — and life, for that matter.

Most beer flavors fall into three loose categories: sweet, bitter and sour. Many sweet flavors come from residual malt sugars that haven't fully converted to alcohol. Corn adjunct (and to a lesser extent, rice) also causes sweetness. Hops boiled with the malt are the major cause of bitterness. Sourness, not often salient in North American beers, but common in many Belgian ales (and quite a seductive characteristic it can be), is often the result of the yeast used. A gross generalization: the Belgians value sourness, the British and the Germans bitterness, and North Americans sweetness.

Interestingly, people are affected by the same beer aromas and flavors in quite different ways. Part of the reason for this is physiological. The tongue is most sensitive for most people just before lunch. Smoking and lack of sleep reduce the ability to detect bitterness. Temperature also affects taste: the colder the beer, the less taste; a warmer beer will also impart more of its sweetness (and many beers seem to sweeten as they warm). Psychological and environmental factors also affect taste.

Your enjoyment of beer will increase as you build your vocabulary for describing it. The flavor and texture words below are ones I find most useful. I try to use plain language.

The terms are organized into five clusters: sweet, bitter, sour, "other," and a list of terms relating to texture or mouthfeel. Some of the terms occur in more than one cluster. "Fruity," for example, is usually a kind of sweetness (and most associated with ales), but is sometimes a good word to describe a kind of low-intensity sourness. Many of the flavor terms also describe aroma.

Sweet *(detected mostly at the tip of the tongue)*

butterscotch
buttery
caramel
chocolate
diacetyl (can be okay or not-so-okay: includes warm milk, lactose, butter-
    scotch, butter, leather, gueuzy, and rancid butter)
fruity (apricot, banana, berry, cherry, currant, date, fig, mango, melon,
    nectarine, peach, pear, prune, raisin)
maizy (corn-like)
malty
mocha
molasses
nutty (almond, brazil nut, hazelnut, pecan, walnut)
port
ricey, sake-like
roasty, roasted grain
sherry
sugary (brown sugar, confectioner's sugar)
toffee
vanilla
vinous

Bitter *(detected mostly at the center-back of the tongue)*

burnt toast
chocolate (baker's chocolate, unsweetened chocolate)
coffee, espresso
earthy
grainy, dry grain
grassy
haylike
heathery
hoppy
licorice
metallic (copper, iron, tin, bloodlike)
mocha
nutshell
oaky
peaty
smoky
sulfury
tannic (astringent oakiness)
toasty
woody

Sour *(detected mostly at the sides of the tongue)*

acerbic

acidic

astringent

cidery

citric

crisp: fresh, clean, sharp (may connote some bitterness)

estery (fruity and/or spicy; banana flavor is a common wheat beer ester)

grapefruit

green (fresh yeasty flavor in young or draft beer)

lactic

lemony

metallic (copper, iron, tin, bloodlike)

orangey

tannic (oaky astringency)

tart: pleasant clean acidity

zesty (citric fruit skin)

Other

alcoholic, warming

biscuity

bready

cereal

dry (absence of sweetness, not lack of flavor)

ethyl

estery

floral, flowery

forest

hay

herbal

hoppy

husky

leathery

medicinal

papery, cardboard (result of poor storage, old age, or overuse of adjunct, particularly corn)

pitchy (tarry)

salty (rare, but sometimes from water used in brewing)

skunky (often from exposure to fluorescent light)

soft

smoky

spicy (allspice, cinnamon, cloves, ginger, nutmeg, pepper)

tarry (pitchy)

vegetal

yeasty

Texture / Mouthfeel

astringent
big
dense
firm
fizzy
full bodied
husky
light bodied
lush
medium bodied
oily
silky
small
soft
thick
thin
unctuous
velvety
viscous (mouthcoating)

BEER WORDS: GLOSSARY

Beer styles are described in chapter 5.

Adjunct: a critical word for beer drinkers. Although adjunct is widely used by the larger brewers, you never see the word in their advertising or public relations. An adjunct is a fermentable sugar other than malted barley or wheat. In Canada, it's typically some form of corn; in the United States, it's either corn or rice. The use of adjunct is historically forbidden in Germany. Mass-market beers such as Blue, Budweiser, Canadian, Coors and Miller are made with, I believe, more than 25 percent adjunct. Some of the cheapest "beers" have over 50 percent adjunct.

Amber: usually denotes little more than color.

Barrel: the standard U.S. unit of production. One barrel equals 37 U.S. gallons.

Bitterness: a collection of flavors critical to many beer styles. Bitterness is detected at the back of the tongue.

Bitterness Units: International Bitterness Units (IBUs) are a conventional measure of the degree of bitterness in a beer. The threshold of detectability is 11 to 12 IBUs. Many mainstream beers have lost their bitterness over the years, and are now at this threshold level. A moderately bitter pale ale or lager might have 20 to 32 IBUs. More than 50 IBUs would make a pale ale or a pilsner taste very bitter, but might be perceived as average bitterness in a stout.

Bottle conditioned: beer on "lees" or yeast sediment. The beer is unfiltered or very loosely filtered so that yeast is still in suspension in the beer. Lees will sediment out, and eventually hard-cake at the bottom of the bottle. Bottle-conditioned beer is still living, still fermenting, albeit slowly. Homebrewers can retrieve and culture the yeast, which is usually still viable. In terms of aroma and taste, bottle conditioning can produce yeasty, bready and woody flavors, and magnify or change other malt and hops flavors. The term bottle conditioned implies that the beer may benefit from some aging or late, slow fermentation in the bottle.

Cask-conditioned beer: see Real Ale.

Draft: draft beer is kegged at the brewery, transported to pubs and served as fresh as possible. Draft beer should not be pasteurized. It has a short lifespan. It's served from a tap, and should have a slightly "green," fresh, sometimes yeasty flavor. Bottled or canned "draft" is a contradiction in terms.

Dry: as a flavor term, dry simply means an absence of sweetness. The modern dry beer has been fermented with a hard-working yeast developed in the

1980s by Japanese brewers. The yeast ferments more of the malt sugars than traditional yeast (called high attenuation), resulting in more alcohol and, because much beer flavor comes from unfermented matter, less malty sweetness and flavor.

Dry hopping: the addition of hops to beer after it has fermented. Dry hopping adds hop taste to beer as well as hop aroma.

Filtering: most microbrewery beer — and increasingly, megabrewery beer — is filtered to gain the shelf life, but not the loss of flavor, associated with pasteurization. All filtered beer is filtered cold: "cold filtered" simply means filtered. Filtration can be loose or tight. The tighter the filtration, the more flavor is lost.

Head: the foam on a glass of beer. It's useful to note the color of the head, the size of the bubbles, the length of time it takes for the head to collapse, and the sound it makes as it does this.

IBUs: see bitterness units.

Ice: Despite the claims of some large breweries, ice beers have a long history. See eisbock in chapter 5.

Lace, lacing, Belgian lace, Brussels lace: the intricate and attractive remnants of the head that cling to the glass after the beer is drunk. A useful term, and sometimes a good indicator of technical quality of a beer, especially of the quantity of malt used. Beers that leave no lace at all may be of poor quality. Lace is often beautiful.

Lees: the yeast sediment in a bottle-conditioned beer.

Krausening: a form of late secondary fermentation with the aim of producing a soft and gentle carbonation, of augmenting "smoothness" without diminishing flavor. Unfermented malt sugars are added late in the fermentation, usually to the conditioning tank, and then slowly fermented out.

Malt: together with water, the main ingredient in beer.

Malting: the process of turning raw barley grain into a ready-to-ferment food, that is, malt. Malting involves soaking the barley grain in water, allowing germination, and then stopping, at a precise point, the germination by drying and roasting the grains. The longer the roast, or the higher the temperature, the darker the malt.

Original gravity (O.G.): the density of the wort relative to water (which has a gravity of 1.000) before the yeast is pitched. An original gravity of 1048 means that the wort is 4.8 percent denser than water. High original gravity means that the wort has a relatively high level of malt sugar, and thus a high potential for conversion to alcohol. The higher the original gravity, the higher the level of resulting alcohol, and/or the greater amount of unfermented matter (the source of much of beer's flavor) in the finished beer. In North America, an O.G. of more than 1052 is higher than average; an O.G.

of less than 1044 is lower than average. When the yeast has done all its work converting fermentable sugars to alcohol, a final gravity (F.G.) reading can be taken. This is apt to be 1004 to 1012. The difference between original and final gravity indicates the alcohol level.

Pasteurization: the killing of bacteria through heat. Pasteurization diminishes flavor because it also kills the beer. (Beer is "living" until it has been pasteurized or had all yeast removed. Beers with a yeast sediment in the bottom of the bottle are "living" beers; the yeast can be reused to ferment another batch of beer.)

Pitching: the activity and the moment of adding yeast to wort.

Real Ale: an ale, usually made with 100 percent barley malt, that is "cask conditioned." See chapter 5.

Reinheitsgebot: the German (Bavarian) beer purity law dating from 1516. The law stipulates that only barley malt, hops and water may be used in the making of beer, with the use of yeast implied. In essence, the law means that no additives, chemicals, adjuncts (other than wheat, which is permitted under an amendment to the law) or preservatives (other than hops) are used. Few, if any, of the heavily advertised, mainstream North American beer brands meet the simple but rigid demands of this law.

Unfiltered: beer is usually filtered prior to packaging. When applied to bottles of beer, unfiltered is the same in terms of process as bottle conditioned; however, the beer may not be designed for aging. Unfiltered beer is often not quite clear (not quite "bright"); it is hazy or cloudy due to yeast residue. Many draft wheat beers are unfiltered or very loosely filtered for greater flavor.

Wort: "pre-beer." The sweet, malty liquid from which beer is made. Wort (pronounced "wert") is about 95 percent water. Yeast is pitched into the wort to convert sugars into alcohol, and the wort is transformed (magically) into beer.

Yeast: a single-celled fungus that breaks down sugar molecules and produces alcohol and carbon dioxide.

Zymurgy: the science and the art of fermentation.

Select Bibliography and Further Reading

Adams, Catherine F. *Nutritive Value of American Foods in Common Units*. United States Department of Agriculture, Washington, 1975.

Baron, Stanley. *Brewed in America: The History of Beer and Ale in the United States*. Little, Brown and Company, Boston, 1962.

Beaumont, Stephen. *Stephen Beaumont's Great Canadian Beer Guide*. MacMillan Canada, Toronto, 1994.

Bellant, Russ. *The Coors Connection: How Coors Family Philanthropy Undermines Democratic Pluralism*. South End Press, Boston, 1991.

Bowering, Ian. *The Art and Mystery of Brewing in Ontario*. General Store Publishing House, Burnstown, Ontario, 1988.

Brewers Publications. *Evaluating Beer*. Brewers Publications, Boulder, Colorado, 1993.

Bussy, Howard. "Chain of Being," in *The Sciences*, March–April, 1996.

Dallas, John and Charles McMaster. *The Beer Drinker's Companion: Facts, Fables and Folklore from the World of Beer*. Edinburgh Publishing Company, Leith, Scotland, 1993.

DeLottinville, Peter. "Joe Beef of Montreal: Working Class Culture and the Tavern" in *Readings in Canadian History Post-Confederation*, R. Douglas Francis and Donald B. Smith, editors. Holt, Reinhart and Winston, Toronto, 1990.

Drummond, J. C. and Anne Wilbraham, *The Englishman's Food*. Pimlico, London, 1991.

Eckhardt, Fred. *The Essentials of Beer Style: A Catalogue of Classic Beer Styles for Brewers and Beer Enthusiasts*. Fred Eckhardt Associates, Portland, Oregon, 1989.

Elkort, Martin. *The Secret Life of Food*. Jeremy P. Tarcher, Los Angeles, 1991.

Gelb, Barbara Levine. *The Dictionary of Food and What's in It for You*. Paddington Press, 1978.

Hernon, Peter and Terry Ganey. *Under the Influence: The Unauthorized Story of the Anheuser-Busch Dynasty*. Simon and Schuster, New York, 1991.

Jackson, Michael. *Pocket Guide to Beer*. Simon and Schuster, New York, 1991.

Jackson, Michael. *The English Pub*. Jackson Morley Publishing; Librairies Classic Bookshops, Rexdale, Ontario, 1976.

Jackson, Michael. *The New World Guide to Beer*. Running Press, Philadelphia, 1988.

MacKinnon, Jamie. *The Ontario Beer Guide*. Riverwood, Sharon, Ontario, 1992.

"Mass-Observation." *The Pub and the People*. Century Hutchinson, London, 1987.

Molson Breweries. "Typical Beer Analysis" (photocopy).

Montanari, Massimo. *The Culture of Food.* (Translated by Carl Ipsen.) Blackwell Publishers, Oxford, England, 1994.

Moore, Thomas. *Care of the Soul.* HarperCollins, New York, 1992.

Papazian, Charlie. *The New Complete Joy of Homebrewing.* Avon Books, New York, 1991.

Piendl, Anton. "Beer as Food," in *Brewers Digest*, January, 1981.

Rinzler, Carol Ann. *The Complete Food Book: A Nutritional, Medical and Culinary Guide.* World Almanac, 1987.

Schermerhorn, Candy. *Great American Beer Cookbook.* Brewers Publications, Boulder, Colorado, 1993.

Schivelbusch, Wolfgang. *Tastes of Paradise: A Social History or Spices, Stimulants, and Intoxicants.* Pantheon Books, New York, 1992.

Smith, C. Anne. *Food and Drink in Britain.* Constable and Company, London, 1973.

Smith, Gregg. *Beer: A History of Suds and Civilization from Mesopotamia to Microbreweries.* Avon Books, New York, 1995.

Saul, John Ralston. *The Unconscious Civilization.* House of Anansi, Concord, Ontario, 1995.

Tannahill, Reay. *Food in History.* Crown Publishers, New York, 1988.

Toussaint-Samat, Maguelonne. *A History of Food.* (Translated by Anthea Bell.) Blackwell Publishers, Oxford, England, 1994.

Vaillancourt, Emile. *The History of the Brewing Industry of Quebec.* G. Ducharme, Montreal, 1940.